THE CRITICAL POINT

IRVING HOWE

THE CRITICAL POINT
on Literature and Culture

HORIZON PRESS  New York

"The City in Literature" and "Philip Roth Reconsidered" are reprinted from
Commentary, by permission; copyright © 1971 and 1972 by the American
Jewish Committee. "Auschwitz and High Mandarin" first appeared as "Review
of George Steiner's *In Bluebeard's Castle*," reprinted from *Commentary*, by per-
mission; copyright © 1972 by the American Jewish Committee. "Zola: The
Poetry of Naturalism" first appeared as an Afterword to Emile Zola's *Germinal*,
translated by Stanley and Eleanor Hochman, copyright © 1970 by The New
American Library, Inc., and is reprinted by arrangement with The New
American Library, Inc., New York, N.Y. "Down and Out in New York and
Chicago" first appeared as "Odysseus, Flat on His Back" and is reprinted by
permission of *The New Republic*, copyright © 1964, Harrison-Blaine of New
Jersey, Inc.

To the Memory of Richard Hofstadter

Contents

Introduction

WRITTEN FOR A VARIETY OF OCCASIONS during the late sixties and early seventies, the literary and cultural essays brought together in this book focus on several centers of concern.

Some of them, like those on Zola and Dostoevsky, are ventures into traditional kinds of literary criticism and history that have only slight relationships to the moment in which they were written. At least one essay, that on Edwin Arlington Robinson, is an "appreciation," a somewhat old-fashioned mode of which I am fond. The "appreciation" has for its purpose the giving of praise to a writer deemed to have suffered neglect, and while proposing to specify the writer's central concerns and qualities, it does not pretend to close analysis.

A number of these essays comprise a response to a phase of our cultural experience—that phase summoned by such tags as the New Left and the counterculture. Though it now seems to be reaching a point of exhaustion, this cultural moment remains of great interest: it would be an error to suppose that we have fully grasped its significance or that we shall not again have to confront any number of variants or modifications of its original thrust. Several of my pieces, then, deal with figures who represent or reflect some of the less attractive elements of this recent cultural period: its frenetic apocalyptism, its infatuation with the violence of word and deed, its "revolutionary" authoritarianism, its reduction of the great tradition of cultural modernism to public display and chic sensation. These are themes that carry further the analysis of my earlier collections of literary, cultural and political essays: *A World More Attractive* (1963), *Steady Work* (1966), and *Decline of the New* (1970). Yet I find scant comfort in the unhappy fate of those social movements and cultural trends which I have criticized. For together with the gross delusions of these movements and trends, there were genuine stirrings of moral outrage, creditable impulses of social rebelliousness and idealism. It would be very sad if the turmoil of the sixties were replaced by a torpor of the seventies, the desperate errors of the New Left by a complacent acquiescence of new conservatives.

In the essay that opens this book I have tried to show, through tentative speculations, some of the characteristics and sources of the social and cultural crisis which lay behind the upheavals of the sixties—and at the same time to trace the possibilities of an authentic radicalism, at once democratic and militant, by means of which to grasp the problems of the period immediately behind us and to act upon those immediately ahead. It is toward this end, the recreation of a vital democratic radicalism in America, that much of my political-cultural criticism is directed.

There remains one other matter to be noticed here. In a good part of whatever reviewing is allotted these days to books of literary criticism, it has become a standard gambit to remark that a collection of critical essays is . . . a collection of critical essays and not a "unified" book. Anticipating this strategy of depreciation or dismissal, critics try to protect themselves by noting in their prefaces that, despite the apparently miscellaneous character of their collection, their pieces nevertheless contain an "underlying unity" of theme, concern, opinion. It is an understandable device of anxiety: I have done it myself.

But let me try, this once, to argue against both the familiar dismissal and the familiar defense. In some cogent if obvious sense, the pieces in this book are characterized by a "unity" of outlook and concern: all were written by the same person, all were written within a period of five or six years so that recurrent preoccupations necessarily show themselves, and all exhibit, no doubt, similar virtues and vices, strengths and weaknesses. Yet, in truth, they were written separately, for separate occasions. They do not have, nor try to have, the kind of unity we expect in a book that claims a continuous argument from start to finish. Which is to say: this is a *different kind* of book, it is a collection of essays. This, or any other such collection, may be judged a distinguished work, a mediocre work, or a mixture; but let it be judged for what it is.

Unless, of course, one cared to argue that critics should, on principle, refrain from collecting their essays into a book. Such a view seems to me arbitrary, fanatical. If obeyed, it would deprive us of some of the best criticism of the past half century. And it would encourage critics toward a disastrous inflation, making bad "full scale" books out of material that might yield good essays. For the essay, a form both flexible and economical, remains the "natural" mode for literary criticism.

Finally, a word of thanks to the editors of the publications in which these essays first appeared. Most of all, to Midge Decter, the editor at *Harper's* with whom I worked during the several years I wrote a bi-monthly literary piece for that magazine. Midge Decter gave me what every writer wants from an editor: complete freedom of expression, encouragement despite differences of judgment, cogent criticism—and space. It was a rare experience and I recall it with pleasure.

WHAT'S THE TROUBLE?

Social Crisis,
Crisis of Civilization,
or Both

We must get it out of our heads that this is a doomed time, that we are waiting for the end, and the rest of it, mere junk from fashionable magazines.

—SAUL BELLOW, *Herzog*

THE RHETORIC OF APOCALYPSE HAUNTS the air and naturally fools rush in to use it. Some of it is indeed "mere junk from fashionable magazines," and even those of us who know that we have lived through a terrible century can become impatient with the newest modes in *fin du mondisme.* Yet people who are anything but fools seem also to yield themselves to visions of gloom, as if through a surrender of rationality and will they might find a kind of peace. And there is a feeling abroad, which I partly share, that even if our cities were to be rebuilt and our racial conflicts to be eased, we would still be left with a heavy burden of trouble, a trouble not merely personal or social but having to do with some deep if ill-located regions of experience. To be sure, if we could solve social problems of the magnitude I have just mentioned, our sense of the remaining troubles would come to seem less ominous. But they would still be there. They would be symptoms of a crisis of civilization through which Western society has been moving for at least a century and a half.

A social crisis signifies a breakdown in the functioning of a society: it fails to feed the poor, it cannot settle disputes among constituent groups, it drags the country into an endless war. If local, a social crisis calls for reform; if extensive, for deep changes in the relationships of power. Yet both those defending and those attacking the society may well be speaking with complete sincerity in behalf of a common heritage of values. Even a major social change doesn't necessarily lead to a radical disruption of the civilization in which it occurs. The American Revolution did not. By contrast, the Russian Revolution not only overturned social arrangements, it also signified a deep rent within the fabric of civilization—or so it seemed only a few decades ago, though today, with the increasing "bourgeoisification" of Russia, we can no longer be certain. Romantic writers like Pilnyak and Pasternak looked upon the Revolution less as a step to proletarian power than as an upheaval within the depths of their country that would force it toward a destiny sharply different from that of the West. Trotsky attacked these writers for this heresy, but in retrospect it does not seem that they were quite as foolish as he made out. They were talking about a crisis of civilization.

Though it may coincide with a social crisis and thereby exacerbate its effects, a crisis of civilization has to do not so much with the workings of the economy or the rightness of social arrangements as it does with the transmission of values, those tacit but deeply lodged assumptions by means of which men try to regulate their conduct. At least in principle, a social crisis is open to solutions by legislation and reform, that is, public policy. But a crisis of civilization, though it can be muted or its effects postponed by the relief of social problems, cannot as a rule be dissolved through acts of public policy. It has more to do with the experience of communities and generations than with the resolution of social conflict. It works itself out in ways we don't readily understand and sometimes, far from working itself out, it continues to fester. A social crisis raises difficulties, a crisis of civilization dilemmas. A social crisis is expressed mainly through public struggle, a crisis of civilization mainly through incoherence of behavior.

To speak of a crisis of civilization is not, of course, to suggest that our civilization is coming to an end: it may be but we have no way of knowing. Nor is it to suggest that every change taking place at the deeper and more obscure levels of our experience should immediately be submitted to moral judgment. There are many things about which we simply cannot know. We can only say that developments occur which occupy a longer time span and are more deeply lodged in the intangibles of conduct than is true for the issues of a given moment.

II

Let us now turn abruptly away from our present concerns and move backward to a point some 75 or 80 years ago, in order to see how an English left-laborite or German Social Democrat might have felt about the experience of his time.[1]

The main historical fact about the nineteenth century—and for socialists, one of the greatest facts in all history—is that the masses, dumb through the centuries, began to enter public life. A Berlin worker had heard August Bebel speak; he was struck by the thought that, for all his limitations of status, he might help shape public policy; and indeed, he might even form or join his "own" party. He would, in the jargon of our day, become a subject of history rather than its object. What the worker came dimly to realize was not merely that history could be made, the lesson of the French Revolution, but that he himself might make it, the message of socialism.

The whole tragic experience of our century demonstrates this to be one of the few unalterable commandments of socialism: the participation of the workers, the masses of human beings, as self-conscious men preparing to enter the arena of history. Without that, or some qualified version of it, socialism is nothing but a mockery, a swindle of bureaucrats and intellectuals reaching out for power. With it, socialism could still be the greatest of human visions. This belief in the autonomous potential of the masses lay at the heart of early Marxism, in what we may now be inclined to regard as its most attractive period: the years in which European social democracy gradually emerged as a popular movement.

[1] The central idea for this section was suggested to me by Max Shachtman, though I cannot say whether he would have approved of the way in which I develop it.

Meanwhile there had flowered in England the theory and practice of classical liberalism. By classical liberalism I have in mind not a particular economic doctrine, as the term has come to be understood in Europe, but rather a commitment to political openness, the values of tolerance, liberties such as were embodied in the American Bill of Rights, and that most revolutionary of innovations, the multi-party system. Among Marxists the significance of this liberal outlook was far from appreciated, and in the Marxist tradition there has undoubtedly been a line of opinion systematically hostile to liberal values. In time that would be one source of the Marxist disaster. So, unless he were the kind of laborite or social democrat who had become a bit skeptical of his received orthodoxies, our observer of 1895 wasn't likely to grasp the revolutionary implications of the liberal premise, or to see it as part of a large encompassing democratic transformation that ideally would link the bourgeois and socialist revolutions.

Our socialist observer might also have noted, in the somewhat reductive terms prevalent on the Left, that science was triumphant and religion in decay. He would surely not have suspected that the weakening of religious belief, a development to which he had contributed, might bring unexpected difficulties to the lives of skeptics. Nor would he have paid attention to the views of, say, Dostoevsky on this matter, for as a rule he felt comfortable in the self-contained world that, together with an ideology proclaiming competence in almost all branches of knowledge, socialism had created for itself.

Finally, he might have become aware of certain trends in Western culture, such as the fierce hostility to bourgeois life shown by almost all writers and artists, including the reactionary ones, and the rapidity of change, indeed the absolute triumph of the principle of change, within European culture. A new sense of time, as Daniel Bell has remarked, came to dominate the arts, and the result would be that thrust toward restlessness and hunger for novelty, that obsession with progress as an end in itself, which has since characterized much of modern culture.

Let us now propose a brutal exaggeration, yet one that has its analytic uses: *by the time the nineteenth century comes to an end, at a point usually agreed to be 1914, the basic direction of world politics starts to be reversed.* The First World War—as it reveals not only the hypocrisies of the European states, including the liberal bourgeois states, but the inability of the social democrats to prevent a global bloodbath—proves to be a terrible blow to the inherited attitudes of the earlier age of progress. If the nineteenth century promised, roughly speaking, an ever-increasing movement toward democracy and liberality, than the twentieth, even while exploiting the catchwords and passions of the nineteenth, would be marked by an overwhelming drift toward various kinds of authoritarianism. This would not of course be the only direction of political change in the twentieth century; vast popular movements, some burned out in defeat and others twisted into betrayals, would also appear in Europe and Asia. But if we remember that ours has been the century of Hitler and Stalin, then my "brutal exaggeration" about the main political drift may not seem . . . well, quite so brutal. The self-activity of the working class, that essential fulcrum of socialist power, would now be replaced in all too many instances by an authoritarian manipulation of plebeian energies (Communism in all its forms) or by an accommodation to the limited goals of the existing society (social democracy in most of its forms). Liberalism as both idea and value came under fierce attack. The expected benefits of Reason were scorned, as being either deceptive or unneeded. Modern culture was recruited as an authority in the assault upon liberal styles of feeling. What I propose to assert is that we have been living not—certainly not merely—in the Age of Revolution about which Trotsky spoke but in an Age of Counterrevolution that has assailed mankind from Right and Left. This, I know, is a view distasteful to what passes today for orthodox Marxism, and so I mean it to be.

The central expectation of Marxism—that by its own efforts the working class could transform history—was called into question. Every political tendency on the Left had to face the question: if the working class turns out not to be the revolutionary force that Marxists had supposed, what then? The spectrum of nominated substitutes, from union bureaucracies to insurgent kindergartens, from technocratic experts to soulful drop-outs, has not been reassuring.

It is still too soon to speak with certainty. Has the vision of the self-activization of the masses, a vision democratic in its essence, proved to be false? Premature? Or merely delayed by historical interruptions and accidents?[2] I shall not try to answer this question, in part because I am not certain how to answer it, except to note the cogency of a remark attributed to Cournot: "The fact that we repeatedly fail in some venture merely because of chance is perhaps the best proof that chance is not the cause of our failure." In any case, for us this failure is the central problem of modern political experience, and it helps explain—even while being far from the sole explanation for—the fact that every mode of politics in our century succumbs in varying degrees to authoritarianism.

People employing another set of categories will no doubt see the politics of this century in other terms; but other terms can often veil similar perceptions. What seems likely is that all who share the view that democratic norms are essential to a tolerable life would be ready to grant some credit to the sketch that has been drawn here.

III

How are we now to relate the two lines of speculation I have thus far advanced—first, that we are experiencing the repercus-

---

[2] In 1948, writing on the occasion of the hundredth anniversary of *The Communist Manifesto*, Jean Vannier, one of Trotsky's close associates, remarked about the working class that

> It has shown itself capable of outbursts of heroism, during which it sacrifices itself without a thought, and develops a power so strong as to shake society to its very foundations. It can rid itself in an instant of the most inveterate prejudices, while there seems to be no limit to its audacity. But by and by, whatever the consequences of its action, whether victory or defeat, it is finally caught up in the sluggish, quotidian flow of things.
>
> The fetid backwaters of the past seep back; the proletariat sinks into indolence and cynicism. And even in its triumphant moments, it exhibits a want of consciousness in its choice of leaders. The "instinctive sense of reality" attributed to it by Auguste Comte, which it so readily reflects in many a circumstance, abandons it at such moments. Its courage and self-sacrifice are not enough to give it what, precisely, is needed in order to act out the role assigned to it by Marx: political capacity.

The question Vannier is raising here is not merely whether the working class can take power—that is an old and well-rehearsed question. He is asking something more troublesome: can a triumphant working class, once in power, display the political "capacity" to rule over a modern society or will it, in effect, cede power to an alliance of bureaucrats, intellectuals, and technocrats?

sions of a crisis of civilization (a few signs of which will shortly be noted) and second, that we are living through the consequences of the failure of socialism? Perhaps by a third line of speculation: that it is precisely the recurrent political-social difficulties of Western capitalism, significantly eased but not removed by the welfare state, which create a fertile ground for the emerging symptoms of a long-festering crisis of civilization. The social-political problems of the moment and the deeper crisis of civilization have, so to say, a habit of collaboration; they even maliciously assume the guise of one another. There follows a terrible confusion in which problems open to public solution become encumbered with metaphysical and quasi-religious issues while efforts are vainly made to bring into the political arena metaphysical and quasi-religious issues beyond the capacity of politics to cope with.

Why we should be experiencing this confusion of realms is a question to which the answers are either too easy or too hard. Let us not rehearse them at length. The atom bomb has made us aware that the very future of the race hangs on political decision. The Nazi and Stalinist concentration camps have raised questions as to the nature of our nature: is there an inherent bestiality in mankind beyond the correction of collective activity? The Vietnam war, in a more recent moment, has been felt by segments of the young as an international trauma, serving to break ties of loyalty with both society and earlier generations. In the West a generation has arisen accustomed to affluence and therefore able to devote itself to problems of life, sometimes merely life-style, as against the problems of making a living. Higher education on a mass scale is becoming a reality in Western society, yet no one quite knows what its purpose, content, or outcome is or should be. A counter society, half-real and half-myth, has appeared as the Third World, imbued by its admirers with a mixture of utopianism and authoritarianism, revolution and primitive nobility: all arising from a revulsion against advanced society. Such are the reasons that might be given for a situation in which the crisis of modern civilization, recurrent for at least a century and a half, is again felt as immediate and pressing; but what we do not really know is the relative weights to assign to these reasons, and that means we do not know very much.

The difficulty—let us say, one difficulty—of living at this moment in history is that we experience, both as *simultaneity and contradiction*, the problems of three stages of modern society. Or to be more modest we experience problems that in our thought we have assigned to three stages of society: precapitalist (race, illiteracy, backwardness); capitalist (class conflict, economic crisis, distribution of wealth); and postcapitalist (quandaries concerning work, leisure, morality, and style, such as are sometimes described as "existential," a term meant to indicate significant imprecision). But it is crucial to note that we experience these three orders of difficulty within the context of an advanced or "late" capitalism. Problems therefore suddenly appear in this late capitalist society that we had supposed would emerge only under socialism—problems not to be described merely or mainly in terms of social class but rather as pertaining to all human beings. (It ought to be said that the more intelligent socialists had foreseen the possibility that by liberating men from material want socialism might impose upon them a severe crisis of civilization, though impose it under circumstances more favorable to the human imagination than had been possible in the past.)

In the industrialized countries capitalism has entered a phase of unprecedented affluence, not justly distributed yet still reaching almost every class in society. Many people, especially those drawn from the upper and middle classes, have thereby come to experience a certain freedom to see their lives in generalized or abstract "human" terms. In the long run this is surely what one hopes for all humanity—that men should free themselves, to the extent that they can, from the tyranny of circumstances and confront their essential being. In the short run, however, this occurs, to the extent that it does occur, within a social context that distorts and frustrates the newly acquired sense of the human. For it occurs within a context of class domination and social snobbism, as well as at a historical moment forcing upon the young ghastly dilemmas. At one and the same time, a young person of middle-class origin can feel free to experiment with his life, yet must also live under the shadow of a war perceived to be unjust and even criminal. He can feel himself free to abandon the norms of bourgeois society, yet in doing so he will often unwittingly reinstate them as self-alienating masks and phantasms.

I am aware here of a possible criticism: that in speaking of these three stages of recent history as they had been thought of by socialists, I am referring not to objective realities but to conceptions nurtured, perhaps mistakenly, by people on the Left, and that there is nothing inherent in modern history which requires that certain problems be correlated with early capitalism or others with socialism. I accept this criticism in advance, but would only add that all of us see, as we must see, historical developments through the lens of our assumptions, and that those who reject socialist categories may come to similar conclusions through their own terms about the mixture of problems I have been discussing. We might, for example, choose to say that during the past decade we have become aware that the religious disputes of the nineteenth and the social anxieties of the twentieth century are related—with the issues that obsessed the nineteenth century, issues that had to do with the desanctification of the cosmos, surviving into our own moment in surprisingly powerful ways. For what should interest us here is not the "rightness" of a particular intellectual vocabulary or tradition, but a cluster of insights that might be reached through different vocabularies and traditions.

In any case, the jumble of interests and needs I have been associating with various stages of modern history could also be regarded as distinctive elements—elements of conflict and tension—within the welfare state. It is in the very nature of the welfare state that through its formal, ideological claims it should arouse steadily increasing expectations which as an economic system still geared mainly to a maximization of profit it does not always or sufficiently satisfy. The welfare state systematically creates appetites beyond its capacity to appease—that, so to say, is the principle of dynamism which keeps it both in motion and off-balance. The welfare state cannot count upon those fierce sentiments of national loyalty which, precisely insofar as it has come to dominate the industrialized portion of the world, it replaces with an array of group and sectional interests—that much-vaunted pluralism of interests often concealing an imbalance of opportunity. The welfare state has small attraction as an end or ideal in its own right, and little gift for inspiring the loyalties of the young. It is a social arrangement sufficiently stable, thus far, to all but eliminate the prospect of revolution in the advanced countries; but it is also a social arrangement unstable enough to encourage the militant arousal of previously silent groups, the intensification of political discontents, and the reappearance, if in new and strange forms, of those tormenting "ultimate questions" with which modern man has beset himself for a century and a half. These "ultimate questions" as to man's place in the universe, the meaning of his existence, the nature of his destiny—that they now come to us in rather modish or foolish ways is cause for impatience and polemic. But we would be dooming ourselves to a philistine narrowness if we denied that such questions do beset human beings, that they are significant questions, and that in our moment there are peculiarly urgent reasons for coming back to them.

IV

How does one know that we, like our fathers, grandfathers and great-grandfathers, are living through a crisis of civilization? What could possibly constitute evidence for such a claim? Even to ask such questions may strike one as both comic and impudent: comic because it seems a little late to be returning to a theme that has been pursued to the point of exhaustion, impudent because it can hardly be approached in a few pages. One is tempted simply to say what Louis Armstrong is supposed to have said when he was asked to define jazz, "If you don't know, I can't tell you." For if felt at all, a crisis of civilization must be felt as pervasive: as atmospheric and behavioral, encompassing and insidious.

How shall we live?—this question has obsessed thoughtful people throughout the modern era, which is to say, since at least the French Revolution, and it has obsessed them with increasing anxiety and intensity. I don't suppose there has ever been a time when the question hasn't been asked, but in those centuries when religious systems were commonly accepted as revealed truth, the problems of existence necessarily took on a different shape and eventuated in a different emotional discipline from anything we know in our time. Some of the more spectacular symptoms of disaffection we are now witnessing ought to be taken not as historical novelties revealing the special virtue or wickedness of a new generation, but as tokens of that continuity of restlessness and trouble which comprises the history of Western consciousness since the late eighteenth century.

One major sign is the decay or at least partial breakdown of the transmission agencies—received patterns of culture, family structure, and education—through which values, norms, and ideals are handed down from generation to generation. It would be self-deceiving, if for some comforting, to suppose that we are going through just another "normal" struggle between generations which "in time" will work itself out through familiar mechanisms of social adjustment. The present conflict between generations or if you prefer, between segments of the generations, is "normal" only insofar as it seizes upon, intensifies and distorts those philosophical, moral and religious themes which we have inherited from the nineteenth century.

The decay or partial breakdown in the transmission of values occurs most dramatically among middle-class and upper-middle-class youth secure enough in the comforts of affluence to feel that in the future our primary concern will be existence rather than survival. Some declare an acceptance of received values but cry out against their betrayal by the system or the men who run it; others reject the received values (sustained work, restraint as a social discipline, postponement of gratifications in behalf of ultimate ends, goals of success, etc.). In practice, it is hard to keep the two kinds of response completely separate. Young protesters often believe they are motivated by a fundamental denial of Western civilization when in reality they are unhappy with their private lot. But more important by far is the fact, as I take it to be, that those who believe they are motivated merely by a revulsion against the betrayal of accepted values are in reality being moved, at least in part and at least with partial consciousness, by the more extreme visions of life-style that we associate with postindustrial society. One result is that in the name of rejecting their elders' betrayal of liberal values they slide into contempt for those values.

The immediate social form through which such young people try to organize their responses is a cluster of distinctively generational groups lying somewhere between family and occupation. Torn between the problems of too much freedom and the problems of too little, between the fear of an endless chaos and the claustrophobia of rigid social definition, they create, in the words of Richard Flacks, "institutions which can combine some of the features of family life with those of the occupational structure. Youth groups, cultures, movements serve this function, combining relations of diffuse solidarity with universalistic values." One immediate cause for establishing these institutions is frustration with the external society: there is less and less socially useful or meaningful labor for young people to do and the consequence is that while the process of socialization is sped up the prospect of maturation is delayed. These fragile institutions of the youth culture also reveal themselves as testing grounds for experiment with, or acting-out for, the crisis of values which long antedates their appearance. Miniature settings serve as laboratories, sometimes mere sickrooms, for dealing with the largest problems of modern life.

Now, it has been argued by writers who are skeptical of the above description that signs of disaffection, whether trivial or profound, are mostly confined to segments of affluent youth and that the blue-collar young, still facing a struggle for economic survival, cannot indulge themselves in such existential luxuries. Perhaps so. But even if true, this hardly minimizes the importance of what has happened within large and significant segments of middle-class youth—especially in the United States where the middle class sprawls across the social map and strongly influences the ways in which adjacent classes live.

If your main concern is to plot out lines of voting behavior, then it is indeed crucial to notice the class limitations of the new youth styles; but if you are concerned with long-range social trends, then you must recognize that by their very nature these are likely first to appear among minorities. (It does not follow that everything to be found among minorities will become a long-range social trend.) What needs, then, to be estimated, or simply guessed, is the extent to which such minorites—in our case, a rather substantial one—may shape the conduct of tomorrow. Clearly, it is too soon to say whether we are witnessing a transient outbreak of malaise reflecting the privileges and disadvantages of middle-class youth or a fundamental revision in the patterns of our life reflecting the emergence of postindustrial society, the loss of faith in traditional values, and the persistence of moral and metaphysical problems thrown up by the crisis of civilization. To insist merely upon the former might be parochial; merely upon the latter, grandiose. But even if we lean toward skepticism, we ought to recognize the possibility that a series of intermittent generational traumas, and the current one is hardly the first, might constitute a long-range historical trend of major importance.[3]

About the gravity of a second major symptom that points to a crisis of civilization there is likely to be less dispute. The whole enterprise of education is in grave trouble. It is marked by anxieties bordering on demoralization and often a retreat from serious purpose that becomes sheer panic. In part this seems due to immediate causes that might let up in a few years; in

[3] A few points about the significance of the new youth styles:

1. It is hard to suppose that the feelings of disaffection or dismay one encounters among young people are confined to those who come from a single class, though it may well be that such feelings are most strongly articulated by them. Even among plebeian segments of our population there are visible strong feelings of rage and resentment, sometimes turned against "the students," but in origin and character often sharing with "the students" sentiments of powerlessness and dismay.

2. Today's middle-class style can become tomorrow's working-class style. In this country, the lines of social and cultural demarcation between the classes are not nearly so firm as in other capitalist societies. Youth mobility is high; working-class children go to college in increasing, if not sufficient, numbers; they are likely to share at least some of the responses of other students; and they do not bring with them a strong sense of class allegiance or definition to which they feel obliged to cling and which might create psychic barriers between them and their middle-class peers.

3. Mass culture quickly provides lower-class equivalents to middle-class styles, and often succeeds in spilling across class barriers. There are overwhelming cultural or pseudo-cultural experiences shared by the young of all classes, certainly more so than in any previous society. Movies, rock music, drugs—these may not figure with equal force in the lives of both working and middle-class youth, but they do create a generational consciousness that, to an undetermined extent, disintegrates class lines.

There have recently appeared reports of widespread and serious drug usage among young workers, both white and black, in major American industries. Whatever this may signify, and I don't pretend to know, it ought to be sufficient evidence to dismiss the claim that somehow the less attractive features of the "counter culture" are unique to disoriented or spoiled middle-class youth. For good or bad, illumination or contamination, young workers in a mass society increasingly share the surrounding general culture.

part it signifies a thread of confusion that has kept recurring throughout the history of modern education. There seems barely any consensus among professors as to what they are supposed to profess, barely any agreement among educators as to what they believe education to be or do. There is little concurrence in our universities, and not much more in our high schools, as to the skills, disciplines, kinds of knowledge, and attitudes of mind we wish to develop. The more education is exalted in our social mythology, the less do we seem to know what it means.

Curricula discussions at faculty meetings are notoriously tiresome, yet they finally do reflect disputes and mirror disorientation concerning the very idea of education and thereby, perhaps, the very nature of our civilization. What, beyond the rudiments of literacy, do people need to know? What, beyond such needs, should they wish to learn? What do we hope to pass on from one generation to the next in regard to moral and cultural values? What is our image of an educated man? Around such questions disputes rage, and rage so harshly that connections can barely be made between the antagonists. For these are disputes that come down to the question of how or whether we shall maintain a vital continuity with traditional Western culture.

When a society does not know what it wishes its young to know, it is suffering from moral and spiritual incoherence. It has no clear sense of the connections it would maintain—or whether it even wishes to maintain them—with the civilization of which presumably it is a part. And when to this incoherence is added the persuasion that young people should be kept in schools for increasing lengths of time (often with the parallel notion that schools should be made to resemble the external society, which is to say, to be as unlike schools as possible), then immediate and long-range troubles are thrust into a dangerous friction.

The United States, and to a lesser extent other advanced countries of the West, have embarked on a project which, we socialists would like to think, might better have coincided with the growth of a democratic socialist order. It is a project that declares every citizen to be entitled to a higher education and soon may enable every citizen to obtain one. Who can fault this premise? But who would deny that there are extremely troubling results from undertaking so revolutionary a task under social circumstances often inhospitable to it? Those of us who spoke for a universalization of culture and education were not, I think, wrong; but we were naive in our sense of how it might be brought about, or what the cost of bringing it about might be. We failed to see that some problems are not open to quick public solution, and we refused to see that the solution of other problems might lead to new and unforeseen ones. In the short run—and who knows, perhaps even the long run—a conflict develops between the values of high culture and the values of universal education, to both of which we are committed but between which we would hardly know how to choose, if choose we had to. Millions of young people are thrust into universities and no one quite knows why or toward what end. The immediate result is social bitterness and clash. One of the few things these millions of young people may discover in the universities is, however, that learning and culture, since they are but faintly credited by many of their teachers, need hardly be credited by them. That expresses and intensifies a crisis of civilization.

Ultimately, one suspects, this crisis has to do with residual sentiments of religion and vague but powerful yearnings toward transcendence. For to the extent that the transmission of values is blocked and a lack of faith in the power of education spreads among the educated classes, there must follow a more pervasive uncertainty as to the meanings and ends of existence. Let me turn to a vocabulary not spontaneously my own and suggest that we are beginning to witness a new religious experience—or, perhaps, an experience of religious feelings. Partly because of the sterility of traditional religious institutions, this experience cannot easily be embodied in religious terms and it must therefore assume the (often misshapen) masks of politics, culture, and life-style. Our socialist of 75 or 80 years ago, smug in his rationalism and convinced that all would be well once "we" took power, could hardly understand such a development; his first inclination would have been to regard it as a sign of reaction. For that matter, it is by no means clear that a socialist of the present moment can understand it, either. Yet, no matter how alien we remain to the religious outlook, we must ask ourselves whether the malaise of this time isn't partly a consequence of that despairing emptiness which followed the breakup in the nineteenth century of traditional religious systems; whether the nihilism every sensitive person feels encompassing his life like a spiritual smog isn't itself a kind of inverted religious aspiration (so Dostoevsky kept saying); and whether the sense of disorientation that afflicts us isn't due to the difficulties of keeping alive a high civilization without a sustaining belief. All questions of the nineteenth century; all returning to plague us at the end of the twentieth.

Richard Lowenthal has remarked on this score:

> We have not yet had a civilization that was not based on a transcendent belief. And what we are trying to do is to maintain our values and move upon the momentum of these values originally created by religion—but after the transcendent belief is gone. The question is: will we succeed?

To such questions a simple answer is neither possible nor desirable. Even if we conclude that the breakdown of religious systems, enormously liberating as in part it was, also yielded unforeseen difficulties for those who might never have stepped into a church or a synagogue, this is not to be taken, of course, as a token of support for those who wish to recreate through will the dogmas that once were supported by faith. Perhaps we have no choice but to live with the uncomfortable aftereffects of the disintegration, aftereffects that range from moving efforts at private spiritual communion to flashy chemical improvisations for pseudoreligious sects. I am convinced, in any case, that the coming era will witness a proliferation of such sects, some betraying the corrupting effects of the very technology they will repudiate, others mixing antinomian ecstasies with utopian visions, and still others seeking to discover through simplicities of custom the lost paradise of love.

Again experience proves far more recalcitrant and complicated than any of our theories has enabled us to suppose. It may indeed be that the religious impulse is deeply grounded in human existence and that men need objects of veneration beyond their egos. "The Golden Age," wrote Dostoevsky, "is the most unlikely of all the dreams that have been, but for it men have given up their life. . . . For the sake of it prophets have died and been slain, without it the peoples will not live and cannot die. . . ." If the impulse Dostoevsky invokes here cannot be expressed through religious channels, then it must turn to secular equivalents. It turns to the fanaticism of ideology (which may explain the continued hold Marxism has on the imaginations of the young). It turns to heretical sects seeking an unsullied pantheism. It turns to communities of the faithful who repudiate technology and civilization itself, a repudiation as old as religion itself.

Who can say? Remembering the certainties of our socialist of 75 or 80 years ago, good, decent, and even heroic fellow that he was, we might be a little cautious in dismissing the needs and aspirations of our fellowmen, especially those we find difficult to understand. All we can say with assurance or good will is that the themes of religious desire appear and reappear in the experience of our epoch, tokens of "the missing All," whether as harmony or dissonance. And they will surely be heard again.

An anxiety,
  A caution,
    And a caution against the caution.

The anxiety: whenever there occurs that meeting of social crisis and crisis of civilization I have sketched here, democratic norms and institutions are likely to be in danger. If we look at the collapse of democratic societies in our century, we must conclude that the usually cited causes—economic depression, unemployment, etc.—are necessary but not sufficient elements; there must also occur some loss of conviction in the animating ethos of the nation or culture, some coming-apart of that moral binder which holds men in the discipline of custom. Anyone observing the intellectual life of the West during the past decade may be struck by the thought that some such loss of conviction, or some such coming-apart of moral binder, seems to be happening, if not among the masses, then certainly among growing segments of the educated classes. The bourgeois mythos has been losing its hold on the bourgeois mind, though nothing has come along to replace it. Nothing, that is, except that vulgarized quasi-Marxism which has been improvised by a small though significant minority of the intellectual young. Nor should this, by the way, come as a surprise, for no other twentieth-century ideology has been so powerfully able to stir or corrupt the nascent religious impulses of sensitive and uprooted people.

By an irony too painful to underscore, it is only in Eastern Europe that intellectuals have come to appreciate the value of liberal institutions. In the West, a mere three decades after the ravages of totalitarianism, there is again visible a strident contempt for the ethic of liberal discourse and the style of rationality. In part this arises from the mixed failings and successes of the welfare state, but in part from an upswell of unacknowledged and ill-understood religious sentiments that, unable to find a proper religious outlet, become twisted into moral and political absolutism, a hunger for total solutions and apocalyptic visions. Impatience with the sluggish masses, burning convictions of righteousness, the suffocation of technological society, the boredom of overcrowded cities, the yearning for transcendent ends beyond the petty limits of group interest, romantic-sinister illusions about the charismatic virtues of dictatorship in underdeveloped countries—all these tempt young people into apolitical politics, at best communes and at worst bombs, but both sharing an amorphous revulsion from civilization itself.

Why then should one suppose that such sentiments can pose a threat to democratic institutions? Because, if carried through to the end, they release yearnings and desires that by their very nature cannot be satisfied through the limited mechanisms of democratic politics. Because, if carried through to the end, they summon moods of desperation and fanaticism which lead to a dismissal of democratic politics.

The caution: nothing could be more disastrous for our political life in the immediate future than to have the modest, perhaps manageable and (as some intellectuals like to suppose) "boring" problems of the welfare state swept aside in behalf of a grandiose, surely unmanageable and (as some intellectuals would feel) "exciting" *Kulturkampf* between the up-tight and the loose, the repressive and the permissive. If, say, in the next decade figures like Spiro Agnew and Jerry Rubin, or to choose less disreputable substitutes, William Buckley and Charles Reich, were allowed to dominate public debate, people would vote according to their prejudices concerning drugs, sex, morality, pornography, and "permissiveness." A bleak prospect; for while such a situation might arise out of spontaneous passions on all sides, it might just as well have been arranged as a political maneuver for the far Right, the only political group that could profit from it. And even if I am wrong in supposing that only the far Right could profit politically from a *Kulturkampf*, how much comfort is that? For the one thing that is entirely clear is that a politics or a social outlook devoted to democratic social change and the style of rationality would lose.

What is required here is a measure of social and intellectual discipline, the capacity for keeping one's various interests distinct and in a hierarchy of importance. Furthermore, we must recognize that at least in a democratic society politics has built-in—and in the long run, desirable—limitations. It may be possible through legislation to remove some of the socioeconomic causes of alienation but it is not possible through politics to cope directly with that seething cluster of emotions we call alienation; it may be possible through legislation to improve the conditions under which men work but it is not possible through politics to cope with the growing uncertainties men have as to work and leisure.

That in a society so beset as ours with ideological noise and cultural clatter we should expect the necessary discipline—give unto the ballot box its due, and leave for your life-style what your taste requires—seems all but utopian. But if we lack that discipline, we will pay heavily.

The caution against this caution: There are limits to common sense and pragmatism, which those who favor these qualities ought to be the first to recognize. The Fabian course to which democratic socialists in the United States are, by and large, committed, seems to me the closest we can come to political realism; but precisely for that reason we ought to recognize the points at which it fails to stir the imagination or speak to the troubles and passions of many people. Such a politics offers a possible way of improving and extending the welfare state, which is about as much as one can hope for in the immediate future, but it has little to say about problems that the welfare state is barely equipped to cope with. A politics of limitation, of coalition, of step-by-step change is desirable; the alternatives are neither real nor attractive; yet we must not allow strategy to blot out vision.

So let us be ready to acknowledge to others and ourselves that between the politics we see as necessary and the imaginative-expressive needs we have as men living in this time, there are likely to be notable gaps. The chaotic but profoundly significant urges and passions that sweep through modern society—at once innocent and nihilistic, aspiring and gloom-ridden, chiliastic and despairing—must touch us as well as those with whom we have political quarrels. How could it be otherwise? Who, looking upon the experience of our century, does not feel repeated surges of nausea, a deep persuasion that the very course of civilization has gone wrong? Who, elbowing his way past the wastes of our cities, does not feel revulsion against the very stones and glass, the brick and towers, all the debris of inhumaneness? Who, thinking of our bombs and our pollution, does not wish, at least on occasion, to join in the jeremiads against all that we are and have?

What we must do is recognize the distance, perhaps the necessary distance, between political strategy and existential response. We are saying that many things requiring remedy are open to social-political solution (provided intelligence and will are present). We are also saying that we live at a moment when problems beyond the reach of politics—problems that *should* be beyond the reach of politics—have come to seem especially urgent and disturbing. We have learned that the effort to force men into utopia leads to barbarism, but we also know that to live without the image of utopia is to risk the death of imagination. Is there a path for us, a crooked path for men of disciplined hope?

A Postscript

To say "No" as one's answer to the question at the end of the above paper would be neither hard nor even foolish. By reasoning alone, or the appearance of it, one can readily conclude that the future humanity can expect, say, fifty or sixty years from now is, mostly, to live in a low-charged authoritarian state, very advanced in technology and somewhat decadent in culture, in which there will be little terror and not much freedom, in which most men will eat fairly well and only a few suffer despair over their condition, and in which order, control, efficiency will coexist with tolerated areas of their opposites.

The famous theory of convergence—which sees the major forms of modern society gradually coming closer to one another, in a kind of eclectic elitism that satisfies none of the traditional social outlooks—has far more defenders than is commonly recognized. It is a theory that easily allows, though it does not necessarily require, a certain bland disdain for political freedom. To believe in such a theory—according to which the trend toward economic collectivism inherent in modern technological conditions comes together with the trend toward authoritarianism inherent either in the sheer complexity of things or the sheer recalcitrance of human nature—it is simply necessary to float with "the given," to accept the effectiveness but not the claims of ideology, and to rid oneself of old-fashioned liberal "illusions."

It hardly seems necessary to elaborate the many ways in which the conditions of modern society militate against the survival or growth of freedom. That technology becomes increasingly complicated, the province of a highly trained elite, and thereby less and less open to democratic controls or social arrangements premised on a high degree of popular participation; that modern urban life tends to create large masses of semi-educated men, vulnerable to the newest modes of manipulation and essentially passive in their responses to political decision; that the steadily exacerbated division between industrialized and backward nations encourages charismatic desperadoes and deracinated intellectuals toward "revolutionary" coups which, whatever else they fail to do, do not fail to destroy all liberties; that the heritage of totalitarian ideology weighs heavily upon us, a poison long settled in the minds of men; that fierce new apocalyptic moods, recklessly blending politics and religion, arise throughout the world, though perhaps most notably in the industrialized nations —all this is by now familiar, commonplace, requiring no detail.

We know that a society which tolerates extreme inequalities of wealth and income runs the risk of revolt that can endanger liberties. But we also know that a society which insists upon enforcing an absolute egalitarianism can do so only by destroying liberties.

We know that a society in which the masses of men, drugged by affluence and the mass media, become passive and inert is one in which liberties may slowly erode. But we also know that a society shaken by the tremors of pseudomessianism, in which wilful idealistic minorities seek to impose their vision upon sluggish majorities, is one in which liberties may be quickly undone.

We know that a society trapped in economic primitivism and clannishness, traditionalist or premodern casts of thought, is not likely to be one in which liberties can flourish. But we also know that it is entirely possible for political tyranny to coexist with an advanced economy.

If, then, we can specify certain conditions—a measure of affluence, the absence of extreme inequalities, a coherent political structure, a high level of education, and perhaps most crucial, a tradition of belief in freedom—which make possible or encourage the survival of liberties, these are at best necessary and not sufficient conditions. In truth, we can only guess at the optimum conditions for the survival and growth of liberties. I think it would be a social democratic society, in which a certain proportion of the central means of production would be socialized, that is, democratically owned and controlled; extremes of inequality in wealth, and thereby, ultimately in power, would be evened out; and liberties, extending from the political to the socioeconomic areas of life, would flourish.

Whether such a society can in fact ever be achieved is an open question: I cannot have the simple faith of my socialist forbears of a century ago. For, as I now see it, such a society would require not merely certain structures of economic relationships and political power—that, by comparison, is *almost* easy to envisage—but also certain structures of shared values, bringing together restraint and cooperativeness, discipline and social initiative. Nor can one believe any longer, as radicals once did, that the mere establishment of the envisaged economic and political structures will necessarily create the required values. I still think it reasonable to suppose that they would *enable* men to create those values, but there is no certainty whatever. For we have learned in recent years that a society can be threatened not merely by external assault or economic breakdown but by something harder to specify yet at least as insidious in effect: namely, the disintegration of those tacit and binding beliefs which enable men to live together. This disintegration, which affects the sons of the bourgeoisie in the West and the sons of the party leadership in the East, can have curiously mixed implications: it can be against gross injustice *and* contemptuous of liberal values, it can be outraged by unjust wars *and* prone to a mystique of violence. At least at this point, Schumpeter seems to have been a better prophet than Marx.

The question that must then follow, and which it would be foolish to try to answer, is this: can a reasonably decent society, liberal in its political style and egalitarian in its socioeconomic outlook, survive in the conditions likely to exist during the next fifty or sixty years? Apart from the factors I have listed a page or two earlier that militate against such a survival, and apart from others that could be added, there is a problem here of the gravest difficulty though one that has come to seem acute only recently. Such a liberal or social democratic society may well provide the best conditions for human beings to live in; but insofar as it comes closer to realization, it may not provide spiritual or psychic goals that will satisfy the people who live in it, at least those most inclined to sentience and restlessness.

To raise this speculation at a moment when most human beings on this globe live in societies that do not satisfy their minimal physical needs and, furthermore, hold them in authoritarian subjection, may seem idle. But it is not. For while intelligent socialists have always said that "the good society" would for the first time make it possible for men to confront freely and with adequate consciousness their metaphysical problems, they hardly could have foreseen the ferocity with which at least some people would try to attack these problems even before reaching, and indeed in the name of reaching, "the good society." If there is in reality a deep, though not always manifest, religious hunger in human beings, or at least the intellectually- and spiritually-aware minority; if this hunger fails in the twentieth century to find outlets through adequate religious institutions, ceremonies, and doctrines; and if it then turns, with a kind of self-alienated violence, into a secular expression, at once apocalyptic, messianic and fanatic—then we may suppose that the closer we approach "the good society," or the more single-mindedly we become preoccupied with approaching it, the more severe the problem will become. The values of a liberal society may indeed be in conflict, immediate or potential, with the religious or quasi-religious impulses among human beings that seem to break out recurrently with varying degrees of passion and force. And insofar as such a society clears away the gross troubles of survival that have afflicted most human beings throughout history, it leaves the way open to what we might call the risks and terrors of the metaphysical.

At this point in our speculations, the intellectuals as a group come straight to center stage. One might hope that they, in the turmoil of a civilization beset by inner doubts and a confusion between political and religious goals, would be the most unyielding, even "unreasonable," in their defense of liberties. Intellectuals, after all, are the single group in society that would seem to have the highest stake in freedom; it is their minimal requirement for professional existence; it is the very element that makes it possible to be an intellectual. But of course, the history of intellectuals in the twentieth century is, not least of all, a history of betrayal and self-betrayal, a history of repeated surrenders to authoritarian and totalitarian ideology and power. The value of freedom stirs only some intellectuals, or it stirs them only at moments when it least needs defense. For this, there are a great many reasons, and I do not pretend to know them all; but let me cite a few. By their very outlook and vocation, intellectuals are peculiarly susceptible to ideological melodrama: it is their form of faith. The grandiosity of the abstract, the wilfulness of schemes of perfection imposed through iron and blood, the feeling that anything short of a total measure is "boring," the refusal to examine the possibility that intertwined with utopian visions can be coarse yearnings for power, the infatuation with charismatic figures who represent decisiveness, rapidity, daring, intuitive authority—these are some of the elements in the experience of intellectuals that make them susceptible to authoritarian movements.

There are also mundane considerations. Modern bureaucratic societies, formally structured as one-party dictatorships, have great need for intellectuals—at least for their skills, if not their vocation. If we take enormous pride in those intellectuals who rebel in the name of freedom, men like Djilas, Solzhenitsyn and Kolakowski, we must also recognize that at least some of those who persecute them are also intellectuals of a sort. And for intellectuals in the underdeveloped countries, dispossessed and estranged, deracinated and unemployed, the prospect of an authoritarian regime resting on ideology signifies a future of prestige, power and privilege. At a certain cost, to be sure. It is therefore silly to expect that in the coming decades the intellectuals as a class will be unconditional defenders of freedom—indeed, it is a notion so silly that only intellectuals could entertain it.

Yet freedom remains our signature. We may know and have to say that many other things are needed if freedom is to exist—a society that satisfies the material and social needs of human beings, a society that gives people a sense of participation and opportunity, a society that does not kill off its young in ghastly wars, etc. But it is freedom that remains the fundament of the intellectual's vocation: he honors or betrays, but he cannot avoid it.

Yet we may ask, what is the historical sanction for this commitment to freedom? what forces in history, what laws of development, what dynamic of the society or the economy?

No doubt, at various points in the future there will be some historical forces enabling or smoothing the way for those persons or groups who will speak in defense of basic liberties. No doubt, it is of the greatest importance to try to estimate the nature and range of those forces, whether they be "impersonal" elements of the social structure or collective movements of classes and groups. But that is not what I propose to do here, partly because I do not feel competent to do it.

I want, instead, to assume that we cannot be "certain," as many of us were in the past, that there is an ineluctable motion within history toward a progressive culmination. I want to discard any faith in the necessary movement of History—even in its much-advertised cunning. Not that I would create instead a gnostic melodrama in which man stands forever pitted against his own history, a promethean loneliness against the run-away of civilization. I simply want to put the question aside, and then to say: the obligation to defend and extend freedom in its simplest and most fundamental aspects is the sacred task of the intellectual, the one task he must not compromise even when his posture seems intractable, or unreasonable, or hopeless, or even when it means standing alone against fashionable shibboleths like Revolution and The Third World.

I am aware that to offer this liberal/social democratic truism as a central idea for the future will not excite many sensibilities or set many hearts beating. Precisely that fact reinforces my conviction that, just as in the perspective of the past two centuries it is the liberal idea that now seems the most permanently revolutionary, so in the world as we know it and are likely to know it the idea of freedom, always perilous, remains the most urgent and therefore the most problematic.

I take as my model Alexander Solzhenitsyn. It seems clear that since publishing his great novels, *The First Circle* and *The Cancer Ward*, Solzhenitsyn has moved to a kind of elemental Christianity, for which there is of course a great tradition in Russia going back to and beyond Tolstoy. This tradition is not mine, though I understand how revolutionary it can be in relation to a total state. But in the Solzhenitsyn novels there is a steady commitment to the idea of freedom, not because it is seen as the logical consequence of history, nor as an unquenchable desire arising from our natures; there is too much evidence against both these views. Solzhenitsyn brings to bear no determinist argument in behalf of freedom. He simply suggests that freedom is the only condition under which people like ourselves can breathe; that freedom is required, as well, by all human beings insofar as they would pursue their particular interests, as groups or classes; that freedom is, for modern man, a supreme good. Let us say—and surely at least a few will still be saying it seventy-five years from now—that it is the name of our desire.

THE CITY IN LITERATURE

SIMPLICITY, *at least in literature*, is a complex idea. Pastoral poetry, which has been written for more than two thousand years and may therefore be supposed to have some permanent appeal, takes as its aim to make simplicity complex. With this aim goes a convention: universal truths can be uttered by plebeian figures located in a stylized countryside often suggestive of the Golden Age. In traditional or sophisticated pastoral these plebeian figures are shepherds. In naive pastoral they can be dropouts huddling in a commune. Traditional pastoral is composed by self-conscious artists in a high culture, and its premise, as also its charm, lies in the very "artificiality" untrained readers dislike, forgetting or not knowing that in literature the natural is a category of artifice. As urban men who can no more retreat to the country than could shepherds read the poems celebrating their virtues, we are invited by pastoral to a game of the imagination in which every move is serious.

With time there occurs a decline from sophisticated to romantic pastoral, in which the conventions of the genre are begun to be taken literally, and then to naive pastoral, in which they *are* taken literally. Yet in all these versions of pastoral there resides some structure of feeling that seems to satisfy deep psychic needs.

Through its artifice of convention, the pastoral toys with, yet speaks to, a nagging doubt concerning the artifice called society. It asks a question men need not hurry to answer: Could we not have knowledge without expulsion, civilization without conditions?

Now, between such questions and pastoral as a genre, there is often a considerable distance. We can have the genre without the questions, the questions without the genre. We can also assume that pastoral at its best represents a special, indeed a highly sophisticated version of a tradition of feeling in Western society that goes very far back and very deep down. The suspicion of artifice and cultivation, the belief in the superior moral and therapeutic uses of the "natural," the fear that corruption must follow upon a high civilization—such motifs appear to be strongly ingrained in Western Christianity and the civilization carrying it. There are Sodom and Gomorrah. There is the whore of Babylon. There is the story of Joseph and his brothers, charmingly anticipating a central motif within modern fiction: Joseph, who must leave the pastoral setting of his family because he is too smart to spend his life with sheep, prepares for a series of tests, ventures into the court of Egypt, and then, beyond temptation, returns to his fathers. And there is the story of Jesus, shepherd of his flock.

Western culture bears, then, a deeply grounded tradition that sees the city as a place both inimical and threatening. It bears, also, another tradition, both linked and opposed, sacred and secular: we need only remember St. Augustine's City of God or Aristotle's view that "Men come together in the city in order to live, they remain there in order to live the good life." For my present purpose, however, the stress must fall on the tradition, all but coextensive with culture itself, which looks upon the city as inherently suspect.

It is a way of looking at the city for which, God and men surely know, there is plenty of warrant. No one can fail to be haunted by terrible stories about the collapse of ancient cities; no one does not at some point recognize the strength of refreshment to be gained from rural life; no one can look at our civilization without at moments wishing it could be wiped out with the sweep of a phrase.

II

Our modern disgust with the city is foreshadowed in the 18th-century novelists. Smollett, connoisseur of sewage, has his Matthew Bramble cry out upon the suppurations of Bath—"Imagine to yourself a high exalted essence of mingled odors, arising from putrid gums, imposthumated lungs, sour flatulencies, rank arm-pits, sweating feet, running sores." In London Bramble feels himself lost in "an immense wilderness . . . the grand source of luxury and corruption." Foreshadowing the late Dickens, Smollett is also a literary grand-uncle of Louis Ferdinand Céline, impresario of Parisian *pissoirs* and New York subway toilets.

Smollett helps create the tradition of disgust, but Fielding, a greater writer, helps set in motion the dominant literary pattern of discovery and withdrawal in regard to the city. It is the pattern of *Tom Jones* and later, in more complicated ways, of those 19th-century novels recording the travels of the Young Man from the Provinces: the youth leaving the wholesomeness of the country and then, on the road and in the city, experiencing pleasures, adventures, and lessons to last a lifetime. Fielding has little interest in blunt oppositions between mountain air and pestilent streets such as Smollett indulges. Smollett's city is more vivid than Fielding's, but Smollett rarely moves from obsessed image to controlled idea: the city, for him, is an item in that accumulation of annoyance which is about as close as he comes to a vision of evil. And thereby, oddly, Smollett is closer to many 20th-century writers than is Fielding. A man of coherence, Fielding knows that the city cannot be merely excoriated, it must be imaginatively transformed. Just as Tom Jones's journey is a shaping into circular or spiral pattern of the picaro's linear journey, so the city of the picaresque novel—that setting of prat-falls, horrors, and what the Elizabethan writer Robert Greene had called "pleasant tales of foist"—becomes in Fielding an emblem of moral vision. The picaro learns the rules of the city, Fielding's hero the rules of civilized existence. In Fielding the city is a necessary stopping-point for the education of the emotions, to be encountered, overcome, and left behind.

It is customary to say that the third foreshadower of the 18th century, Daniel Defoe, was a writer sharing the later, 19th-century vision of the city, but only in limited ways is this true. For Defoe's London is bodiless and featureless. Populated with usable foils, it provides less the substance than the schema of a city; finally, it is a place where you can safely get lost. The rationality of calculation Max Weber assigns to capitalism becomes in *Moll Flanders* an expert acquaintance with geographic maze. Moll acts out her escapade in a city functional and abstract, mapped out for venture and escape—somewhat like a ballet where scenery has been replaced by chalk-marks of choreography. Defoe anticipates the design of the city, insofar as it is cause and token of his heroine's spiritual destitution, just as Kafka will later dismiss from his fiction all but the design of the city, an equivalent to his dismissal of character psychology in behalf of metaphysical estrangement.

III

The modern city first appears full-face—as physical concreteness, emblem of excitement, social specter, and locus of myth—in Dickens and Gogol. Nostalgic archaism clashes with the shock of urban horror, and from this clash follows the myth of the modern city. Contributing to, though not quite the main component of this myth, is the distaste of Romanticism for the machine, the calculation, the city.

"The images of the Just City," writes W. H. Auden in his brilliant study of Romantic iconography, "which look at us from so many Italian paintings . . . are lacking in Romantic literature because the Romantic writers no longer believe in their existence. What exists is the Trivial Unhappy Unjust City, the desert of the average from which the only escape is to the wild, lonely, but still vital sea."

Not all Romantics go to sea, almost all bemoan the desert. Wordsworth complains about London in *The Prelude*:

The slaves unrespited of low pursuits,
Living amid the same perpetual flow
Of trivial objects, melted and reduced
To one identity, by differences
That have no law, no meaning, and no end.

This Romantic assault upon the city continues far into our century. Melville's Pierre says, "Never yet have I entered the city by night, but, somehow, it made me feel both bitter and sad." "I always feel doomed when the train is running into London," adds Rupert Birkin in *Women in Love*. Such sentences recur endlessly in modern writing, after a time becoming its very stock in trade. And the assault they direct against the modern city consists of more than sentimentalism, or archaism, or *Gemeinschaft*-nostalgia. The Romantic attack upon the city derives from a fear that the very growth of civilization must lead to a violation of traditional balances between man and his cosmos, a Faustian presumption by a sorcerer who has forgotten that on all but his own scales he remains an apprentice. Nothing that has happened during this past century allows us easily to dismiss this indictment.

Darkened and fragmented, it is an indictment that comes to the fore in Dickens's later novels. In the earlier ones there is still a marvelous responsiveness to the youthfulness of the world, an eager pleasure in the discoveries of streets. Almost every *idea* about the city tempts us to forget what the young Dickens never forgot: the city is a place of virtuosity, where men can perform with freedom and abandonment. And it is Dickens's greatness, even in those of his books which are anything but great, that he displays London as theater, circus, vaudeville: the glass enlarging upon Micawber, Sarry Gamp, Sam Weller. If the city is indeed pesthole and madhouse, it is also the greatest show on earth, continuous performances and endlessly changing cast. George Gissing notes that Dickens seemed "to make more allusions throughout his work to the *Arabian Nights* than to any other book," a "circumstance illustrative of that habit of mind which led him to discover infinite romance in the obscurer life of London." Continues Gissing: "London as a place of squalid mystery and terror, of the grimly grotesque, of labyrinthine obscurity and lurid fascination, is Dickens's own; he taught people a certain way of regarding the huge city."

In Dickens's early novels there are already ominous chords and frightening overtones. The London of *Oliver Twist* is a place of terror from which its young hero must be rescued through a country convalescence, and the London of *The Old Curiosity*

Shop, as Donald Fanger[1] remarks, "impels its victims . . . to flee to the quasi-divine purity of the country . . . repeatedly identified with the remote springs of childhood, innocence and peace." Yet throughout Dickens's novels London remains a place of fascination: he is simply too great a writer to allow theory to block perception.

In his earlier novels sentimental pastoral jostles simple pleasure in color and sound; and the pattern toward and away from the city, as classically set forth by Fielding, is used in a somewhat casual way until it receives a definitive rendering in *Great Expectations.* But it is in his three great novels—*Bleak House, Little Dorrit,* and *Our Mutual Friend,* with their commanding images of fog, prison, dust-heap—that Dickens works out that vision of our existence which has so brilliantly and oppressively influenced later writing. Here the by-now worn notions of our culture—alienation, depersonalization, forlornness—are dramatized with an innocence of genius. That in cities men become functions of their function; go crazy with the dullness of their work; transform eccentricities into psychic paralysis; soon come to look as if they themselves *were* bureaucracies; and die without a ripple of sound —all this Dickens represents with a zest he had not yet learned to regard as ill-becoming. He enlarges his earlier comic gifts into the ferocious splendor of the Smallweeds, the Guppys, the Snagsbys, so that even as the city remains a theater, the play is now of a hardening into death.

Not only, as Edmund Wilson remarks, does Dickens develop the novel of the social group; he becomes the first to write the novel of the city as some enormous, spreading creature that has gotten out of control, an Other apart from the men living within it. By the time he writes his last complete novel, the savage and underrated *Our Mutual Friend,* Dickens sees London as "a hopeless city, with no rent in the leaden canopy of its sky . . . a heap of vapour charged with muffled sounds of wheels and enfolding a muffled catarrh."

We have learned to speak lightly of "society" as something pressing and enclosing us, but imagine the terror men must have felt upon first encountering this sensation! Reading these late

---

[1] Let me here record my debt to the brilliant writings on the theme of the city and literature by Donald Fanger and John Raleigh.

novels of Dickens we seem to be watching a process like that of the earth being buried beneath layers of ice: a process we now can name as the triumph of the Collective. And to this process Dickens's most intimate response is a bewilderment he projects onto an alienated space, in that multiplying chaos where Mr. Krook, double of the Lord High Chancellor, reigns and the dust-heap becomes a symbol of the derangements of exchange value. The indeterminacy of urban life, for Dostoevsky a frightening idea, is for Dickens a frightening experience.

As if in echo, one of Gogol's clerks cries out, "There is no place for me." Not in Petersburg there isn't nor in the grotesque emblem of Petersburg Gogol created. Meek spiritual cripples, his clerks lure us for a moment into sympathy with the smallness of their desires. But perhaps out of that awe at the endlessness of suffering which leads Faulkner and Leskov into harshness, Gogol treats pathos not as pathetic but as the material for comedies of irreducible disorder. The grander the city, the more wormlike its creatures. Socially fixed, the clerks are personally erased. Reduced to clerkness, one of them takes home documents to copy for pleasure—this zero reveling in his zero-ness recalls another zero, Peretz's Bontche Shveig, who when asked in heaven to name his ultimate desire, requests a hot roll with butter each morning.

How can one bear such a world, this Gogol-city of innumerable petty humiliations? By a gesture signifying the retribution of arbitrariness. In "The Overcoat" Akaky Akakievich (in Russian a name with cloacal associations) affirms himself only after death, when Petersburg is haunted by an Akakyish specter: an excremental cloud hanging over this excremental city. In "The Nose" a character finds that his nose has simply quit his face, with a sauciness he would not himself dare. But how can a nose quit a face? (As like ask Kafka how a man can turn into a cockroach.) When the weight of the determined becomes intolerable, the arbitrary gesture that changes nothing yet says everything may come to seem a token of freedom. The nose leaves the face because Gogol *tells* it to.

The figures and atmospheres of Dickens and Gogol are appropriated by Dostoevsky, but in his novels men appear as conscious beings, their alienated grotesqueness elevated to psychological plenitude. The life of man in the city becomes a metaphysical question, so that in those airless boarding houses into which Dostoevsky crams his characters there is enacted the fate of civilization. Raskolnikov's ordeal relates to Petersburg and Christianity: Can man live in this world, is there a reason why he should? *Crime and Punishment* offers a wide repertoire of city sensations, not as a catalogue of display but as a vibrant correlative to Raskolnikov's spiritual dilemmas. God and the Devil still live in this city, the former as idiot or buffoon, the latter as sleazy good-natured petit-bourgeois. That is why in Dostoevsky the city of filth retains a potential for becoming the city of purity. The city brings out Raskolnikov's delusions: it is the locale of the modern fever for mounting sensations, for the modern enchantment with the sordid as a back-alley to beatitude. The city is also the emblem of Raskolnikov's possible redemption: it is the locale of men who share a community of suffering and may yet gain the ear of Christ. Never does Dostoevsky allow the attractions of nihilism to deprive him of the vision of transcendence. In "Notes from Underground" the city bears a similar relation, what might be called a dialectical intimacy, with the narrator: each of his intellectual disasters is publicly reenacted as a burlesque in the streets. More than social microcosm or animated backdrop, the city provides Dostoevsky with the contours and substance of his metaphysical theme.

IV

Let us abruptly turn from what literature may tell about the city to what the city does in and to literature.

The city as presence brings major changes in narrative patterns. Abandoning the inclusive tourism of the picaresque, the 19th-century novel often employs a spiral-like pattern; first a pull toward the city, then a disheartened retreat to some point of origin (the blacksmith shop in *Great Expectations*, the chestnut tree in *The Charterhouse of Parma*). Elements of pastoral seem still attached to this narrative configuration, for one of its tacit ends is to retain in the novel clusters of feeling that flourished best in earlier genres. Lionel Trilling describes this kind of narrative:

. . . equipped with poverty, pride and intelligence, the Young Man from the Provinces stands outside life and seeks to enter . . . It is his fate to move from an obscure position into one of considerable eminence in Paris or London or St. Petersburg, to touch the life of the rulers of the earth. He understands everything to be "a test."

And then? Always the same denouement: the Young Man's defeat or disillusion, and his retreat to the countryside where he can bind his wounds, cauterize his pride, struggle for moral renewal. Even more striking than its presence in novels as explicitly hostile to the city as *Great Expectations* and *Sentimental Education* is the way this pattern dominates novels in which the author seems consciously to intend a celebration of the city. For Balzac Paris is a place of "gold and pleasure," and the central portion of *Lost Illusions* evokes a stormy metropolis of excitement and sheer animatedness. Yet even this most cosmopolitan of novels follows the pattern of attraction and withdrawal, bringing its hero Lucien back to the countryside in bewilderment and thereby offering a distant nod to pastoral. At the end, to be sure, Balzac's cynicism triumphs (one almost adds, thank God) and Lucien is seen in the tow of the devil, who will take him to the city where life, naturally, is more *interesting*: the city, as Balzac said, that "is corrupt *because* it is eminently civilized."

If the pattern of 19th-century fiction forms a spiral to and away from the city, it is in the sharpest contrast to later novels in which the city becomes a maze beyond escape. In *Ulysses* and *The Trial* the traditional journeys of the hero are replaced by a compulsive backtracking: there is no place else to go, and the protagonist's motions within the city stand for his need, also through backtracking, to find a center within the self.

The city allows for a more complex system of social relationships than any other locale. Sociologists keep repeating that the city impels men into relationships lacking in warmth, often purely functional and abstract; and from this once-revolutionary perception they slide into nostalgia for an "organic community" located at notoriously imprecise points in the past. For the novelist, however, the city's proliferation of casual and secondary relationships offers new possibilities: the drama of the group and the

comedy of the impersonal. The experiences of Ulysses for which
Homer had to arrange complicated journeys, Joyce can pack
into a day's wandering through a single city. There follows the
possibility of fictions constructed along the lines that the Soviet
critic M. M. Bakhtin calls a "polyphonic" structure, in which
social loss may yield literary advance. Dostoevsky's novels, writes
Bakhtin, "caught intact a variety of social worlds and groups
which had not [yet] . . . begun to lose their distinctive apartness"
and thereby "the objective preconditions were created for the
essential multilevel and multivoice structure of the polyphonic
novel."

To which I would add two observations: 1) The rise of the
city is a blessing for minor characters who might otherwise never
see the light of day; and 2) The inclination of some novelists
to employ a multiplicity of narrative points of view has much
to do with the rise of the city.

As the city becomes a major locale in literature, there occur
major changes in regard to permissible subjects, settings, and
characters. The idea of literary decorum is radically transformed,
perhaps destroyed. Literature gains a new freedom; everything,
which may be too much, is now possible. Out of the dogmas
of anti-convention, new conventions arise. The city enables the
birth of new genres: who could imagine surrealism without Paris?

In the novel of the city, a visit to a slum can serve as a shorthand
equivalent to a descent into hell, as in *Bleak House* or *Redburn*.
An address, a neighborhood, an accent—these identify the condition of a man, or the nature of an act, quite as much as social
rank or notations of manners once did. So powerful, at first
liberating and then constricting, do these new conventions
become that in *The Waste Land* their rapid evocation permits
a summary vision of an entire culture. The typist's life as a
familiar barrenness, the dialogue in the bar as a characteristic
plebeian mindlessness, the conversation between upper-class husband and wife as a recognizable sterility—these serve as the
terms of an overarching spiritual assessment.

As the city breaks down traditional rankings, there emerges
the plebeian writer or the writer of fallen circumstances. The
city erases family boundaries, in one direction toward those root-
less wanderers of the streets first imagined by Edgar Allen Poe,

and in the other direction toward the extended families pictured by Dostoevsky. The city yields stunning and rapid juxtapositions: "In Paris," gloats Balzac, "vice is perpetually joining the rich man to the poor, and the great to the humble."

The city thereby offers endless possibilities of symbolic extension. In Gissing's *New Grub Street* it becomes a place of paralyzing fatigue, a grayness of spirit that finds its extension in the grayness of a London winter. To Flaubert in *Sentimental Education*, as if to anticipate Max Weber's fear that we are entering "a long polar night of icy darkness and hardness," Paris comes to represent a collective yielding to *acedia* and nihilism, and as we read we have the sensation of watching men turn slowly into stone, a whole civilization in process of quiet petrifaction.

The city affects literature in still another way: it provides a new range of vocabularies, from the street argot of a Céline to the ironic urbanities of the early Auden, from the coarse eloquence of Balzac's Parisians to the mixture of racy street-Jewishness and intellectual extravaganza of Bellow. The city also encourages that flavorless language, the language of sawdust, we associate with naturalism, as if the denial of will must be reflected in the death of words; yet the city also yields writers like Dickens and Gogol new resources for grotesquerie and mockery. Language can be reduced to bureaucratic posture, as in Guppy's proposal to Esther Summerson in *Bleak House*, employing the terms of a brief for a small-claims court. Or it can be used by Gogol in a style the Russians call *skaz*, described by Yevgeny Zamyatin as "The free, spontaneous language of speech, digressions . . . coinages of the street variety, which cannot be found in any dictionary . . . [and in which] the author's comments are given in a language close to that of the milieu depicted."

One of the great temptations for the writer dealing with city life is to think of it as a "creature" or "being" independent from and looming over the people who live in it. Apostrophes to London and Paris are frequent in Dickens and Balzac, but these are only feeble rhetorical intimations of what they are struggling to apprehend. The sense that somehow a city has "a life of its own" is so common, it must have some basis in reality; but precisely what we mean by such statements is very hard to say. For Dickens and Gogol, as for Melville, such metaphors become ways of expressing the sense of littleness among people forming the anonymous masses. For other writers, such as Zola, Andrey Biely and Dos Passos, these metaphors prepare the way for an effort to embody the life of the group in its own right, to see the collective as an autonomous and imperious organization.

The city as presence in modern literature gives rise to a whole series of new character types, and these come to be formidable conventions in subsequent writing. A few of them:

The clerk, soon taken to represent the passivity, smallness, and pathos of life in the city: Gogol, Melville, Dickens, Kafka.

The Jew, bearer of the sour fruits of self-definition: Joyce, Proust, Mann.

The cultivated woman, one of the triumphs of modern writing, inconceivable anywhere but in the city, a woman of femininity and intelligence, seductiveness and awareness, traditional refinement and modern possibilities: Tolstoy's Anna, James's Madame Vionnet, Colette's Julie.

The underground man, a creature of the city, without fixed rank or place, burrowing beneath the visible structure of society, hater of all that flourishes aboveground, meek and arrogant, buried in a chaos of subterranean passions yet gratified by the stigmata of his plight: Dostoevsky and Céline.

"The psychological basis of the metropolitan type of individual," writes Georg Simmel in his essay, "The Metropolis and Mental Life," "consists in the intensification of nervous stimulation which results from the swift and uninterrupted change of outer and inner stimuli. . . . Lasting impressions . . . use up, so to speak, less consciousness than does the rapid crowding of changing images, the sharp discontinuity in the grasp of a single phrase, and the unexpectedness of onrushing impressions." Dostoevsky and Joyce best capture this experience in the novel, Baudelaire and Hart Crane in verse.

In *Crime and Punishment* Raskolnikov is assaulted by repeated impressions during his dazed wanderings through Petersburg. He walks along the street and sees a coachman beating his horse with gratuitous brutality. He watches a street entertainer grinding out a tune on a barrel organ, tries to strike up a nervous conversation with a stranger and frightens the man away. Another man approaches him and without warning mutters, "You are a murderer." At still another moment he notices a woman in front of him, "at first reluctantly and, as it were, with annoyance, and then more and more intently"; he supposes her a victim of a seduction; the terribleness of the city seems flaringly vivid to him. Each of these apparently stray incidents becomes a tonal equivalent to Raskolnikov's condition, and the seemingly chaotic business of the city is transformed into a map of the protagonist's turmoil.

V

Together with what I have called the myth of the modern city —enemy of man: pesthole, madhouse, prison—there appear in modern literature at least two other significant visions of urban life. The first is benign, fairly frequent among American writers who have grown up in a culture devoted to the virtues of the countryside. For Henry James the city serves as a token of the possibilities of a high civilization. The Paris of *The Ambassadors* is a mixture of Balzac's Paris (without Balzac's greasepaint, vulgarity, and financial delirium) and an American dream of a European City of Beauty. Paris becomes the shining gloss of man's history, the greatness of the past realized in monuments and manners. Paris stands for the Jamesian vision of a culture far gone in sophistication yet strangely pure, as if no dollar were exchanged there or loyalty betrayed. James was not a naif, he knew he was summoning a city of his desire; and in an earlier novel, *The American*, he had shown himself capable of presenting a Paris sinister and shabby. But now Paris has become the home of civilization, with the splendor of its history yielding the materials for his myth of idealization.

Quite as benign is Whitman's vision of New York. His poems do not capture the terrible newness of the industrial city, for that he does not really know. Whitman's city flourishes in harmony with surrounding forests and green; it figures modestly in the drama of democracy; there is still psychic and social roominess, so that this bohemian singing of the masses can easily knock about in the streets, a New World *flâneur*, without feeling crowded or oppressed. Between the noisy groping city and Whitman's *persona* as the Fraternal Stranger there are still large spaces, and this very spaciousness allows him to celebrate the good nature and easy style of his "camerados" in New York. Not many 19th-century writers can share that comfort.

The second and by far more influential vision of the city proceeds in a cultural line from Baudelaire through Eliot and then through Eliot's many followers. In the smudge of our time, this vision of the city has come to seem indistinguishable from the one I have attributed to the 19th-century masters; but it is distinguishable. There is in Baudelaire little of that recoil from the city about which I have spoken and little, if any, pastoral indulgence. He accepts the city as the proper stage for his being; he apprehends, better than anyone, the nervous currents that make cosmopolitan life exciting and destructive; he writes in the *Tableaux Parisiens* not only of ugliness and debauchery but also, in Proust's words, of "suffering, death, and humble fraternity." A famous passage celebrates the public concerts, "rich in brass," that "pour some heroism into the hearts of town dwellers."

Walter Benjamin notes that "Baudelaire placed the shock experience at the very center of his artistic work," and he remarks also on the relation between that "shock experience" and Baudelaire's "contact with the metropolitan masses . . . the amorphous crowd of passers-by" with whom he "becomes an accomplice even as he dissociates himself from them." In Baudelaire's poems shock serves more than a social end; it has to do with his struggle for a scheme of moral order, a struggle conducted, *in extremis*, through images of disorder. Baudelaire's fear is not, as others had already said before him, that the city is hell: his fear is that it is *not* hell, not even hell. His strategy of shock comes to seem a modernist terror-raid in behalf of classical resolution—not always so, of course, since poets can become secret sharers of the devils they grapple with. It hardly matters whether Baudelaire is seen as a figure of urban satanism or inverted Christianity; he moves in the orbits of both, emanating, in Mallarmé's wonderful line, "a protective poison that we must go on breathing even if we die of it." For Baudelaire, Paris embodies the fear of a life reduced from evil to the merely sordid, a life sinking into the triviality of nihilism.

This is the side of Baudelaire that Eliot appropriates in *The*

Waste Land: "Unreal City . . . I had not thought death had undone so many." Eliot lacks Baudelaire's capacity for surrendering himself to the quotidian pleasures of a great city, but he narrows the Baudelairean vision into something of enormous power, perhaps the single most powerful idea of our culture. Eliot's idea of the city has become assimilated to that of the great 19th-century writers, though it is imperative to insist on the difference between madhouse and wasteland, even prison and wasteland. Eliot's vision is then taken up, more and more slackly, by the writers of the last half-century, charting, mourning, and then—it is unavoidable—delectating in the wasteland. Life in the city is shackled to images of sickness and sterility, with a repugnance authentic or adorned; and what seems finally at the base of this tradition is a world view we might designate as *remorse over civilization.* "When one has a sense of guilt after having committed a misdeed," says Freud gloomily, "the feeling should . . . be called remorse." Our guilt, almost casual in its collective sedimentation, proceeds from the feeling that the whole work of civilization—and where is that to be found but in cities?—is a gigantic mistake. This remorse appears first as a powerful release of sensibility, in imaginative works of supreme value, and then as the clichés of *kitsch,* Madison Avenue modernism. The strength of the masters remains overwhelming, from Baudelaire to Eliot to Auden, as they fill their poems with forebodings of the collapse of cities, the crumbling of all man's works. Auden writes in "The Fall of Rome":

> *Private rites of magic send*
> *The temple prostitutes to sleep;*
> *All the literati keep*
> *An imaginary friend.*
>
> *Caesar's double-bed is warm*
> *As an unimportant clerk*
> *Writes* I DO NOT LIKE MY WORK
> *On a pink official form.*

And the Greek poet Cavafy writes about a city waiting, with impatient weariness, for the barbarians to take over:

> *What does this sudden uneasiness mean,*
> *And this confusion? (How grave the faces have become!)*

Why are the streets and squares rapidly emptying,
and why is everyone going back
home lost in thought?

Because it is night and the barbarians have not come,
and some men have arrived from the frontiers
and they say there are no barbarians any more
and now, what will become of us without barbarians?
These people were a kind of solution.

VI

The suspicion of the city and all it represents seems to run so deep in our culture that it would be impossible to eradicate it, even if anyone were naive enough to wish to. In its sophisticated variants it is a suspicion necessary for sanity. And perhaps, for all we know, it is a suspicion emblematic of some ineradicable tragedy in the human condition: the knowledge that makes us cherish innocence makes innocence unattainable.

In traditional pastoral, suspicion of the city is frequently contained through a discipline of irony proceeding through a sequence something like this: game of the shepherds, seriousness of the game, recognition of how limited are the uses of that seriousness. In modern literature, which can have but little interest in shepherds, there is a violence of response to the city which breaks past the discipline of irony—our experience demands that. But then, just as traditional pastoral suffers the corruptions of literalism, so must the modernist assault upon the city. How, we ask ourselves, can we bring together, in some complex balance of attitude, our commitment to the imaginative truth in what the modern writers show us about the city and our awareness that it may no longer be quite sufficient for us?

We are the children, or step-children, of modernism. We learned our *abc*'s lisping "alienation, bourgeoisie, catastrophe." As against those who brushed aside the 20th century, we were right in believing our age to be especially terrible, especially cursed, on the rim of apocalypse. But today loyalty to the tradition of modernism may require a rejection of its academic and marketplace heirs, and far more important, a questioning of its premises and values.

To deride the epigones of modernism who have reduced it

from a vision to a fashion, is no great intellectual risk. We should go farther and ask whether the masters must, in some sense, be held responsible for their corrupted followers, if only insofar as the corruption may point back to some little-noticed or half-hidden flaw in the world-view of the masters. Our problem then becomes to ask whether the visions of the great modernist writers can retain for us the moral urgency and emotional command they so powerfully exerted only a few decades ago.

Clearly this is not à question to be answered in a few paragraphs, though I have tried on an earlier occasion to indicate some opinions.[2] What matters, in behalf of a serious confrontation with our dominant literary heritage, is to move past (which is not to say abandon) both the authentic pieties we retain from an earlier moment and the false ones that have followed them.

I propose a hypothesis: We have reached the point in our cultural history where it seems both possible and useful to remove ourselves from the partisanship that cultural modernism evoked throughout the past century. Modernism is no longer threatened, nor in question. Its achievements are solid and lasting, its influence is incalculable. It is beginning to take a place in the development of Western culture somewhat like that which Romanticism can be said to have taken by the last two or three decades of the 19th century. *Modernism is beginning to become part of history*, and thereby, for those of us responsive to history, a complex of styles and values we can accept through the mediation of its classical works. Modernism can now enter our moral experience complicated by that awareness of historical distance which is a mark of a cultivated sensibility, and thereby it remains a crucial part of our experience, as Romanticism does too. But if we ask ourselves questions as to the truth of the vision of a Lawrence or an Eliot or a Yeats—and I have some awareness of how tricky such questions can be—then we are no longer likely, and younger people are certainly no longer likely, to answer them with an unbroken passion, that total assent or denial elicited by a cultural movement both contemporary and embattled.

If we lose much by no longer seeing modernism as a contemporary cultural presence, we may gain something too. We may

---

[2] In my essay, "The Culture of Modernism," *Decline of the New.*

gain a certain detached perspective upon its nature and its achievements, as in recent decades, through discovery, polemic, and
reassessment, we have been gaining such a perspective upon
the nature and achievements of Romanticism. And if we do
approach modernism in this way—as a major component of our
culture which the motions of history are transporting into that
segment of our experience we call the past—then we may discover
that a good many of our earlier enthusiasms will have to be
qualified. Not repudiated; qualified. The famous "revolutionary"
aspect of modernism may come to have for us an ambiguous
value: in part an authentic response to the terribleness of the
age and in part a nostalgia for a historically unlocatable and
morally dubious "organic past"; in part a profound engagement
with the inner nerves of city life and in part a snobbism of
the fastidious embraced by those who look down upon the commonplace desires of commonplace mankind; in part an assault
upon the calculation that lies at the heart of the bourgeois ethic
and in part a cruel dismissal of those fragmented solutions and
moderate comforts which it has become easy to dismiss as bourgeois. And we may then have to conclude that the now established
hostility to the idea of the city, which is one portion of the
modernist legacy, will no longer serve as well as in the past.
The vision of the city we inherit from Eliot and Baudelaire,
Céline and Brecht—with its ready nausea, packaged revulsion,
fixed estrangement—will have to be modulated and itself seen
as a historical datum. If we ask ourselves whether we accept
the ideas of Shelley or the vision of Blake, their very distance
allows us to answer with a sense of ironic qualification that
would be difficult to summon for an embattled contemporary.
Something of the sort should soon be true in regard to the great
figures of modernism.

To remain faithful to its tradition means to call it sharply
into question. Can we not, for example, say, yes, the city remains
the pesthole and madhouse, the prison and setting of spiritual
void that you have shown it to be, nevertheless we can no longer
be satisfied with this perception and this perception alone.

Nor is it as if we lack an inspiring model from within literary
modernism itself. No writer has portrayed the city with such
severity as James Joyce. Every assault that the modernist literary
tradition can make upon the city appears in *Ulysses*, magnified

in scope and feverish with intensity. Yet that assault is also, in *Ulysses*, transcended through a skeptical humaneness, a tolerance beyond tolerance, a recognition that man was not put on this earth to scratch his eyes out. Of all the writers who render the modern city, it is Joyce who engages in the most profound struggle with nihilism, for he sees it everywhere, in the newspaper office and the church, on the street and in the bed, through the exalted and the routine. Joyce, says Richard Ellmann, shows that "the world of cigars is devoid of heroism only to those who don't understand that Ulysses' spear was merely a sharpened stick . . . and that Bloom can demonstrate the qualities of man by word of mouth as effectively as Ulysses by thrust of spear." The theme of *Ulysses*, says Ellmann, is simply that "casual kindness overcomes unconscionable power." Does it? In reality? In Joyce's book? I hardly know but cherish Ellmann's sentence, as I believe Joyce would have too.

We may destroy our civilization, but we cannot escape it. We may savor a soured remorse at the growth of civilization, but that will yield us no large or lasting reward. There is no turning back: our only way is a radical struggle for the City of the Just.

The City of the Just . . . the phrase rings a little hollow right now, so far do we seem to be from it. Still, we shall create genuine cities, which means vital civilizations, or we shall perish. We shall create a high culture, serious and gay, or we shall sink into a rocklike, mainline stupor. Assault upon the city is now to be valued only when understood as the complex play of men who live in cities and would live nowhere else. It is too late for tents and sheep and lutes, or whatever surrogates we may invent. "Perhaps the best definition of the city in its higher aspects," says Lewis Mumford, "is that it is a place designed to offer the widest facilities for significant conversation."

So we must turn again, to build the Just City where men can be decent and humane and at ease, that ease Wallace Stevens speaks of:

> *One's grand flights, one's Sunday baths,*
> *One's tootings at the wedding of the soul*
> *Occur as they occur . . .*

And what will we do in the city? Take our Sunday baths, toot at "the wedding of the soul," read Colette, marvel at Balanchine, and with proper modulations of irony, realize the claims of pastoral, that indestructible artifice of the urban imagination. More than 400 years ago Barnaby Googe understood it all: "God sends me Vittayles for my nede, and I synge Care awaye."

ZOLA: THE POETRY
OF NATURALISM

EACH LITERARY GENERATION fashions its own blinkers and then
insists that they allow unimpeded vision. My generation grew
up with a mild scorn for the writers of naturalistic fiction who
flourished in the late nineteenth and early twentieth centuries.
Some of them we took to be estimable and others talented: we
did not mean to be unfair. Many naturalists had a strong feeling
for social justice, and if irrelevant to their stature as writers,
this seemed to their credit as men. Zola's great cry during the
Dreyfus Affair could still rouse us to admiration. His great cry
could stir even those of us who had reached the peak of sophistication where Flaubert was judged superior to Balzac, Stendhal
to Flaubert, and all three, it need hardly be said, to Zola—for
Zola was tendentious, Zola was rhetorical, Zola was coarse,
Zola knew little about the new psychology. With such wisdom,
we entered the world.

Everyone had of course read Zola earlier, in those years of
adolescence when all that matters in our encounter with a novel
is eagerly to soak up its experience. Then *Germinal* had stirred
us to the bone. But later we learned that literary judgment must
not be defiled by political ideas, and Zola, that damp and clumsy
bear of a novelist, became an object of condescension.

It was wrong, hopelessly wrong—like those literary fashions

of our own moment which two or three decades from now will also seem wrong. Reading *Germinal* again, and reading it with that emotional readiness which middle age can sometimes grant, I have been overwhelmed by its magnitude of structure, its fertility of imagination, its reenactment of a central experience in modern life.

Still, it should be admitted that if we have been unjust to Zola these last few decades, some of the blame must fall on his own shoulders. He talked too much, he pontificated too much about Literature and Science, he advertised himself too much. We are accustomed in America to bemoaning the redskin dumbness that overcomes so many of our writers when confronted with a need to theorize about their craft, and behind this complaint of ours there is often a naïve assumption that European writers have commonly possessed the range of culture we associate with, say, a Thomas Mann. It is not true, of course. What had Dickens or Balzac to say about the art of the novel? As for Zola, there can hardly have been a modern writer so confused about the work he was doing. Consider the mechanical scientism to which he clung with the credulousness of a peasant in a cathedral; the ill-conceived effort to show forces of heredity determining the lives of his characters (so that a reader of *Germinal* unaware of the other volumes in the Rougon-Macquart series can only with difficulty understand why Etienne Lantier should suddenly, without preparation or consequence, be called "a final degenerate offshoot of a wretched race"); the willful absurdity of such declarations as "the same determinism should regulate paving-stones and human brains"; the turgid mimicry with which Zola transposed the physiological theories of Dr. Claude Bernard into his *Le Roman expérimental*. About this side of Zola—the journalist preening himself as scientist-philosopher—Angus Wilson has remarked:

> . . . he must present his artistic method as though it were a solid intellectual scheme, lend that air of culture and education—of which in reality he knew himself to be deficient—to present as a logical theory what was in fact the form in which his individual genius expressed itself.

Yet we ought not to be too hasty in dismissing Zola's intellectual claims. His physiological determinism may now seem crude, but his sense of the crushing weight which the world can lower upon men remains only too faithful to modern experience, perhaps to all experience. If his theories about the naturalistic novel now seem mainly of historical interest, this does not mean that the naturalistic novel itself can simply be brushed aside. What remains vital in the naturalistic novel as Zola wrote it in France and Dreiser in America is not the theoretic groping toward an assured causality; what remains vital is the massed detail of the fictional worlds they establish, the patience—itself a form of artistic scruple—with which they record the suffering of their time.

In looking back upon the philosophical improvisations of those late nineteenth-century writers who were driven by conscience to surrender their Christian faith and then to improvise versions of rigid mechanism and spiritualized secularism, we like to suppose that their "ideas," once so earnestly studied by literary scholars, were little more than impediments they had to put aside, dead weight on the tissue of their work. You ignore Dreiser's pronouncements about "chemisms"; you agree with Huysman's remark about Zola: "Thank God he has not carried out in his novels the theories of his articles, which extol the infusion of positivism in art." There is of course something to be said for this view of the matter, but less than we commonly suppose, for the announced ideas behind a novel, even those thrust forward by the author as direct statement, ought not to be confused with the actual play of his intelligence. We may judge these announced ideas as tiresome or inert or a mere reflex of fashion; we may be irritated by their occasional appearance, like a mound of fossil, along the path of the narrative; yet in the novel itself the writer can be engaged in a play of intelligence far more supple than his formal claims lead us to suppose. A reductive determinism is what Zola flaunts, as when he places Taine's not very brilliant remark, "Vice and virtue are products like sugar and vitriol," on the title page of *Thérèse Raquin;* but a reductive determinism is by no means what controls *Germinal* and *L'Assommoir.* When we say that a work of literature "takes on a life of its own," we mean in part that the process of composition has brought textural surprises, perhaps fundamental shifts in perspective, which could not have been foreseen by studying the author's original intention.

Even among ideas we regard as mistaken, sharp discriminations must be made when trying to judge their literary consequences. A writer infatuated with one or another kind of psychic charlatanism is hard to take seriously. A writer drawn to the brutalities of fascism rouses a hostility that no creed of aesthetic detachment can keep from spilling over into our feelings about his work. But when writers like Zola and Hardy and Dreiser were attracted to the thought of Darwin and Huxley, or to popular versions of their thought, they were struggling with serious and urgent problems. They may have succumbed too easily to the "advanced ideas" of the moment—precisely the kind that date most quickly. Still, they were grappling with questions that gave them no rest, just as a half-century later Sartre and Camus would be grappling with the questions raised by existentialism, a school of philosophy that may not last much longer than deterministic scientism but which has nevertheless helped to liberate valuable creative powers. As Harry Levin[1] has said in partial defense of Zola:

> Surely no comparable man of letters, with the exception of Poe, had tried so hard to grasp the scientific imagination. His contemporary, Jules Verne, led the way for writers of science fiction to tinker with imaginary gadgets. Science for them has been an Aladdin's lamp, a magical fulfillment, an easy trick. . . . For Zola it was much tougher than that; it was behavior under pressure; and the literary experimenter was both the witness of the behavior and the gauge of the pressure.

Insofar as a writer's ideas enter his literary work, they matter less for their rightness or wrongness than for their seriousness. And at least with some writers, it is their seriousness which determines whether the ideas will release or block the flow of creative energies. Zola shared with many late nineteenth- and early twentieth-century writers a lust for metaphysics. Christianity might be rejected, Christianity might be remembered, but its force remained. Among those who abandoned it there was still a hunger for doctrine, a need for the assuagements of system.

---

[1] From Professor Levin's scholarly study of French nineteenth-century fiction, *The Gates of Horn*, I have borrowed several citations, and wish here to record my debt to his valuable book.

They wished to settle, or continuously to worry, the problem of their relation to the cosmos. To us this may seem a curious need, since we are more likely to be troubled by our relation to ourselves; but in the last half of the nineteenth century the lust for metaphysics was experienced by people whose moral and intellectual seriousness cannot be questioned.

One large tendency in nineteenth-century literature, coursing through but not confined to romanticism, is an impulse to spiritualize the world, to distribute the godhead among numberless grains of matter, so that in a new if less tidy way, purpose can be restored to the cosmos and the sequence of creation and recreation be made to replace the promise of immortality. Toward the end of the nineteenth century men like Zola could no longer accept transcendental or pantheist derivatives from Christianity, yet they wanted some principle of order by means of which to locate themselves in the universe; whereupon they proceeded to shift the mystery of the creation onto the lawfulness of the determined. What then frightened reflective people was something that we, in our benumbed age, seem to accept rather easily: the thought of a world without intrinsic plan or point.

The transfer from *telos* to causality, insofar as it preserved a premise of meaning, enabled writers like Zola and Dreiser to make their lives into a heroic discipline—heroic because radically at variance with the ideas they expounded. It was almost as if they were reenacting in secular charade the paradox of Calvinism: that a belief in the utter worthlessness of man, living in a world blinded by God's grace, could yet drive the faithful to zeal and virtue.

Zola went still further than those writers who transferred the dynamic of faith into a fixity of law. Like Balzac before him, he yielded to the brilliant impiety of transforming himself into a kind of god, a god of tireless fecundity creating his universe over and over again. The nineteenth-century novelist—Dickens or Balzac, Hardy or Zola—enacts in his own career the vitalism about which the thought of his age drives him to a growing skepticism. Zola's three or four great novels are anything but inert or foredoomed. He may start with notions of inevitability, but the current of his narrative boils with energy and novelty. *Germinal* ends with the gloom of defeat, but not a gloom predestined. There is simply too much appetite for experience in Zola, too much sympathy and solidarity with the struggles by which men try to declare themselves, too much hope for the generations always on the horizon and always promising to undo the wrongs of the past, for *Germinal* to become a mere reflex of a system of causality. Somehow—we have every reason to believe—Zola's gropings into the philosophy of determinism freed him to become a writer of energy, rebellion, and creation.

II

Germinal releases one of the central myths of the modern era: the story of how the dumb acquire speech. All those at the bottom of history, for centuries objects of manipulation and control, begin to transform themselves into active subjects, determined to create their own history.

Now we cannot say that this myth has gained universal acceptance in our culture, nor that those of us who register its moral claims can do so with the unquestioning credence and mounting awe we suppose characteristic of men in ancient cultures. Still, we might remember that insofar as we know Greek myth through Greek drama, we know it mediated by individual artists, and with the passage of time, mediated in directions increasingly skeptical. The myth in *Germinal*—if we agree, however hesitantly, to call it a myth—is one that may have some parallels in earlier cultures, but it takes its formative energies from the French Revolution. It is the myth of the people and more particularly, of the proletariat. They who had merely suffered and at times erupted into blind rebellion; they who had been prey to but not part of society; they who had found no voice in the cultures of the past—they now emerge from the sleep of history and begin the task of a collective self-formation. This, of course, is a schematized version of historical reality, or at least a perspective on historical reality—which may indeed be the distinctiveness of whatever modern myths we have. Where traditional myths appear to us as transhistorical, a frieze of symbolic representation, our own take their very substance from the materials of history, magnifying and rendering heroic the actions of men in time. Some idea of this kind may have led Thomas Mann to write that "in Zola's epic," made up as it is of events taken from everyday life, "the characters themselves are raised up to a plane above that of everyday life."

The myth of *Germinal* as I have been sketching it is close to the Marxist view of the dynamics of capitalism, but to yield ourselves to Zola's story is not necessarily to accept the Marxist system. Zola himself does not accept it. At crucial points he remains a skeptic about the myth that forms the soul of his action. His skepticism is not really about the recuperative powers of the miners, for it is his instinctive way of looking at things that he should see the generations crowding one another, pushing for life space, thrusting their clamor onto the world. His skepticism runs deeper. Zola sees the possibility that in the very emergence of solidarity—that great and terrible word for which so many have gone smiling to their death!—there would be formed, by a ghastly dialectic of history, new rulers and oppressors: the Rasseneurs, the Plucharts, and even the Lantiers of tomorrow, raised to the status of leaders and bureaucrats, who would impose their will on the proletariat. Zola does not insist that this must happen, for he is a novelist, not a political theoretician. What he does is to show in the experience of the Montsou workers the germ of such a possibility. As it celebrates the greatest event of modern history, the myth of emergence contains within itself the negation of that greatness.

(Is it not this note of prescience, this intuition all too painfully confirmed by recent history, which explains why Georg Lukacs —the east European Marxist critic who always starts with heterodox insights and ends with orthodox dogmas—should attack Zola's work as mechanistic and passive, lacking in revolutionary dynamism? We have here a confrontation between a writer's honesty and an ideologue's tendentiousness, between Zola's myth of a collective entry into consciousness and Lukacs's pseudomyth of "socialist realism." The true myth is a story arising from the depths of common experience; the pseudomyth, a manipulation of that story in behalf of a false collective declaring itself the "vanguard of the proletariat.")

At the center of the novel is the mine. Dramatic embodiment of exploitation, the mine nevertheless makes possible the discipline through which to overcome exploitation. But for the moment, man's nature still bows to his history, personal need

to the workings of the market. The mine has a "natural" awesome-
ness, with its crevices and alleys, depths and darkness: its symbolic power arises organically, spontaneously, and not as a willed
imposition of the writer. And then, in a stroke that does bear
the mark of will, Zola creates an astonishing parallel to the miners.
The mine-horses share the misery of the men, but without the
potential for motivated rebellion; the mine-horses represent, as
a gruesome foreshadowing and with an expressionist grossness
that defeats critical scruples, what the men may yet accept or
sink to.

The mine is voracious and unappeasable, a physical emblem
of the impersonality of commodity production. It "seemed evil-
looking, a hungry beast crouched and ready to devour the world."
It "kept devouring men . . . always ravenous, its giant bowels
capable of digesting an entire nation." But this suggestion of
a force bursting out of the control of its creators gains its strength
not merely from the intrinsic properties of the mine. Here Zola
does come close to the Marxist notion that men must beware
of fetishizing their predicaments; they must recognize that not
in mines or factories lie the sources of their misery but in the
historically determined relations between contending classes.
And here surely historical associations come into play, associations which even the least literate reader is likely to have with
mining—a major industry of early industrialism, notorious for
its high rate of exhaustion and accident. As always in *Germinal*,
the mythic and symbolic are of the very substance of the historical. And thereby Zola can fill out his myth with the evidence
of circumstantiality. The more he piles up descriptions of the
mine's tunnels, shafts, timbering, airlessness, and dampness, the
more are we prepared to see it as the setting for the apocalypse
with which the book reaches its climax.

In a fine piece some years ago William Troy remarked that
the great scene in which Etienne and Catherine are trapped in
the mine

> . . . brings us back to an atmosphere and a meaning at least
> as old as the story of Orpheus and Eurydice. For what is the
> mine itself but a reintegration of the Hades-Hell symbol? The
> immediate and particular social situation is contained within the
> larger pattern of a universal recrudescence . . . . Etienne emerges

from his journey underground to *la vita nuova* of his own and of social experience.

The Orpheus-Eurydice motif is there, Etienne experiences a recrudescence, though of a somewhat ambiguous kind, and the mine is surely the symbolic center of the book. Yet we should be clear as to how Zola achieves these effects. Zola controls his narrative with one overriding end in mind, and that is to show not the way men are swallowed by their work (surely not new) nor how a hero can emerge healed from the depths (also not new) but the gradual formation of a collective consciousness. When Maheu, that superbly drawn worker, begins to speak to the manager, "the words were coming of themselves, and at moments he listened to himself in surprise, as though some stranger within him were speaking." The stranger is his long-buried self, and this transfiguration of Maheu is at least as morally significant as that of the individual protagonist gaining access to self-knowledge in the earlier nineteenth-century novel.

Etienne reads, Maheu speaks, La Maheude cries out: everything is changed. Gathering their strength and for a time delirious with fantasies of freedom, almost childlike in the pleasures of their assertiveness, the workers become what Marx called a class for itself. And then, with his uncanny gift for achieving mass effects through individual strokes, Zola begins to individualize his characters. He does this not to approximate that fragmentized psychology we associate with nineteenth-century fiction but toward the end of preparing the characters for their new roles: Etienne in the pride and exposure of leadership, Maheu in the conquest of manhood, La Maheude as the voice of ancient grievance, and even the children, led by the devilish Jeanlin, who in their debauchery release the spontaneous zest that the overdisciplined life of the miners has suppressed.

The strike becomes the central action, and thereby the myth of emergence takes on the sharp edge of conflict. The workers are shown in their rise to a noble solidarity and their fall to a brutal mob—better yet, in the ways the two, under intolerable stress, become all but indistinguishable. ("Do not flatter the working class nor blacken it," Zola told himself in notes for *L'Assommoir.*) And nothing is more brilliant than Zola's intuition—it speaks for his powers of insinuating himself beneath the skin of the miners—that after the horrible riot with which Part Five closes, he sees the men continuing their strike, digging in with a mute fatalism, "a great somber peacefulness," which rests far less on expectations of victory than on a common yielding to the pathos of standing and starving together. Defeat comes, and demoralization too, but only after Zola has charted with a precise objectivity the rhythms of struggle, rhythms as intrinsically absorbing for the novelist (and at least as difficult to apprehend) as those of the individual psyche in turmoil.

Again, it should be stressed that the myth Zola employs is not the vulgar-Marxist notion of an inevitable victory or of a victory-in-defeat ending with noble resolves for the future. True, he shows as no other European novelist before him, the emergence of a new historical force, and he reveals the conflict that must follow; but its outcome remains uncertain, shadowy, ambiguous. The more serious versions of Marxism speak of historical choice: freedom or barbarism. It is a choice allowing for and perhaps forming the substance of tragedy. *Germinal* shares that view.

III

A work of modern literature may employ a myth and perhaps even create one, as I think *Germinal* does, but it cannot satisfy its audience with a composed recapitulation of a known, archetypal story. With theme it must offer richness of variation, often of a radical kind, so as slyly to bring into question the theme itself. The hieratic does not seem a mode easily accessible to modern literature. We want, perversely, our myths to have a stamp of the individual, our eternal stories to bear a quiver of nervous temporality.

The picture Zola draws of Montsou as a whole, and of Montsou as a microcosm of industrial society, depends for its effectiveness mainly on the authority with which he depicts the position of the miners. Just as the novel is a genre that gains its most solid effects through accumulation and narrative development, so the action of Zola's book depends on his command of an arc of modern history. If he can persuade us that he sees this experience with coherence and depth, then we will not be excessively troubled by whatever intellectual disagreements we may have with him or by our judgment that in particular sections of the novel he fails through heavy exaggeration and lapses of taste. Two lines out of tune in a sonnet can spoil our pleasure, since a short lyric depends for its success on verbal unity; but in a novel whole episodes can be out of tune without necessarily spoiling our pleasure, since an extended prose fiction depends mainly on such large-scale effects as narrative thrust and character development.

Again we reach an interpenetration of commanding myth and historical material—what I take to be Zola's great achievement in *Germinal*. A stranger arrives, slightly removed from the workers because of superior intellect, yet required to enter their lives and ready to share their troubles. So far, the pattern of the story is not very different from that of much fiction composed earlier in the nineteenth century. But then comes a radical shift; the stranger, now on the way to being a leader, remains at the center of the book, but his desires and reflections do not constitute its central matter. What engages us primarily is the collective experience of the miners, the myth of their emergence. In Part Five of *Germinal*, both the most original and the most exciting portion of the novel, this entry into consciousness is shown in its two-sidedness, and with a complexity of tone that unites passionate involvement and dispassionate removal. In his notes for the book Zola understood that he must remain faithful to his story as archetype:

> To get a broad effect I must have my two sides as clearly contrasted as possible and carried to the very extreme of intensity. So that I must start with all the woes and fatalities which weigh down the miners. Facts, not emotional pleas. The miner must be shown crushed, starving, a victim of ignorance, suffering with his children in a hell on earth—but not persecuted, for the bosses are not deliberately vindictive—*he is simply overwehelmed by the social situation as it exists.* On the contrary I must make the bosses humane so long as their direct interests are not threatened; no point in foolish tub-thumping. The worker is the victim of the facts of existence —capital, competition, industrial crises.

For this perception to be transformed into a dramatic action, Zola relies mainly on the narrative increment that follows from his myth of the speechless and the symbolic suggestiveness of the mine. In saying this I don't mean to imply that everything which occurs in the novel is necessary or appropriate. The narrative is frequently flawed by cheap and lurid effects. Zola, as someone has remarked, had an overwhelming imagination but only an uncertain—and sometimes a corrupted—taste. That the riot of the miners should be a terrifying event seems entirely right; that it should end with the ghastly *frisson* invented by Zola is a sign of his weakness for sensationalism. Zola tries hard to present his middle-class characters, the Hennebeaus and Grégoires, with some objectivity and even sympathy, but he usually fails. Not, I think, for the reason William Troy gives: ". . . the inherent unsuitability of naturalism, a system of causality based on quasi-scientific principles, to the practice of literature." I doubt that local failures in a novel are ever to be traced so directly to philosophical conceptions. Zola fails because in this novel he is not interested in such people at all. They are there because his overall scheme demands it, because he feels an obligation to "fill out the picture." Sensing as much, we read these inferior portions with a certain tolerance, assuaged by the likelihood that further great scenes with the miners lie ahead. The mediocre intervals come to serve as "rests" helping Zola create or regather suspense. M. Hennebeau, the mine manager, is a partial exception, if only because he is a figure of power and power is always fascinating for Zola. Still, the subplot of Hennebeau's personal unhappiness and his envy of what he takes to be the miners' unsoiled virility is obviously weak—just how weak one can see by comparing it to D. H. Lawrence's treatment of similar material. And again, the immersion of Etienne and Catherine in the mine, once the strike has been lost, is both a scene of considerable power and a scene marred by Zola's lack of discipline when he has the body of Chaval, the girl's former lover, float horribly up to them in the darkness. Zola does not know when to stop.

To notice such flaws can be damaging, and to write as if *Germinal* were no more than the sum of local incidents could be a strategy for dismissing the book entirely. But this seems a poor way of dealing with a novel. *Germinal*, like many works of fiction, depends upon effects that are larger, more gross, and less open to isolated inspection than picking out scenes of weakness would suggest; it depends upon the large-muscled rhythms of the narrative as a whole. We are dealing here with a writer of genius who, in both the quality of his imagination and the occasional wantonness of his prose, can sometimes be described as decadent. One remembers T. S. Eliot's remark that Dickens was "a decadent genius," a remark accurate enough if the noun is stressed at least as much as the modifier. The decadence of Zola, which has points of similarity to that of Dickens, comes through in the excesses of local episodes, the vulgarities of particular paragraphs, the flushed rhetoric with which Zola seeks to "reinforce" material that has already been presented with more than enough dramatic vitality. The genius comes through in the mythic-historical sweep of the narrative as a whole. And at least this once, Zola himself knew exactly what he was doing:

> Everyone in the world [he wrote] analyzes in detail nowadays, I must react against this through the solid reaction of masses, of chapters, through the logic, the thrust of the chapters, succeeding each other like superimposed blocks; by the breath of passion, animating all, flowing from one end to another of the work.

If what I have been saying has validity, it follows that there will also be frequent episodes of brilliance—else how could the novelist achieve his large rhythms of narration? And there are, of course, such episodes. Two kinds may be distinguished: those persuading us of Zola's authority as imaginative historian (substantiating detail) and those persuading us of his psychological penetration into a given moment of the action (illuminating detail).

The first kind is to be found mainly in his treatment of the miners at the peak of crisis. Etienne reading a Belgian socialist weekly, hastily and poorly absorbing its contents, seeking to make up for years of waste as he is "gripped by the uneducated man's methodless passion for study" and then overcome by "the dull dread that he had shown himself unequal to the task"—all this bears the thick circumstantiality of the actual. Zola knew the kind of men who were drawn to socialist politics: not merely learned bourgeois intellectuals like Marx and Kautsky, but self-educated workers like Bebel, straining with ambition and stumbling into knowledge. This command of his material is shown even more subtly in the portrayal of the inner relationships among his three radicals: Rasseneur, the most cautious and experienced, clearly on the way to becoming a classical social democrat;

Souvarine, also a classical figure, though of the anarchist-terrorist kind who declares the need "to destroy everything . . . no more nations, no more governments, no more property, no more God or religion" and then to return to "the primitive and formless community,"[2] and Etienne, the sincere unformed worker, open to a wide range of possibilities but determined—his aspiring intellectuality prods his ambition—to make a place for himself on the stage of history.

The second and more striking kind of detail shows Zola's imagination at work somewhat more freely, releasing incidents which do not depend directly on the overall design of the novel. On the simplest level there is the pathos of the mine girl Mouquette, hopelessly generous with all she has (her body to the men, her affection to almost anyone, her bared bottom to the strikebreakers), who offers Etienne a dozen cold potatoes to still the hunger of the Maheu household. It is a trifle, but from such trifles affecting novels are made. On a level hard to apprehend in strictly rational terms, there is Etienne finding himself a place to hide, after the riot, in one of the hated mines. But the greatest of such imaginative strokes concerns the strange old Bonnemort, introduced at the outset as a ghost of a man embodying the exhaustion of the workers' lives. He has nothing to say, he is barely alive, until at the strike meeting, amid the predictably rousing speeches

> . . . everybody was surprised to see old Bonnemort standing on the tree trunk and trying to make himself heard. . . . No doubt he was giving way to one of those sudden fits of babbling that would sometimes stir up the past so violently that old memories would rise from his depths and flow from his lips for hours. It had become very quiet, and everybody listened to the old man, so ghostly pale in the moonlight; as he was talking about things that had no obvious connection with the discussion, long stories

[2] The reader of *Germinal* may be tempted to see Souvarine as a remarkable anticipation of certain contemporary figures, and indeed he does talk as if he belonged to an esoteric New Left faction. But it should be remembered that by the late nineteenth century the anarchist-terrorist, often a popular stereotype, had become a familiar presence in European culture. Zola was here drawing upon a fund of common material, and what is notable about Souvarine is not the conception behind him but the detachment, even the ironic coolness, with which he is presented.

that nobody could understand, their astonishment increased. He
spoke of his youth, told of his two uncles who had been crushed
to death at Le Voreux, then went on to the pneumonia that had
carried off his wife. Through it all, however, he never lost hold
of his one idea: things had never been right and they never would
be right.

Without rhetorical strain, this passage summons the losses
of the past, the whole unreckoned waste that forms our history.
The mode is grotesque, but for readers with a measure of historical imagination, Zola achieves something far beyond the limits
of what that descriptive usually suggests.

IV

Zola's style aspires toward a rich and heavy impasto rather
than toward a lucid line-drawing, and it is often marred by
excess. In *Germinal* the writing is nevertheless effective at two
points: first, the passages describing the mine with that wary
respect for the power of the actual a novelist must have, and
second, the episodes in which he evokes the surge of conflict
and the passions of enraged men. In these episodes the prose
can be extremely effective, combining mass and speed—as long
as Zola stays with his central purpose, which is to depict the
sensations of men who have thrown off the discipline of society
but not yet discovered the discipline of self. Nor need we succumb
to any version of "the imitative fallacy"—that in its internal
qualities a style must reflect the matter it is trying to convey—in
order to recognize at least some correspondences as proper to
the relation between style and subject. One does not write about
the collapse of a mine in the style of James analyzing an exquisite
heroine.

Zola achieves the effect of speed, but not the light or nervous
speed of a Stephen Crane or an Isaac Babel. Especially in Part
Five of the novel, his style is that of a rumbling and heavy
speed—a leaden speed. The writing is rarely nimble or graceful;
the sentences are weighted with qualifiers and prepositional
phrases, as well as with accumulating clauses which repeat and
magnify the matter of their predecessors. Admittedly, this prose
is highly rhetorical: it employs organic metaphors of anger,
release, and cataclysm ("Nature," says Zola, "is associated with

our griefs"), and it depends heavily on Zola's hoarse and rasping
voice. For what he is trying to do seems decidedly risky, even
from the vantage-point of eighty-five years later: he is giving
dramatic embodiment to a collective as it disintegrates into a
mob, and since he must keep his attention mainly on the group,
which has of course no individuality of consciousness or will,
he finds himself forced to speak in his own voice. That, in the
actuality of composition, is the paradox the novelist must face
when he tries to dramatize the conduct of a group. His effort
to create an action of extreme objectivity, a plot of collective
behavior, leads the novelist to a style of extreme subjectivity in
which he finds himself driven to "impersonate" the group. At
its worst, this kind of writing can seem willed—an effort to
do for the action through rhetoric what film-makers try to do
for their stories through music. At its best, the writing has a
coarse strength and even splendor—what might be called the
poetry of naturalism.

Still, it would be foolish to claim for Zola that his prose can
yield the kind of sentence-by-sentence pleasure that can be had
from the prose of a writer like James or Flaubert. Zola is often
careless as a stylist, sometimes wanton, occasionally cheap. His
trouble, however, is not that his prose lacks nicety of phrasing
or epigrammatic neatness; it is that he does not content himself
with a utilitarian plainness but must reach out for the ornamental
and exalted, seeking through rhetorical fancy-work to establish
his credentials as a literary man. Like other half-educated novelists and journalists of the late nineteenth century, Zola was painfully susceptible to those charms of the "literary" that he claimed
to dismiss.

His style, like almost everything else in *Germinal*, is interesting
mainly when considered in the large. One then encounters a
phenomenon I do not pretend to understand, and which seems
an essential mystery of literature. For long portions of the novel
Zola yields himself entirely to the passions of the miners,
and his prose becomes strongly, even exorbitantly, passionate.
We are swept along, as we are meant to be, by the surge of
men in revolt; we are with them, the starving and the hunted,
and the language heaves and breaks, sweeping across us with
torrents of rhetoric. But let us not be frightened by that word

"rhetoric": it bears the strength, not only the weakness, of Zola's novel.

Rhetoric, yes; but a rhetoric which accompanies and sustains a remarkably strong evocation. The passion Zola pours out finds its match, its justification, in the incidents he imagines. Yet, as we read into the depths of the book, we grow aware that there is another Zola, one who draws back a little, seeing the whole tragedy as part of an eternal rhythm of struggle and decision. This Zola, as if writing from some timeless perch, is finally dispassionate, withdrawn from his own commitments, and capable of a measure of irony toward the whole human enterprise. Zola the partisan and Zola the artist: for those who like their "commitment" straight such ambivalence is detestable. But I take it to be a sign of Zola's achievement. If there has ever been a novel concerning which one might forgive a writer his unmodulated passions it is *Germinal*; yet precisely here Zola's "scientism" proves to be an unexpected advantage, enabling him to achieve an aesthetic distance that gives the book its ultimate austerity.

There is still another doubleness of response in *Germinal*. Hardly a Zola critic has failed to note the frequency with which images of fecundity occur in the book—repeated scenes in which, along and beyond the margin of his central narrative, Zola displays the unplanned and purposeless creativity of existence. Henry James, in his essay on Zola, remarks:

> To make his characters swarm, and to make the great central thing they swarm about "as large as life," portentously, heroically big, that was the task he set himself very nearly from the first, that was the secret he triumphantly mastered.

Now for many nineteenth-century novelists, this "swarming" can be a source not merely of narrative energy but also of a mindless and pseudoreligious sentimentalism. Everyone has encountered it as a special kind of fictional cant: the generations come, the generations go, etc. Asserted without irony, such declamations often constitute a kind of psychic swindle, convenient enough for novelists who fear the depressing logic of their own work or who need some unearned lilt in their final pages. That Zola does approach this kind of sentimentalism seems beyond doubt, but again and again he draws back into a baffled stoicism, evading the trap his romantic heritage has set for him. "A black avenging army" is "germinating in the furrows"; "soon this germination would sunder the earth." But even as such sentiments fill Zola's final pages there is no simple assurance—indeed, no assurance of any kind. Despite the sense of a swarming procreation which keeps the race alive, Zola ends on a note of anguish; he does not propose an easy harmony between the replenishments of nature and the desires of men. Etienne, clumsily balancing his idealism and his ambition, goes out into the world. To one reader at least, he enters neither upon personal triumph nor the "final conflict" promised by the dialectic of history, but upon a journey into those treacherous regions of the unknown where sooner or later all men find themselves.

THE STRUGGLE
FOR CREATION
A View of Dostoevsky's Notebooks

FOR SOME YEARS NOW, Professor Edward Wasiolek has been issuing, under the imprint of the University of Chicago Press, the Notebooks Dostoevsky kept while composing his major novels. The original Russian volumes first came out in the Soviet Union during the thirties; scrupulously edited by Wasiolek, the English versions contribute enormously to our understanding of Dostoevsky's genius, and in some important respects, require us to change received notions as to its development. I know of nothing else that shows a great writer so fully, painfully and—it's no mere rhetoric to say—heroically at work as do these Notebooks. Once and for all they should destroy the widespread notion that Dostoevsky was some sort of genius-desperado, an inspired madman who, between epileptic fits and gambling orgies, dashed off chapters of his novels for serial publication. The Notebooks make it clear, on the contrary, that Dostoevsky was a highly self-conscious craftsman, doggedly pursuing the true and false (mostly false) leads his imagination yielded him and worrying his unclarified conceptions and glimmers of characterization with the feverish energy that marks the novels themselves.

The Notebooks for *The Possessed* are, for me, especially absorbing, since they seem distinctively "Dostoevskyian," repeatedly approaching the fierce intellectual drama that comprises the heart of his fiction. Among Dostoevsky's four masterpieces, *The Possessed*, with its buffoonish phantasmagoria of radical conspiracies and metaphysical improvisations, seems the most urgent; there is even a danger, mostly to be resisted, of reading this novel as if it were written about the chaos of our own day. It is also, of all Dostoevsky's novels, the most problematic: it has the richest but least accessible group of characters, the most abandoned display of his jolly-vicious humor, and the most insistent jumble of everything one both admires and deplores in his thought. It is an ill-made novel, mostly because the two ideas with which Dostoevsky starts out—the Life of the Great Sinner, transformed into the story of Prince Stavrogin, and the conspiracy of the Russian revolutionist Nechaev, transformed into the story of Peter Verhovensky—were never completely integrated, either in his own mind or in the book itself. With a bewildering wealth of detail, the Notebooks show Dostoevsky laboring at, modifying and recasting his impressions in order to satisfy both his needs as ideologist and his self-demands as artist.

Dostoevsky wrote most of *The Possessed* between August 1869 and summer 1871, while wandering across Europe from one resort town to another. It was a time of misery for him. He was heavily in debt. He was in poor health: epileptic fits, shortness of breath, hemorrhoids. "Paris," remarks Professor Wasiolek, "is under siege by the Prussians, and Dostoevsky is under siege by penury, delays, nonunderstanding editors, and lost letters." Occasionally he breaks past the impersonal surface of the Notebooks with a thrust of complaint, as in this entry for June 1870:

> *The weather keeps changing; it is rainy and relatively cold. The money has not arrived, and I don't know if I'll get any at all. I've completed the fifth chapter of my novel.*

> *. . . at night (two nights in a row) I can hardly work: the blood rushes to my head, I feel torpid, sleepy, I'm afraid of the bad consequences of working at night (a stroke, or something of that kind?).*

He studies his physical disease with the harsh scrutiny which, in the novels, he reserves for moral and psychological disorders:

> *The fit occurred during an almost full moon. . . . I did not feel it, awoke after 8 o'clock, with a feeling that I had had a fit. I had a headache*

and my body was aching all over. N.B. Altogether, the aftereffects of my fits, i.e., nervousness, shortness of memory, an intensified and foggy, quasi-contemplative state, persists longer now than in previous years. They used to pass after three days, while now it may take six. Especially at night, by candlelight, an indefinite hypochondriac melancholy, and as if a red, bloody shade (not color) upon everything. Almost impossible to work these days.

But he does work. He rewrites endlessly, trapped in the maze of his unclarified intentions and hoping to break out of it by the sheer act of repetition. In January 1871 he complains that he has revised his novel twenty times! That same month he begins to serialize it in a St. Petersburg monthly, where it will run a full two years: a work paid for with blood, bone, nerves.

How did he begin? When a great writer plans a novel of major scope which he intends as an assault on the disorders of modern life, how does he go about arranging his materials? How does he integrate his ideological preconceptions with his projected action? And how does he learn to accept the risks of seeing his story take on a life of its own, apart from and even in opposition to his first intentions?

The answer, at least for Dostoevsky, seems to be that he works in a fever of imaginative chaos and for a time yields himself to—in fact, deliberately enlarges the scope of—that chaos. He subjects his fixed ideas and ready-made novelistic formulas to the shattering pressures of his imagination, so that at first the chosen result seems a breakdown of his entire scheme. Only later, through a gradual reconstruction of character and plot, does he reassert the rationality of intent and the claims of discipline. Everything he has brought to this struggle for creation is transformed but not, as the cliché has it, "beyond recognition" or even beyond the authority of his will; it is transformed from static to dynamic, from idea to image, from notation to vignette. Then vignettes move into incidents and incidents fall into place as elements of a coherent action, yet always with character, rather than plot, at the center of his awareness. It may be argued that Dostoevsky's novels conform to Aristotle's formula, but he himself works consciously against it.

The writer—let us be more cautious and say, this writer—begins with a *donnée*, as Henry James called it: an anecdote overheard, an item in the paper, a figure observed or imagined. The *donnée* matters, however, only insofar as it leads him to *discover* his true subject. In the very course of submitting himself to the chaos, even the blockage, of his imagination, Dostoevsky nevertheless retains, with a completely imperious will, the ideological bias with which he began.

In all his novels Dostoevsky starts with two seemingly unrelated elements: a pressing ideological purpose, such as his assault on the superman cult in *Crime and Punishment*, and an intrigue envisioned, as in the early Notes for *The Possessed*, through embarrassingly trite and melodramatic images (the Prince, the Usurer, the Beauty locked into a triangle). The ideological purpose recharges his ability to work; in the Notes, as he develops plot schemes and sketches for characters, this purpose seems slowly to be loosened and thereby to allow more freedom to the foreplay of creation; yet it never does relax entirely, since for Dostoevsky pure art, the novel as game or caprice, is a frivolity that must always yield to a *Weltanschauung*. Salvation hovers across every phrase.

Very much like Balzac, Dostoevsky turns habitually to stock devices, the most weary clichés of nineteenth-century melodrama. Such conventions—triangles, murders, family conflicts —are useful to the novelist, providing him with a protective casing in which to nourish his personal vision. Without these rituals of convention, there might not be individual sensibility. But the stock devices of melodrama have a deeper use for Dostoevsky: they correspond not to the everyday-ness of human existence but to a kind of shorthand morality, yielding versions of disaster and fatality with which to order the flux and dribble of experience. Melodrama is essential to Dostoevsky, as the "objective correlative" for his sense of menace inherent in the nature of things. To his heterodox Christian imagination, it serves as emblem of the evil conditioned by the very presence of matter and flesh. And as a reduced or petrified morality making everything too sharp and clear, melodrama gives Dostoevsky a base from which to move toward his own radical variants of moral exploration and judgment.

The Notes begin, then, with creaky outlines of an intrigue dominated by the familiar Dostoevskyan heroine, the beautiful, haughty, icy-hot Byroness who keeps searching for sensation and salvation, or better yet, for each through the other. Soon, however, she fades into the background: Dostoevsky is after bigger game. The loose-tongued progressive intellectual (in the novel, Stepan Trofimovitch Verhovensky) appears as Granovsky, a real-life Russian professor whom Dostoevsky despised. Next comes the revolutionary nihilist who will be at the center of *The Possessed*, Peter Verhovensky, dimly anticipated at this point and cast only in his generic role as The Student. What to do with The Student Dostoevsky does not yet know; he sees him as handy for the romantic intrigue and as a spokesman for detested ideas, but not yet with the full ominous brilliance, as the central agent of disorder, he will assume in the novel.

In December 1869 Dostoevsky reads in a newspaper the story of an obscure Russian revolutionist, Nechaev, leader of an underground cell who had murdered one of his comrades, Ivanov, seemingly out of fear that Ivanov would betray the group but also in order to bind his co-conspirators with a chain of guilt. The incident makes a shattering impression on Dostoevsky, providing him with an action which for the first time can dramatize his political bias. Now he must go a step farther and, while elaborating the character of Nechaev-Peter Verhovensky, find a way of connecting the political theme with the romantic intrigue to which he stubbornly clings. I doubt that Dostoevsky really makes this connection very persuasive in the novel itself, but it is a book so feverish and brilliant that one can easily be distracted from its flaws.

Even as Nechaev comes quickly to life in the Notes—through a marvelous set of speeches that establish him more as a voice than a person—Dostoevsky remains trapped in his struggle to develop a coherent plot. Again and again he tries to bludgeon his way through, simply by developing his plot as pure intrigue; but some profound instinct of self-criticism steadily frustrates the effort. Intrigue, in Dostoevsky's novels, must always be at the ultimate service of an idea; and indeed—paradox as it may seem—it is precisely his tendentiousness which finally drives him to complicate his action. So eager is he to do in the radicals, he must first bring them to incomparable life. He connects Nechaev with the Beauty, preparing thereby a compact of destruction; he hits upon the idea of presenting Nechaev as the son of Granovsky (in the novel, Peter the son of Stepan

Trofimovitch), so as to demonstrate the supposed lineal descent of murderous nihilism from sentimental liberalism.

Yet something is missing, something wrong. With the hindsight of a century we can see that what is missing is Dostoevsky's special use of the double plot yoking melodrama and metaphysics. Nechaev, Granovsky, the Beauty, and all the complications rehearsed in the Notes provide in embryo the familiar Dostoevskyan action, even a portion of the familiar Dostoevskyan setting; but not yet the Dostoevskyan tone. His motivating idea seems still too mundane, too close to ordinary social reality; the imaginative transposition into his distinctive world has not yet been completed.

For this to happen, at least two more novelistic elements are needed, the full timbre of the Dostoevskyan voice and the clarification of what he means to do with Prince Stavrogin, the Great Sinner.

Professor Wasiolek tells us that he

> *first conceived of "The Life of a Great Sinner"* . . . *about December 1868, and then reconceived it and worked on it between December 1869 and May 1870.* . . . *Dostoevsky planned to take his hero in the [eighteen] thirties and forties through the suffering of childhood, boarding school, flight and complicity in murder, life in a monastery* . . . *exposure to the world and interest in various contemporary political and philosophical movements such as atheism and positivism, and, finally, after much sin, cruelty, suffering and ambivalent feeling, to a religious crisis and regeneration in love, humility, faith and Christ.*

> . . . *the "great Sinner" is characterized by tumultuous passions and contradictory drives. He attempts to find what he is looking for in debauchery, in the accumulation of wealth, in science, art and letters, and in the monastery.* . . . *What drives him most of all is a desire for despotic power over others.*

The Stavrogin we know from *The Possessed*, however, is far more original and enigmatic a figure than the familiar Dostoevskyan type sketched out by Wasiolek. Nothing gave Dostoevsky more trouble than the shadowy Stavrogin and it has been a constant subject for debate among his critics whether Stavrogin does in fact cohere into an achieved character. At the beginning Dostoevsky sees Stavrogin's function in the novel, but not Stavrogin as a more or less autonomous being:

> *Stavrogin flings himself into a spree of debauchery in a terrible fit of rage and pride.* THAT IS THE MAIN THING.

> *In his fantastic vagaries, boundless dreams, to the point of dethroning God and putting himself in His stead . . .*

With the other characters Dostoevsky moves rapidly into fragments of representation, but almost until the end Stavrogin resists all efforts at focusing. Dostoevsky sees him, but at a distance; knows he is a crucial figure, but not quite why. Even abstractly, Dostoevsky has great trouble in explaining to himself the growing sense he has that Stavrogin is a creature new to his imaginative universe. In the Notes for late 1869 and early 1870 he assigns Stavrogin long-winded speeches, bristling with the rhetoric of sin and salvation; but this is all wrong, for the Stavrogin we know in the novel is beyond rhetoric. One of the crucial entries describes Stavrogin not as a person but rather as a kind of natural energy:

> *This immense, instinctive force, seeking nothing but peace, yet agitated to the point of suffering, does in the course of its searchings and wanderings veer into monstrous deviations and experiments, until it will finally come to rest upon so powerful an idea as to be fully proportional to their instinctive animal strength. . . .*

By the spring of 1870 Dostoevsky's conception has developed to the point where he begins to grasp what is so remarkable about Stavrogin—and I phrase this deliberately, to stress the fact that the writer struggles to apprehend a character he feels already to exist:

> *Yet there remains for him the question: what is he himself? The answer for him is "Nothing." He finds no solid basis whatsoever within himself and is bored.*

By August the picture comes into sharper focus:

> *. . . a somber, passionate, demoniac, and dissolute character who knows no moderation; facing the ultimate question he has reached "to be or not to be?"*

A few entries later there occurs the tantalizing sentence, "STAVROGIN IS EVERYTHING," but so far as I can tell, this is not yet the "everything"—that is, the "everything" of nothingness—he is to be in the novel. But by now all the pieces are at hand, and they are summed up in the polarity: everything—nothing.

What was it, then, that Dostoevsky wanted Stavrogin to be, and that Peter Verhovensky, in his brilliant deranged fashion, recognizes as present in Stravrogin when he calls him the "fairy-tale prince" and the future "pope" of Russia? Stavrogin finally emerged in Dostoevsky's imagination as a gigantic projection of the unfilled spaces, the vast frightful emptiness, which he saw as the source and condition of disbelief. Peter Verhovensky is the public consequence or symptom of disbelief; Stavrogin, the embodiment of its animating nullity. And if the wish to dramatize nothingness may be in principle unrealizable, this helps explain the enormous difficulties Dostoevsky had with Stavrogin.

Stavrogin can also be understood as the opposite of Prince Myshkin, the inspired messiah-epileptic of *The Idiot*. Dostoevsky calls Myshkin "the wholly beautiful man." Harold Rosenberg sees Myshkin descending into the world of Dostoevsky's novel "like a divine messenger in Homer or the Old Testament, and also a figure who seems about to turn into the abstract person of a religious or political tract." Stavrogin, by contrast, is a counter-messiah, a messenger from below bearing the gift of emptiness. Yet his role in *The Possessed* is analogous to that of Myshkin in *The Idiot*, about whom Rosenberg says that "his function is not to alter the course of the action but to disseminate the aura of a new state of being." Precisely: it is Stavrogin's "new state of being," a being emptied-out and drained of the will to live, that makes Peter Verhovensky possible. Stavrogin is the ultimate source of the chaos that streams through the characters of *The Possessed*—intellectually, Dostoevsky persuades us of this option, but dramatically he does not fully achieve it. In a half-mad but dazzling scene, Peter rushes after Stavrogin, kissing his hand and saying to him, "Without you I'm a zero, a fly in a glass jar, a bottled thought, a Columbus without America."

There is something bolder still, if again not fully realized, in the completed novel. Dostoevsky believed in a potential identity of opposites: that nihilism might turn out to be faith *in extremis*, that nothing could become the token of everything, that the draining of energy might prove to be an equal sign to the flooding of the soul with grace, perhaps even that Satan might melt into God. People expect Stavrogin to lead, he himself "seeks a burden." Admittedly, this side of him never emerges into full clarity; by its very nature, it cannot. Yet Dostoevsky, out of attraction to the depths of nihilism and his passion for some ultimate reconciliation of all the moral forces at war in the universe, shares in his own way Peter Verhovensky's expectations concerning Stavrogin. That in neither the Notes nor the novel can he fully bring these into dramatic view, or even abstract articulation, is hardly surprising. To make credible the goodness of a Myshkin is hard enough, but to create in a Stavrogin an anti-Myshkin who yet bears in his burnt-out soul the violated potential of everything Myshkin stands for . . .

With the other characters Dostoevsky has no equivalent difficulties. Shatov the god-seeker and Kirillov the god-denier come through rapidly, the two halves of Dostoevsky given independent life. Stepan Trofimovitch, the old liberal windbag, Dostoevsky keeps taunting and mocking throughout the Notes, as in the novel too; but only toward the end does he hit upon his most inspired idea: that Stepan Trofimovitch, buffoon, coward and toady, should nevertheless be the one character decisively to repudiate the Nechaevism of his son:

> *Details aside, the essence of Stepan T. lies in the fact that though ready at first to compromise with the new ideas, he breaks with them in the end, and indignantly so (preferring to go begging), and alone refuses to succumb to these new ideas, remaining true to his old idealistic muddle.*

Old idealistic muddle—but that is the sentimental liberalism Dostoevsky has so mercilessly ridiculed. Some deep sense of justice, the sense that allows him to *become* his most despised characters, drives Dostoevsky to allot to Stepan Trofimovitch, though with a full share of jibes and jeers, the single act which in the deranged world of *The Possessed* approaches redemption.

With Nechaev-Peter, Dostoevsky has little trouble, for as an "old Nechaevist"—so Dostoevsky called himself and he did not lie—he feels a spidery kinship with the revolutionist. Professor Wasiolek believes that Dostoevsky never fully understood Peter, but I doubt that it matters: Dostoevsky created him. Some of the speeches he works out for Nechaev-Peter in the Notes—like a true political man, he *hears* Nechaev before seeing him—are used almost verbatim in the novel. Others he discarded. In one of them, Dostoevsky has Peter say, as if in touch with twentieth-century madness, "You know: the worse the better." At another point he remarks with great insight:

> *Nechaev is not a socialist but a rebel . . . his new world lies in aiming everything at insurrection, "but let it be a live one," and "the more rioting, disorders, bloodshed and collapse, fire and destruction of traditions, the better." "I don't care what will be later: what's most important is that the existing order be shaken, shattered, and exploded."*

Fascinating as these Notebooks are, both as illuminations of the novel and in their own right, they finally persuade one that between even the most sustained entries and the equivalent portions in *The Possessed* there is an enormous gap. Something happens which I do not understand and have never seen explained, something to which we give the unilluminating name of "the creative process," and this mysterious event creates a new order, a unity, indeed a self-sufficient universe which the Notes do not reach. Perhaps what one misses in the Notes is the Dostoevskyan speaker, the malicious-reflective "I" who plays almost no role in the action and whose presence one is inclined to forget, yet who provides a tone at once viciously deflating and ultimately humane. In the Notes Dostoevsky seldom bothers to approximate this tone of voice, or perhaps it is only in the novel that he can achieve it. Instead, as if to remind himself what he will be able to do once he has released his full powers, he merely jots down stage directions:

> *. . . show them all, as well as all of their society,* through little stories.

> *Think up many more details.*

> *Characters are the only thing that matters.*
> *And most valuable of all:*

> *The tone consists in not explaining Nechaev or the Prince.*

Testifying as they do to the dedication and cost of Dostoevsky's struggle for creation, these Notebooks yet persuade one that only in the course of writing the novel itself could that struggle be won.

THE STRAIGHT
AND THE CROOKED
Solzhenitsyn and Lukacs

FOR MOST OF HIS LIFE Georg Lukacs, the intellectual heresiarch of Communism, was unable to write freely. During the years he spent under Stalin in Russia and Rakosi in Hungary he had no freedom at all; under Kadar in Hungary, he was granted a measure of intellectual independence but only in a cautious, limited way. Lukacs made one major bolt from the bounds of political orthodoxy by joining the Nagy government during the Hungarian revolution of 1956, but once the Russian troops destroyed it he gradually came back into the fold. He had always to keep looking over his shoulder, sometimes literally and more often figuratively, so as to measure the latitude allowed him by the Party. Long ago he had chosen the role of the (at times) semi-dissident Communist, but never an openly oppositionist Communist and certainly not a public opponent of the party-state dictatorship.

Lukacs's reasons for this choice were clear: the locomotive of history had gone badly astray, the best passengers had been killed, the engineer had turned out to be a homicidal maniac, yet somehow that locomotive chugged in the direction of "progress." To have declared a clear opposition to totalitarianism, he believed, would have meant to isolate himself from History. It was a choice like that of the old Bolshevik Nikolai Bukharin, who in the early thirties paid a secret visit to some Mensheviks in Paris, trembling with fright and horror at the excesses of Stalin yet unable to face the prospect of exile. For Bukharin the result was death; for Lukacs a captivity sometimes grating, sometimes silken.

The course they chose, whatever its political merits, was not likely to encourage moral strength or forthrightness, since "if you always look over your shoulder," as a character in Solzhenitsyn's *The First Circle* remarks, "how can you still remain a human being?" Not a good Communist or adept dialectician, but "a human being." That Lukacs, in the little book he wrote about Solzhenitsyn at the very end of his life, should have cited with seeming approval these words—and Lukacs was a man who knew his way around his shoulder—is a matter of high intellectual drama.

It is a remarkable book,[1] far more so than the theoretical writings of Lukacs's earlier years, which in their recent translations have given rise to a wavelet of Marxist scholasticism. Perhaps because he found it easier or more prudent to express his deepest convictions through the mediated discourse of literary criticism than through direct political speech, Lukacs releases, with a fervor he had never before shown in print, the disgust he felt for Stalinism, at least Stalinism as the terrorist phase of the party-state dictatorship, if not as an integral sociopolitical system.

In *One Day in the Life of Ivan Denisovich*, writes Lukacs, "*the concentration camp is a symbol of everyday Stalinist life.*" Remarkable; especially when one remembers the rebukes from both left and right delivered to those of us who have been saying exactly the same thing for some years now. Still more remarkable is Lukacs's reference, obviously made with an eye toward the Khrushchev and Brezhnev regimes, to "the new era with all its changes which preserve *the essential methods of Stalinism* with only superficial modifications" (emphasis added—I.H.). Such passages, and there are a number of them, are at least as revealing of Lukacs's inner thoughts as they are of Solzhenitsyn's books.

Lukacs's admiration for Solzhenitsyn clearly went beyond the latter's literary achievement; it had much to do with his moral

[1] Solzhenitsyn, by Georg Lukacs (Cambridge, MIT Press, 1971).

stature, his independence and courage. And it is precisely here
that we encounter a painful problem. For between the absolute
candor of Solzhenitsyn's work and the deviousness of Lukacs's
career there is a startling difference, so much so that one senses
in this little book a measure of discomfort and defensiveness.
A man as intelligent as Lukacs could hardly have been unaware
that he kept praising Solzhenitsyn for precisely the virtues he
himself had rarely shown.

Completely fascinating in this respect is Lukacs's attitude
toward one of the characters in *The First Circle*, the prisoner
Rubin who is portrayed by Solzhenitsyn as a very decent man but
intellectually still in the grip of Communist orthodoxy. For
Rubin, writes Lukacs,

> friendship . . . is an indispensable part of life, and here [in the
> special camp for scientists] he cannot befriend like-minded persons,
> while all his friends reject his views. . . . In order to be able to exist
> accordingly, he repeatedly recites humorous parodies of poems
> . . . the only effect of which is that he must subsequently be
> ashamed of the role he has played.

Yet what have a good many of Lukacs's own writings been during
the last few decades but parodies of Marxism composed under
the pressures of the Party, for which he must subsequently have
felt ashamed? One source of his admiration for Solzhenitsyn
seems to be the Russian novelist's deliberate refusal of "tactics,"
the whole stale jumble of "dialectics" by which thinkers like
Lukacs have persisted in justifying their submission to the Party
dictatorship.

Precisely this uncomfortable mixture of responses may account
for the fact that in discussing Solzhenitsyn's novels Lukacs turns
to a theme that has long preoccupied independent critics in the
West (and secretly, no doubt, in the East) but has hardly figured
in Lukacs's own work. I refer to the problem of integrity as
a trait not reducible to political opinion or class status. It is
the problem of how men under tyranny struggle, as Lukacs
well puts it, "to preserve their own human integrity even here."
And still more striking is Lukacs's remark that "in the camps"
—which you will remember he has described as "a symbol
of everyday Stalinist life" such as he himself experienced for

years—"a refusal to compromise in all human and social essentials thus forms a prerequisite for anyone wishing to remain really human." Strong words!

Stronger still is the remark of Nerzhin, the central character of *The First Circle*, which Lukacs quotes with evident approval: there "is no better place" than prison "to understand the part of good and evil in human life." Good and evil! What is Lukacs doing with these "trans-historical," these quite undialectical, these perhaps neo-Kantian categories? Not "progressive and reactionary," but "good and evil!" Something, one can only surmise, must have been fermenting in Lukacs's mind during his last years which the appearance of Solzhenitsyn's novels helped bring to fruition, something more heretical than he ever dared express in his own right.

About the social world portrayed by Solzhenitsyn, Lukacs comments:

> Should bureaucracy become the dominant mode of life of those participating in it, should the decisions dictated by it determine their way of life entirely, then inevitably the tactics of the apparatus, dictated by its day-to-day needs, become the ultimate judge of all decisions between good and evil.

It really begins to look as if, in the end, Lukacs was badly torn between such admirable sentiments, elicited and brought to sharp articulation by Solzhenitsyn's books, and his continuing persuasion, part canniness and part habitual abjectness, that he had to remain faithful to the Party.

II

One reason Lukacs admires Solzhenitsyn the novelist is that he sees him as a realist in the nineteenth-century tradition who does not fiddle about with experimental techniques, clearly has large moral-historical scope, and puts at ease a programmatically antimodernist critic like himself. To some extent—I can't pretend to exactitude—this seems to me a misunderstanding of Solzhenitsyn's fiction, just as some years ago there was a similar misunderstanding of Pasternak's novel. Each of these writers chose to go back to the capacious forms of the nineteenth-century realistic novel, with its interweaving of themes, narrative elements, and characters, but not, I think, because of a deliberate or ideological rejection of literary modernism. Their decisions rested, instead, on moral-political grounds that can be inferred from their novels themselves, namely, a persuasion that genuinely to return to the Tolstoyan novel, which the Stalinist dogma of "socialist realism" had celebrated in words but caricatured in performance, would constitute a revolutionary act of the spirit. It would signify a struggle for human renewal, for the reaffirmation of the image of a free man as that image can excite our minds beyond all ideological decrees. Pasternak had already been for many years a modernist poet, and Solzhenitsyn, forced by circumstances to live apart from all literary tendencies or groups, seems not to have been interested in the question of modernism. He had apparently reached the "instinctive" conclusion that in an authoritarian society the role of the writer is to recover fundamental supports of moral existence, direct intuitions of human fraternity, encompassing moments of truth. A writer seized by such a vision—which in some sense must be regarded as religious in urgency and depth—is not likely to think first of all about innovations of technique, though there is reason to suppose that he may nevertheless achieve them.

The first task of such a writer, as he takes upon himself the heavy and uncomfortable mantle of moral spokesman, is to remember, to record, to insist upon the sanctity of simple fact and uncontaminated memory. That is why Solzhenitsyn's apparent indifference to literary modernism which so pleases Lukacs would seem to be less a deliberate repudiation than a step beyond the circumstances that had first led to modernism. It is a step that prompted Solzhenitsyn to revive—though with significant modifications—the Tolstoyan novel, a step taken out of the conviction that in our time the claim for freedom is inseparable from the resurrection of history. To be free means in our century, first of all, to remember.

Simply as a literary critic, Lukacs often writes well in this book. He compares *One Day in the Life of Ivan Denisovich* with by now classical novellas of Conrad and Hemingway in order to work out a rough schema for the novella, or short novel, as a form:

It does not claim to shape the whole of social reality, nor even to depict that whole as it appears from the vantage point of a fundamental and topical problem. Its truth rests on the fact that an individual situation—usually an extreme one [but has not modernism just entered here, through the back door?—I.H.]—is possible in a certain society at a certain level of development, and just because it is possible, is characteristic of this society and this level.

If not quite original, this is very keen. More original and illuminating is Lukacs's notion that in the twentieth century there has appeared a kind of novel that takes over and enlarges upon the central structure of the novella. Lukacs notices this, first of all, in *The Magic Mountain*, whose "compositional innovation"

> may be described . . . in a purely formal way, namely that the uniformity of the setting is made the immediate foundation of the narrative. The characters of this novel are removed from the "natural" location of their lives and movements, and are transplanted into new and artificial surroundings (here the sanatorium for consumptives). The major consequence of this is that the characters do not come into contact with each other, as so often in life and even more frequently in art, in "normal" ways . . .; rather this "chance" common terrain of their present existence creates new fundamental forms of their human, intellectual and moral relations with each other.

What such a literary structure then does is to sustain a prolonged interval of crisis in which the characters are put to a test. In *The Magic Mountain* Thomas Mann enforces the test through a confrontation with the reality of the characters' own death. In *The First Circle* Solzhenitsyn has the prisoners confronted "not only by the slender hope of liberation, but by a very real threat of a more infernal region of hell" (that is, shipment to the worst camps in Siberia).

Clearly this is the kind of analysis that serious readers can respect, since it makes an effort to see works of literature in their own realm of being and ventures upon comparisons in regard to structure and technique that leap across the dull hurdles of "socialist realism." Yet it seems utterly characteristic of Lukacs that just as he shows his mind at its liveliest he should also show it still unfree. Having analyzed the relation of the structural principle in Solzhenitsyn's novels to that which he locates in the work of Mann, Lukacs must then come up with a preposterous remark that "Solzhenitsyn's works appear as a rebirth of the noble beginnings of socialist realism." But this is sheer nonsense. Whatever Solzhenitsyn's novels may be, they really have nothing in common with "socialist realism," not even with the one, rather frayed instance offered by Lukacs of its "noble beginnings," the fiction of the Soviet writer Makarenko which he overrates simply in order to show that publicly he does, still, adhere to a version of "socialist realism."[2]

III

The central criticism Lukacs makes of Solzhenitsyn is that the Russian novelist writes from the strong but limiting perspective of the plebeian mind, rather than from a socialist consciousness. Lukacs grants that Solzhenitsyn's criticism of Soviet society is "rooted in a genuine plebeian hatred of social privilege"; it is tied by numerous filaments of attitude to the "plebeian social view" of such Tolstoyan characters as Platon Karatayev in *War and Peace;* but it lacks, as it must, the historical perspective, the theoretical coherence that can alone be provided by the "socialist" outlook.

This point is of considerable literary and political interest, since it marks quite clearly the limits within which Lukacs, for all his on-again, off-again hatred of Stalinist society and the "new era" which "preserves the essential methods of Stalinism," nevertheless continued to function.

Lukacs refers to a striking phrase of Marx, the *"ignorant perfection"* of ordinary people, a perfection of healthy social impulse, a moral rightness that can spontaneously arise among the masses. It is "perfection" because it immediately sniffs out frauds and tyrants, but "ignorant" because it has not been raised to a level of generality or fortified with "dialectics." It remains a healthy

---

[2] Not one in a hundred of Lukacs's readers are likely to have read Makarenko, and that may lend his claim plausibility. But having struggled with an English translation of Makarenko's *The Road to Life*, which Lukacs praises so highly, I can testify that it is a characteristic exercise in agit-prop, though perhaps a shade better than most Soviet writing. Perhaps Lukacs was indulging in some sort of inside joke, with those in Eastern Europe who do know Makarenko being tipped off not to take this standard reference very seriously.

reaction to what exists, but by itself cannot lead to action in behalf of what might be. The vocabulary of Leninism made a parallel distinction between ordinary trade-union consciousness, which the masses can reach by themselves, and revolutionary consciousness, which the vanguard party must bring to (or impose upon) the masses.

Now, historically Lukacs is being more than a little ingenuous in confining the dominant vision of Solzhenitsyn's work, as well as that represented in Tolstoy by the character Platon Karatayev, to the level of the "plebeian." Plebeian these certainly are, as in the wonderful remark of Solzhenitsyn's character Spiridon who, when asked to describe the difference between the guilty and the innocent, answers, "Sheepdogs are right and cannibals are wrong." But in reality, as any student of Russian literature must know, the plebeian stress in Tolstoy and Dostoevsky, which one hears again in Solzhenitsyn, draws upon a strand of Christian belief very powerful in Russian culture, a strand that favors egalitarianism and ascetic humility, as if to take the word of Jesus at face value. Platon Karatayev may himself be an example of "ignorant perfection," but Tolstoy's act in creating him is anything but that. It follows from a major world view,[3] in its own way at least as comprehensive as that of Marxism. And the same might hold in regard to Solzhenitsyn's "plebeian" sentiments.

It should also be stressed that at a time when the "socialist" vocabulary is used for oppressive ends, the "plebeian" response, even if undecorated with ideology and "world views," takes on a liberating, indeed a revolutionary character. And the same, I would say, holds for certain religious responses. That Lukacs could write a book about Solzhenitsyn without so much as mentioning the problem of his religious inclinations, let alone those

[3] On the component of heretical Christianity in Tolstoy and its political significance, Trotsky's essays on Tolstoy are far more illuminating than Lukacs's, perhaps because Trotsky writing under the Czar was less inhibited than Lukacs under the reign of the Party. If, by the way, it is Marxist literary criticism that interests some young intellectuals these days, they will find it—to the extent that it can be said to exist—far more brilliantly, clearly, and elegantly achieved in Trotsky than in Lukacs. I sometimes suspect that the current fad of Lukacs has something to do with his imposing verbal opacity.

of the Tolstoy to whom he links Solzhenitsyn, is indeed a "dialectical" feat.

Let us nevertheless stay with Lukacs's argument for a moment, even granting, for the sake of that argument, the evident justice in his remark that "the inner 'ignorant perfection' of the common people is not sufficient to develop in man a positively effective and critical attitude toward the reform of his alienated society." Yet precisely these cogent words are likely to raise a tremor of distrust among readers experienced in the politics of Marxism. For Lukacs is speaking not merely in the abstract about the need for theoretical vision and generality; he writes from his own version of Marxism-Leninism. And when he contrasts Solzhenitsyn's "plebeian" limitation with the largeness of "socialist" perspective, we can't avoid translating this into a contrast between, let's say, Solzhenitsyn's "moral-social criticism of Communist society from the standpoint of freedom" and Lukacs's "criticism directed toward the resurrection of the Party within the framework of orthodox belief." What then becomes evident is that Solzhenitsyn's criticism of Russian society—even if limited by the "ignorant perfection" of the "plebeian" outlook—is far more revolutionary and far closer to the needs of a genuine socialism than that of Lukacs. Neither the dissident nor oppositionist label really fits Solzhenitsyn. Plebeian, yes. Plebeian, in that he has become the voice of all those who silently suffered through the decades of the terror and beyond. Brushing past the cant of Lukacs's world ("the leading role of the Party," "the Leninist heritage," etc.), Solzhenitsyn embodies in his fiction that empathy with the lowly and the mute which links him both to the great masters of the nineteenth century and the still-uncreated future of free man.

A GRAVE AND SOLITARY VOICE

An Appreciation of
Edwin Arlington Robinson

THE CENTENNIAL OF EDWIN ARLINGTON ROBINSON passed several years ago—he was born on December 22, 1869—with barely a murmur of public notice. There were a few academic volumes of varying merit, but no recognition in our larger journals and reviews, for Robinson seems the kind of poet who is likely to remain permanently out of fashion. At first, thinking about this neglect, I felt a surge of anger, since Robinson seems to me one of the best poets we have ever had in this country. But then, cooled by reflection and time, I came to see that perhaps it doesn't matter whether the writers we most care about receive their "due." Only the living need praise. Writers like Robinson survive in their work, appreciated by readers who aren't afraid to be left alone with an old book.

Robinson himself would hardly have expected any other fate, for he was not the sort of man to make demands on either this world or the next. Shy of all literary mobs, just managing to keep afloat through a workable mixture of stoicism and alcohol, he lived entirely for his poetry. Most of the time he was very poor, and all of the time alone, a withdrawn and silent bachelor. He seems to have composed verse with that single-mindedness the rest of us keep for occasions of vanity and profit. As a result he wrote "too much," and his *Collected Poems*, coming almost to 1,500 crowded pages, has a great deal of failed work. But a small portion is very fine, and a group of fifteen or twenty poems unquestionably great.

This, to be sure, is not the received critical judgment—though a few critics, notably Conrad Aiken in some fine reviews of the 1920s and Yvor Winters in a splendid little book published in 1946, have recognized his worth. The public acclaim of a Robert Frost, however, Robinson could never hope to match; the approval of the *avant-garde*, when it came at all, came in lukewarm portions, since T.S. Eliot had declared his work to be "negligible" and that, for a time, was that. Robinson stood apart from the cultural movements of his day, so much so that he didn't even bother to *oppose* literary modernism: he simply followed his own convictions. He was one of those New England solitaries—great-grandsons of the Puritans, nephews of the Emersonians—whose lives seem barren and pinched but who leave, in their stolid devotion to a task, something precious to the world.

The trouble in Robinson's life was mostly interior. Some force of repression, not exactly unknown to New England character, had locked up his powers for living by, or articulating openly, the feelings his poems show him to have had. Even in the poems themselves a direct release of passion or desire is infrequent; they "contain," or emerge out of, enormous depths of feeling, but it is a feeling pressed into oblique irony or disciplined into austere reflection. He was not the man to yield himself to what Henry James once called "promiscuous revelation."

Robinson lived mainly within himself, and sometimes near a group of admiring hangers-on who, as he seems to have known, were unworthy of him. Among his obsessive subjects are solitude and failure, both drawn from his immediate experience and treated with a richness of complication that is unequaled in American poetry. For the insights Robinson offered on these grim topics, in poems such as "The Wandering Jew" and "Eros Turannos," he no doubt paid a heavy price in his own experience. But we should remember that, finally, such preoccupations are neither a regional morbidity nor a personal neurosis: they are among the permanent and inescapable themes of literature. In his own dry and insular way, Robinson shared in the tragic vision that has dominated the imagination of the West since the Greek playwrights. By the time he began to write, it had perhaps become impossible for a serious poet to compose a tragedy on the classical scale, and as a result his sense of the tragic, unable to reach embodiment in a large action, had to emerge—one almost says, leak through—as a tone of voice, a restrained and melancholy contemplativeness.

At the age of twenty-two, Robinson could already write, half in wisdom and half in self-defense, sentences forming an epigraph to his whole career:

> Solitude . . . tends to magnify one's ideas of individuality; it sharpens his sympathy for failure where fate has been abused and self demoralized; it renders a man suspicious of the whole natural plan, and leads him to wonder whether the invisible powers are a fortuitous issue of unguided cosmos. . . .

Like Hawthorne and Melville before him, Robinson came from a family that had suffered both a fall in circumstances and a collapse of psychic confidence. To read the one reliable biography, by Herman Hagedorn, is gradually to be drawn into a graying orbit of family nightmare, an atmosphere painfully similar to that of a late O'Neill play. Tight-lipped quarrels, heavy drinking, failing investments, ventures into quack spiritualism and drugs—these were the matter of his youth. Hagedorn describes the few months before the death of the poet's father:

> [The elder Robinson's] interest in spiritualism had deepened and, in the slow disintegration of his organism, detached and eerie energies seemed to be released. There were table rappings and once the table came off the floor, "cutting my universe . . . clean in half." . . . Of these last months with his father, he told a friend, "They were a living hell."

Not much better were Robinson's early years in New York, where he slept in a hall bedroom and worked for a time as a subway clerk. He kept writing and won some recognition, including help from President Theodore Roosevelt, who was impressed by one of Robinson's (inferior) poems but had the honesty to admit he didn't understand it. Toward the end of his career Robinson scored his one commercial success with *Tristram*, the least interesting of his three lengthy Arthurian poems. This success did not much affect his life or, for that matter, his view of life. He died in 1935, a victim of cancer. It is said that as Robinson lay dying one of his hangers-on approached him for a small loan: life, as usual, trying to imitate art.

II

The imprint of New England on Robinson's sensibility is strong, but it is not precise. By the time he was growing up in the river-town of Gardner, Maine (the Tilbury Town of his poems), Puritanism was no longer a coherent religious force. It had become at best a collective memory of moral rigor, an ingrained and hardened way of life surviving beyond its original moment of strength. Yet to writers like Hawthorne and Robinson, the New England tradition left a rich inheritance: the assumption that human existence, caught in a constant inner struggle between good and evil, is inherently dramatic; and the habit of intensive scrutiny, at once proud and dust-humble, into human motives, such as the old Puritans had used for discovering whether they were among the elect. Writers like Hawthorne and Robinson were no longer believers but since they still responded to what they had rejected, they found themselves in a fruitful dilemma. They did not wish entirely to shake off the inflexible moralism of the New England past; yet they were fascinated by the psychological study of behavior that would come to dominate twentieth-century literature and, meanwhile, was both a borrowing from nineteenth-century European romanticism and a distillation of Puritan habits of mind. The best of the New England writers tried to yoke these two ways of regarding the human enterprise, and if their attempt is dubious in principle, it yielded in practice a remarkable subtlety in the investigation of motives. As for Emersonianism, by the time Robinson was beginning to think for himself it was far gone in decay, barely discernible as specific doctrine and little more than a mist of genteel idealism.

Robinson borrowed from both traditions. His weaker poems reveal an Emersonian yearning toward godhead and transcendence, which is an experience somewhat different from believing in God. His stronger poems share with the Puritans a cast of mind that is intensely serious, convinced of the irreducibility of moral problems, and devoted to nuance of motive with the scrupulosity his grandfathers had applied to nuance of theology. Even in an early, unimpressive sonnet like "Credo," which begins in a dispirited tone characteristic of much late nineteenth-century writing,

> *I cannot find my way: there is no star*
> *In all the shrouded heavens anywhere*

Robinson still felt obliged to end with an Emersonian piety:

> *I know the far-sent message of the years,*
> *I feel the coming glory of the Light.*

Whenever that "Light" begins to flicker, so tenuous a symbol for the idea of transcendence, it is a sure sign of trouble in Robinson's poems. A straining toward an optimism in which he has no real conviction, it would soon be overshadowed, however, by Robinson's darkening fear, as he later wrote in a long poem called *King Jasper*, that

> *No God,*
> *No Law, no Purpose, could have hatched for sport*
> *Out of warm water and slime, a war for life*
> *That was unnecessary, and far better*
> *Never had been—if man, as we behold him,*
> *Is all it means.*

Such lines suggest that Robinson's gift was not for strict philosophizing in verse; he was eminently capable of thinking as a poet, but mainly through his arrangement of dramatic particulars and the casual reflections he wove in among them. What makes Robinson's concern with God and the cosmos important is not its doctrinal content, quite as vague in statement and dispirited in tone as that of other sensitive people of his time, but the way in which he would employ it as the groundwork for his miniature dramas. Fairly conventional doctrine thereby becomes the living tissue of suffering and doubt.

It is an advantage for a writer to have come into relation with a great tradition of thought, even if only in its stages of decay, and it can be a still greater advantage to struggle with the problem of salvaging elements of wisdom from that decayed tradition. For while a culture in decomposition may limit the scope of its writers and keep them from the highest achievement, it offers special opportunities for moral drama to those who can maintain their bearing. The traps of such a moment are obvious: nostalgia, on the one extreme, and sensationalism, on the other. Most of the time Robinson was strong enough to resist these temptations, a portion of the old New England steel persisting in his soul; or perhaps he could resist them simply because he was so entirely absorbed in his own sense of the human situation and therefore didn't even trouble about the cultural innovations and discoveries of his time. He made doubt into a discipline, and failure into an opening toward compassion. The old principles of his culture may have crumbled, but he found his subject in the problems experienced by those to whom the allure of those principles had never quite dulled.

III

Many of Robinson's shorter poems—lyrics, ballads, sonnets, dramatic narratives—are set in Tilbury Town, his Down East locale where idlers dream away their lives in harmless fantasy, mild rebels suffer the resistance of a community gone stiff, and the tragedy of personal isolation seems to acquire a universal character, as if speaking for Robinson's vision of America, perhaps all of life. Other nineteenth-century writers had of course employed a recurrent setting in their work, and later Faulkner would do the same with Yoknapatawpha County. Yet Robinson's use of Tilbury Town is rather different from what these writers do: he makes no attempt to fill out its social world, he cares little about details of place and moment, he seems hardly to strive for historical depth. Tilbury Town is more an atmosphere than a setting, it is barely drawn or provisioned, and it serves to suggest less a vigorous community than a felt lack of historical continuity. The foreground figures in these poems are drawn with two or three harsh, synoptic strokes, but Tilbury Town itself is shadowy, fading into the past and no longer able to bind its people. Robinson eyes it obliquely, half in and half out of its boundaries, a secret sharer taking snapshots of decline. To illuminate a world through a glimpsed moment of crisis isn't, for him, a mere strategy of composition; it signifies his deepest moral stance, a nervous signature of reticence and respect. He seems always to be signaling a persuasion that nothing can be known with certainty and the very thought of direct assertion is a falsehood in the making.

Some of these Tilbury pieces, as Robinson once remarked, have been "pickled in anthological brine." Almost "everybody" knows "Miniver Cheevy" and "Richard Corey," sardonic vignet-

tes of small-town character, Yankee drop-outs whose pitiable
condition is contrasted—in quirky lines and comic rhymes—
with their weak fantasies. These are far from Robinson's best
poems, but neither are they contemptible. In the sketch of poor
Miniver, who "loved the days of old," there are flashes of
cleverness:

> *Miniver mourned the ripe renown*
> *That made so many a name so fragrant;*
> *He mourned Romance, now on the town,*
> *And Art, a vagrant.*

Such pieces lead to better ones of their kind, such as the
tautly written sonnets about Reuben Bright, the butcher who
tears down his slaughterhouse when told his wife must die, and
Aaron Stark, a miser with "eyes like little dollars in the dark."
My experience in teaching these poems is that students trained
to flounder in *The Waste Land* will at first condescend, but when
asked to read the poems again, will be unsettled by the depths
of moral understanding Robinson has hidden away within them.

The finest of Robinson's sonnets of character is "The Clerks."
Describing a return to Tilbury Town, the poet meets old friends,
figures of "a shopworn brotherhood," who now work as clerks
in stores. The opening octet quietly evokes this scene, and then
in the closing sestet Robinson widens the range of his observation
with a powerful statement about the weariness of slow defeat:

> *And you that ache so much to be sublime,*
> *And you that feed yourselves with your descent,*
> *What comes of all your visions and your fears?*
> *Poets and kings are but the clerks of Time,*
> *Tiering the same dull webs of discontent,*
> *Clipping the same sad alnage of the years.*

Without pretending to close analysis, I would like to glance
at a few of the perceptual and verbal refinements in these six
lines. The opening "ache . . . to be sublime" has its workaday
irony that prepares for the remarkable line which follows: to
"feed" with "your descent" is a characteristic Robinsonian turn,
which in addition to the idea of consuming oneself through age

suggests more obliquely that indulgence in vanity which claims distinction for one's decline. Poets and kings who are "clerks of Time" are helplessly aligned with the Tilbury clerks, yet Robinson sees that even in the democracy of our common decay we cling to our trifle of status. For in the "dull webs of discontent" which form the fragile substance of our lives, we still insist on "tiering" ourselves. Coming in the penultimate line, the word "tiering" has enormous ironic thrust: how long can a tier survive as a web? And then in the concluding line Robinson ventures one of his few deviations from standard English, in the use of "alnage," a rare term meaning a measure of cloth, that is both appropriate to the atmosphere of waste built up at the end and overwhelming as it turns us back to the "shop-worn" clerks who are Robinson's original *donnée*.

Now, for readers brought up in the modernist tradition of Eliot and Stevens, these short poems of Robinson will not yield much excitement. They see in such poems neither tangle nor agony, brilliance nor innovation. But they are wrong, for the Tilbury sonnets and lyrics do, in their own way, represent a significant innovation: Robinson was the first American poet of stature to bring commonplace people and commonplace experience into our poetry. Whitman had invoked such people and even rhapsodized over them, but as individual creatures with warm blood they are not really to be found in his pages. Robinson understood that

> *Even the happy mortals we term ordinary or commonplace act their own mental tragedies and live a far deeper and wider life than we are inclined to believe possible. . . .*

The point bears stressing because most critics hail poets like Eliot and Stevens for their innovations in metrics and language while condescending toward Robinson as merely traditional. Even if that were true, it would not, of course, be a sufficient reason for judgments either favorable or hostile; but it is not true. Robinson never thought of himself as a poetic revolutionary, but like all major poets he helped enlarge for those who came after him the possibilities of composition. The work of gifted writers like Robert Lowell, James Dickey, and James Wright was enabled by Robinson's muted innovations.

His dramatic miniatures in verse—spiritual dossiers of American experience, as someone has nicely called them—remind one a little of Hawthorne, in their ironic undercurrents and cool explorations of vanity, and a little of James, in their peeling away of psychic pretense and their bias that human relationships are inherently a trap. Yet it would be unjust to say that Robinson was a short-story writer who happened to write verse, for it is precisely through the traditional forms he employed—precisely through his disciplined stanzas, regular meters, and obbligatos of rhyme—that he released his vision. Robinson's language seldom achieves the high radiance of Frost, and few of his short poems are as beautifully complexioned as Frost's "Spring Pools" or "The Most of It." But in Robinson there are sudden plunges into depths of experiences, and then stretches of earned contemplativeness, that Frost can rarely equal. Here, for example, is the octet of a Robinson sonnet, "The Pity of the Leaves," that deals with an experience—an old man alone at night with his foreboding of death—which in "An Old Man's Winter Night" Frost also treated memorably but not, I think, as well:

> *Vengeful across the cold November moors,*
> *Loud with ancestral shame there came the bleak*
> *Sad wind that shrieked and answered with a shriek,*
> *Reverberant through lonely corridors.*
> *The old man heard it; and he heard, perforce,*
> *Words out of lips that were no more to speak—*
> *Words of the past that shook the old man's cheek*
> *Like dead remembered footsteps on old floors.*

It is always to "the slow tragedy of haunted men" that Robinson keeps returning. One of his greatest lyrics on this theme, the kind of hypnotic incantation that *happens* to a poet once or twice if he is lucky, is "Luke Havergal": a grieving man hears the voice of his dead love and it draws him like an appetite for death, a beauty of death quiet and enclosing.

The greatest of these Tilbury poems, and one of the greatest poems about the tragedy of love in our language, is "Eros Turannos." Yvor Winters aptly calls it "a universal tragedy in a Maine setting." It deals with a genteel and sensitive woman, advancing in years and never, apparently, a startling beauty, who has married or otherwise engaged herself to a charming wastrel with a taste for the finer things of life:

> *She fears him, and will always ask*
> *What fated her to choose him;*
> *She meets in his engaging mask*
> *All reasons to refuse him. . . .*

With a fierce concentration of phrase, the poem proceeds to specify the entanglements in which these people trap themselves, the moral confusions and psychic fears, all shown with a rare balance of exactness and compassion. The concluding stanza reaches a wisdom about the human lot such as marks Robinson's poetry at its best. Those, he writes, who with the god of love have striven,

> *Not bearing much of what we say,*
> *Take what the god has given;*
> *Though like waves breaking it may be,*
> *Or like a changed familiar tree,*
> *Or like a stairway to the sea*
> *Where down the blind are driven.*

Thinking of such poems and trying to understand how it is that in their plainness they can yet seem so magnificent, one finds oneself falling back on terms like "sincerity" and "honesty." They are terms notoriously inadequate and tricky, yet inescapable in discussing poets like Robinson and Thomas Hardy. It is not, after all, as if one wants to say about more brilliant poets like Eliot and Yeats that they are insincere or lacking in honesty; of course not. What one does want to suggest is that in poems like Robinson's "Eros Turannos" and "Hillcrest," as in Hardy's "The Going" and "At Castle Boterel," there is an abandonment of all pretense and pose, all protectiveness and persona. At such moments the poet seems beyond decoration and defense; he leaves himself vulnerable, open to the pain of his self; he cares nothing for consolation; he looks at defeat and does not blink. It is literature beyond the literary.

IV

Robinson was also a master of a certain genre poem, Wordsworthian in tone and perhaps source, which Frost also wrote but not, in my judgment, as well. These are poems about lost and aging country people, mostly in New England: "Isaac and Archibald," "Aunt Imogen," and "The Poor Relation." The very titles are likely to displease readers whose hearts tremble before titles like "Leda and the Swan," "The Idea of Order at Key West," and "The Bridge." A pity!

"Isaac and Archibald" is the masterpiece of this group, a summer idyll tinged with shadows of death, told by a mature man remembering himself as a boy who spent an afternoon with two old farmers, lifelong friends, each of whom now frets that the other is showing signs of decay. The verse is exquisite:

> So I lay dreaming of what things I would,
> Calm and incorrigibly satisfied
> With apples and romance and ignorance,
> And the still smoke from Archibald's clay pipe.
> There was a stillness over everything,
> As if the spirit of heat had laid its hand
> Upon the world and hushed it; and I felt
> Within the mightiness of the white sun
> That smote the land around us and wrought out
> A fragrance from the trees, a vital warmth
> And fulness for the time that was to come,
> And a glory for the world beyond the forest.
> The present and the future and the past,
> Isaac and Archibald, the burning bush,
> The Trojans and the walls of Jericho,
> Were beautifully fused; and all went well
> Till Archibald began to fret for Isaac
> And said it was a master day for sunstroke.

Another kind of poem at which Robinson showed his mastery, one that has rarely been written in this country, is the dramatic monologue of medium length. "Rembrandt to Rembrandt," "The Three Taverns" (St. Paul approaching Rome), and "John Brown" are the best examples. The pitfalls of this genre are notorious: an effort to capture the historic inflections of the speaker's voice, so that both conciseness of speech and poetic force are sacrificed to some idea of verisimilitude; a tendency toward linguistic exhibitionism, blank verse as a mode of preening; and a lack of clear focusing of intent, so that the immediate experience of the speaker fails to take on larger resonance. Robinson mostly transcends these difficulties. He chooses figures at moments of high crisis, Rembrandt as he plunges into his dark painting, St. Paul as he ruminates upon his forthcoming capture, and John Brown as he readies himself for hanging. The result is serious in moral perception, leading always to the idea of abandonment of the self, and dignified in tone, for Robinson had little gift for colloquial speech and was shrewd enough to maintain a level of formal diction.

It is Frost who is mainly honored for this kind of dramatic poem, but a sustained comparison would show, I think, the superiority of Robinson's work. Though not nearly so brilliant a virtuoso as Frost, Robinson writes from a fullness of experience and a tragic awareness that Frost cannot equal. Frost has a strong grasp on the melodramatic extremes of behavior, but he lacks almost entirely Robinson's command of its middle ranges. Frost achieves a cleaner verbal surface, but Robinson is more abundant in moral detail and insight.

There remains finally a word to be said about Robinson's Arthurian poems, *Merlin*, *Lancelot*, and *Tristram*, the first two of which are very considerable productions. I am aware of straining my readers' credulity in saying that *Merlin* and *Lancelot*, set in the court of King Arthur and dealing with the loves and intrigues of his knights, are profound explorations of human suffering.

Tennyson's *Idylls of the Kings*, dealing with the same materials, is mainly a pictorial representation of waxen figures, beautiful in the way a tapestry might be but not very gripping as drama. Robinson's Guinevere and Lancelot, however, are errant human beings separated from us only by costume and time; his Merlin is an aging man of worldly power and some wisdom who finds himself drawn to the temptations of private life. Long poems are bound to have flaws, in this case excessive talk and a spun-thin moral theorizing that can become tedious. There is the further problem that any effort at sustained blank verse will, by now, lead to padding and looseness of language. Still, these are poems for mature men and women who know that in the end we are all as we are, vulnerable and mortal. Here Merlin speaks at the end of his career, remembering his love:

> *Let her love*
> *What man she may, no other love than mine*
> *Shall be an index of her memories.*
> *I fear no man who may come after me,*
> *And I see none. I see her, still in green,*
> *Beside the fountain. I shall not go back . . .*
> > *If I come not,*
> *The lady Vivian will remember me,*
> *And say: 'I knew him when his heart was young.*
> *Though I have lost him now. Time called him home,*
> *And that was as it was; for much is lost*
> *Between Broceliande and Camelot.'*

In my own experience Robinson is a poet who grows through rereading, or perhaps it would be better to say, one grows into being able to reread him. He will never please the crowds, neither the large ones panting for platitude nor the small ones supposing paradox an escape from platitude. All that need finally be said about Robinson he said himself in a sonnet about George Crabbe, the eighteenth-century English poet who also wrote about commonplace people in obscure corners of the earth:

> *Whether or not we read him, we can feel*
> *From time to time the vigor of his name*
> *Against us like a finger for the shame*
> *And emptiness of what our souls reveal*
> *In books that are as altars where we kneel*
> *To consecrate the flicker, not the flame.*

THE CASE OF
EZRA POUND

THE CASE OF EZRA POUND, it begins to seem, will be with us forever. Like a bad dream, it keeps coming back, prodding us to struggle with difficult, perhaps insoluble problems: the relation of art to morality; the terms of aesthetic judgment when confronting literary works with a heavy ideological freight; the reasons a good many major twentieth-century writers succumbed to totalitarianism. Painful as it may be, this return to old issues has a positive value: It forces us to remember what might be more pleasant to forget.

Twenty-three years ago, in 1949, the Bollingen Award was given to Ezra Pound. The jury included such distinguished writers as T. S. Eliot, Robert Lowell, W. H. Auden, and Allen Tate. There followed a harsh dispute, in *Partisan Review* and elsewhere, concerning the ethical propriety of honoring a poet who, only a few years earlier, had been making wartime speeches on Mussolini's radio in praise of fascism and anti-Semitism. Now, this past summer, we have had a replay. The American Academy of Arts and Sciences decided to reject a subcommittee's recommendation that Pound be given its Emerson-Thoreau Award, whereupon followed a spate of resignations, statements, and letters to the editor almost as heated as those of 1949. Clearly this issue presses on a sensitive nerve, and just as clearly, neither side has succeeded in persuading the other of its rightness.

When the Bollingen Award to Pound was announced in 1949, he was a mental patient at St. Elizabeth's Hospital in Washington, D.C. At the end of the war Pound had fallen into the hands of the U.S. Army in Italy and by all accounts been badly mistreated; the result was a nervous breakdown. Brought back to the United States, he faced a possible charge of treason for his wartime broadcasts.

In 1949 he was put on trial and judged to be of "unsound mind." He was then confined to St. Elizabeth's, where he would remain in benign captivity for twelve years. Though cruelly prolonged, this sentence was perhaps a desirable evasion of what might otherwise have been the excruciating spectacle of a great or once-great poet being tried for conduct that could have brought far more severe punishment.

Some of Pound's defenders would later use the juridical verdict of "unsound mind" to dismiss or minimize the significance of his wartime broadcasts. Rarely, however, were they prepared to accept the consequences of their argument—first, that his speeches on the Italian radio were consistent with, if more extreme than, what he had been saying earlier, especially in his book *Guide to Kulchur*; and second, that if the verdict of "unsound mind" is to be seen as relevant to Pound's wartime activities (Prof. Harry Levin says that the "psychiatrists would seem to have absolved him" from "responsibility for antisocial behavior"), then that same verdict becomes embarrassingly relevant to the writings composed directly after the war and for which the Bollingen Award was honoring him. For how, one wonders, could a man of "unsound mind" have written a considerable quantity of verse without imprinting on it the marks of his condition?

Historical memory is painfully short; new horrors pile up on the old ones; younger generations prefer not to remember. So it may be useful to cite a few passages from Pound's wartime broadcasts:

> [April 23, 1942] Any man who submits to Roosevelt's treason to the public commits a breach of citizen's duty. . . . Had you the sense to eliminate Roosevelt and the Jews . . . at the last election, you would not now be at war.

[May 10, 1942] England will certainly have nothing whatever to say about the terms [of the next peace]. Neither, I think, will simplehearted Joe Stalin, not wholly trusted by the kikery which is his master.

[May 26, 1942] Every sane act you commit is committed in homage to Mussolini and Hitler. . . . They are your leaders, however much you think you are conducted by Roosevelt or told up by Churchill. You follow Mussolini and Hitler in every constructive act of your government.

"Sound mind" or not, Pound was here repeating the standard line of the Hitler-Mussolini axis. If there was any doubt as to his sentiments, he put it to rest with an interview on May 25, 1945, in which he told a reporter that Hitler was "a Jeanne d'Arc, a saint . . . a martyr."

What makes the Pound case especially complicated is that in *The Cantos*, to which he has kept adding over the years, Pound included some decidedly similar sentiments, ranging from a number of anti-Semitic passages to expressions of tenderness for Mussolini to such sickening lines as "Pétain defended Verdun while Blum / was defending a bidet." It therefore becomes difficult to make a clear-cut distinction of the kind urged by his supporters between the man who spoke in behalf of the Fascist powers, and the poet who is to be judged solely on literary grounds.

The first major anti-Semitic passages occur in "Canto XXXV," published in the thirties:

The tale of the perfect schnorrer: a peautiful chewisch poy
wit a vo-ice dot woult
meldt dh heart offa schtone
and wit a likeing for to make arhtvoiks
and ven dh oldt ladty wasn't dhere any more
and dey didn't know why, tdhere
     ee woss in the
oldt antique shop and nobodty knew how he got dhere

There are people, I suppose, who find this sort of thing amusing and perhaps deaf-mutes who praise the accuracy of the poet's ear. But even if we grant that Pound's intentions may not have been vicious, this passage shows that a highly cultured man can be as sensitive as a street bum. "There is no point in denying,"

writes Prof. Donald Davie in his sympathetic study of Pound,
that such material in "Canto XXXV" is anti-Semitic; indeed,
there is a point in asserting it. By the *Pisan Cantos*, published
after the war and the immediate occasion for the Bollingen
Award, the anti-Semitism is blunter and the intent behind it
utterly vicious:

> the yidd is a stimulant, and the goyim are cattle
> in gt / proportion and go to saleable slaughter
> with the maximum of docility.

There are other anti-Semitic passages in *The Cantos*, including
a statement fraudulently attributed to Benjamin Franklin by an
American Fascist newspaper, which in 1934 Pound picked up
without checking and threw into his poem:

> Remarked Ben: better keep out the jews or yr/ grand children
> will curse you

How important, one may ask, are these anti-Semitic passages
in *The Cantos?* Are they central to the whole thrust of the work
or mere incidental blemishes? It is hard to answer this question
with complete assurance, since *The Cantos*, at least in my reading,
are a chaos of reflections, diatribes, vignettes, reminiscences,
arguments, visions, and self-contained lyrics, a grab bag of
incoherence in which the mind of the poet reveals itself without
the benefit of disciplined form. Quantitatively the percentage
of anti-Semitic passages is small, but thematically they are closely
related to the whole political drift of the poem, which at some
points is explicitly Fascist and at other points supportive of the
Fascist myth. In any case, how many outbursts of anti-Semitic
venom would be required for Pound's defenders to acknowledge
that they constituted more than an "incidental blemish"?

That Pound was a major force in the development of modern
poetry; that he performed wonders in the chastening of the English language; that he often displayed a gift for metrical
innovation; that he showed himself a teacher and colleague
remarkably kind and helpful—all this, attested to in numerous
memoirs and histories, is beyond challenge. But it does not tell
us very much about the nature and quality of his major work.

Here I would call upon the testimony of Allen Tate, a poet who voted for giving the Bollingen Award to Pound in 1949 and who then passionately defended his position:

> As a result of observing Pound's use of language in the past thirty years, I had become convinced that he had done more than any other living man to regenerate the language, if not the imaginative forms, of English verse. I had to face the disagreeable fact that he had done this even in passages of verse in which the opinions expressed ranged from the childish to the detestable.

Now it seems to me possible to accept Tate's judgment while still disagreeing with him as to the propriety of the award—but of that more later. Let me quote from Tate what is, I believe, a crucial statement about *The Cantos:*

> The work for which I voted is formless, eccentric, and personal. *The Cantos* are . . . "about nothing at all." They have a voice but no subject. . . . Pound is incapable of sustained thought in either prose or verse. His acute verbal sensibility is thus at the mercy of random flights of "angelic insight," an Icarian self-indulgence of prejudice which is not checked by a total view. . . . .

And still more cogent:

> I have little sympathy with the view that holds that Pound's irresponsible opinions merely lie alongside the poetry, which thus remains uncontaminated by them. The disagreeable opinions are right in the middle of the poetry. And they have got to be seen for what they are . . . unrelated to a mature and coherent conception of life.

This seems to me an accurate description: "the disagreeable opinions are right in the middle of the poetry"—more accurate, I think, than Prof. Harry Levin's reference to "an artistic achievement flawed by certain problematic commitments."

Ezra Pound summed up in his work and career the wrenching contradictions of modernist culture. He was a generous man committed to murderous ideology. A midwestern provincial let loose in the inferno of twentieth-century Europe, he pretended—with an arrogance too many other writers of his generation shared—to universal knowledge on everything from Chinese cul-

ture to economics and began to preach in verse and prose grandiose schemes for monetary reform that were marked by a simplistic illiteracy. His mind contained large amounts of historical
information, but he had no ordered sense of European history—
small wonder he could be taken in by a buffoon like Mussolini
or suppose Stalin to be "simplehearted." *The Cantos*, with their
linkage of Jefferson and Mussolini, their absurd portrait of
Martin Van Buren, their rantings against the Rothschilds, are
a junk shop of intellectual debris. (How morally bracing, by
contrast, is James Joyce's sardonic remark in 1934, "I am afraid
poor Mr. Hitler will soon have few friends in Europe apart
from my nephews, Masters W. Lewis and E. Pound.") Yet there
are also superb passages in *The Cantos*, brilliantly recorded
dialogue, keen fragments of action, affecting lyrics. It is a work
of that distinctly American type, the Crank as Genius—or near-
Genius.

Here, for example, is a passage that brings together Pound's
lyrical gifts with his obsession about usury—though it is important to note that "usura" figures in this passage as a quite abstract
category, so that one could easily substitute for it another term
or concept, and what really matters is Pound's evocation of human
dismay:

> With usura hath no man a house of good stone
> each block cut smooth and well fitting
> that design might cover their face,
> with usura
> hath no man a painted paradise on his church wall
>
> with usura, sin against nature,
> is thy bread ever more of stale rags
> is thy bread dry as paper,
> with no mountain wheat, no strong flour

And there is the single greatest passage in *The Cantos*, much
quoted but not thereby any the less pleasurable:

> What thou lovest well remains,
>   the rest is dross
> What thou lov'st well shall not be reft from thee
> What thou lov'st well is thy true heritage

The ant's a centaur in his dragon world.
Pull down thy vanity, it is not man
Made courage, or made order, or made grace,
Pull down thy vanity, I say pull down.

Written while Pound was a prisoner of the U.S. Army in
Pisa, these lines reflect a softening of temper, the single boon
of defeat. Toward individual persons Pound grew more merciful,
his sufferings taught him that "No man who has passed a month
in the death cell / believes in cages for beasts." And at the end:

If the hoar frost grips thy tent
Thou wilt give thanks when night is spent.

When the Bollingen judges announced their decision, they
were aware that it might stir up a quantity of protest, and they
therefore wrote: "To permit other considerations than that of
poetic achievement to sway the decision would destroy the significance of the award and would in principle deny the validity
of the objective perception of value on which any civilized society
must rest."

Now, in principle, this is a statement with which anyone
at all concerned for literature must surely be inclined to agree.
The bitter experiences of our century have taught us that literary
judgments should not be at the service of political movements
or ideologies. Just as we are appalled at the Soviet government's
persecution of Solzhenitsyn because of his anti-Communist opinions, so we should not allow, say, our distaste for Pablo Neruda's
Communist opinions to impede our appreciation of his poetry
or prejudice us against him in case he were being considered
for an award. (But notice a crucial difference. The issue in the
Soviet Union is not whether the government should honor
Solzhenitsyn but whether it should allow his books to be published; while in the Pound controversy the issue is not whether
Pound should be censored, something that no responsible person
has advocated, but whether he should be honored.)

We are all, or should all be, committed to the value of autonomous aesthetic judgment; but to say that is not yet to cope with
the difficulties raised by a work like *The Cantos*. For in this
case there can be no clear separation between the man and the

poet, or his opinions and his creative work. Any effort to weigh Pound's "poetic achievement" must take into account the kinds of anti-Semitic passages I have quoted—passages that involve not only political beliefs with which one may or may not disagree but something far more fundamental in our moral life, emotions of hatred utterly repugnant. "How far is it possible," asked William Barrett in the Bollingen discussion, "for technical embellishments [or even, one might add, integral technical accomplishments—I.H.] to transform vicious and ugly matter into beautiful poetry?"

If we look at the anti-Semitic and Fascist passages in isolation, then there should be little difficulty in advancing a negative *literary* judgment, since they have no distinction of thought or language. If we ask what the weight of such passages may be in the work as a whole, then the problem becomes trickier: We must rely on our intelligence, our sense of tact, our view of the relation between the parts and the whole.

But perhaps I have gone too fast. There is a possible judgment suggested by Allen Tate, the most complicated of all, that might go like this: "Yes, these passages are indeed odious but even in them, as in *The Cantos* in their entirety, language is employed with such power and vividness that we have no choice but to overlook the detested content and praise the verbal achievement." This view, pushing the separation between form and content to an extreme, is one that I find hard to accept. Yet in honesty I must admit that it points to a fact in our experience of literature: the fact that we can at times find moving and significant a poem or novel that we may also find, in its controlling ideas, deplorable or offensive.

The question then becomes, how far can we push this kind of analysis? I confess that I have no general answer, only an appeal to a common experience of tact. Perhaps a few examples will help. I am greatly moved by John Donne's *Holy Sonnets*, even though I am not a Christian—but here it is simply a matter of reaching imaginatively the power of a religious outlook that is not mine yet has behind it an enormous penetrative grasp of human existence. I deeply admire Louis-Ferdinand Céline's novels, though I detest his fascism—but here it is simply a matter of making a neat distinction between his novels, authentic works of art almost entirely free of ideology, and his tracts, which are mere rubbish. I read with pleasure the poems of Bertolt Brecht, although I am repelled by his Stalinism—but here, not so simply, it is a matter of seeing how his subtlety of mind breaks past, complicates, and sometimes undercuts his ideological stance.

But—to turn to a writer of far less consequence—when I read LeRoi Jones calling for "dagger poems in the slimy bellies of the owner-jews" or urging black people to say "the magic words . . .: Up against the wall mother fucker this is a stick up!" to "Sears, Bambergers, Klein's, Hahnes', Chase, and the smaller joosh enterprises," then I know I am in the presence of a racist hoodlum inciting people to blood. And I am not going to be deflected from that perception by talk about rhythm, metaphor, and diction.

Ezra Pound's *Cantos* fall somewhere between the two kinds of writing I have just noted, those in which intellectual disapproval does not significantly affect one's appreciation of a literary work and those in which the destestable matter is so gross, so ugly that there is nothing to appreciate. The truth is, then, that almost any literary statement about *The Cantos* is likely to have some validity and that the problem is to rank particular judgments into a proper discipline.

Let us therefore grant the "poetic achievement" of *The Cantos*. That still does not settle the problem of whether an award should have been given to its author. The argument put forward by Clement Greenberg in 1949 is a very serious one:

> I do not quarrel here with the aesthetic verdict, but I question its primacy in the affair at hand, a primacy that hints at an absolute acceptance of the autonomy not only of art but of every separate field of human activity. Does no hierarchy of value obtain among them? Would Mr. Eliot, for instance approve of this for his "Christian society"?

It was considerations of this kind that led some of us to feel that even if the *Pisan Cantos* were indeed the best poetry of 1948, the award to Pound should still not have been given and that an appropriate response would have been: "Yes, Pound wrote the best poetry of this past year, but on those occasions when aesthetic standards and our central human values clash in fundamental ways, the latter can be more important. We do not wish in any way to harm Ezra Pound, but because of what he has done as both poet and man, we cannot extend to him the hand of admiration that a prize would signify."

Something, if only a word or two, needs to be said about "the autonomy of literature," the standard that has been raised as the main reason for favoring an award to Pound. The matter is very complicated, and all I wish to do here is to suggest that it is possible for a reasonable man to believe in the autonomy of literature while nevertheless holding to any one of several views on the Pound case.

By the autonomy of literature we mean, I would say, that a poem or novel has properties distinctive to itself; that such a work must be perceived, analyzed, and judged with categories distinctive to its kind; that it is an imaginative verbal composition, which cannot be reduced to other kinds of communication since it involves a use of language different from the ways language may be used in exposition, argument, or exhortation. So far, with necessary verbal corrections, most critics would probably agree.

Difficulties arise when we try to discover the relations between this literary work and the external world of familiar experience. How are we to relate our experience of the literary work, an experience distinctive and irreducible, to the larger flow of human experience of which it is presumably a part?

Some critics, including myself, would say that even as they recognize that the work of literature constitutes a distinctive object, qualitatively different from any others, it also shares elements of valuation and perception with those employed both in our common experience and in our response to other kinds of verbal composition. The poem or novel is not a tract or a case study, but the materials it employs and the criteria by which it organizes them are drawn from experiences and perceptions that can also pertain to the tract or the case study. As a result, there cannot be a total discontinuity between the way we use precepts of morality and norms of social valuation in literary analysis and the way we use them in direct experience.

There is, however, another view, very powerful among literary people. This view insists that the work of literature is not merely autonomous in the sense of being distinctive but also, one might say, "separate" in kind, "self-sufficient" in its very being. It cannot really be understood by references back to external reality; it is not an "imitation" of the world we know; it inhabits a universe of its own. Consequently statements in a poem may not be understood or judged as if they had been made in direct speech, for the "aesthetic transaction" has its own norms and justifications.

Now, even this hurried description ought to suggest the ways in which contrasting aesthetic premises may lead to sharply varying responses to the Pound case—as it also suggests that a belief in the autonomy of literature does not automatically confirm any response. Granted that a poem is not, in any ordinary sense, a statement, what are we to make of the statements that occur within the poem? That is the question with which we end and it is perhaps just as well to leave it at that. I would only add that Pound himself has never taken shelter in any aestheticist defense, but has always insisted on the continuity of his life, his thought, and his work.

There remains one argument, a troubling argument, for granting Pound an award in 1972, though not in 1949: "It was right to refuse in 1949 to join in honoring Pound, but now time has passed, the old poet has endured enough suffering, so that we should be ready to forgive him. What is more, in a 1968 interview with Allen Ginsburg, Pound expressed his regret for having made anti-Semitic statements." This argument appeals to one's humane impulses—who would not like to think himself capable of forgiving those who have wronged him? But I wonder whether it is pertinent here.

Insofar as I am concerned, or anyone else in the Pound dispute, there is nothing to forgive. Pound has not wronged me in any direct way, and I am ready to suppose that if I had chanced to visit him a few decades ago, as a fledgling critic eager to talk to a master poet, he would have been as generous to me as he was to many others—even though I happen to be a Jew.

Yet that is precisely what makes one feel so complete a despair about literary anti-Semitism. Pound wished none of us personal harm; his rantings against the Jews were utterly *abstract*, a phantasm of ideology that is a major dimension of their terribleness. It was a theological hatred that he was releasing, a hatred that never sought a particular victim or even envisaged the consequences of its rhetoric; all one can charge him with—all!—is a blind complicity in the twentieth century's victimization of innocents.

We may then wonder: Does anyone have the right to forgive Ezra Pound? Who could grant me or any other person the right to speak for those millions who paid the final price for anti-Semitism? It might be said by way of reply that neither have I nor has anyone else been granted the right to refuse Pound forgiveness. And I would entirely agree with that, too.

But the question of whether to honor Pound involves neither the granting nor the refusal of forgiveness. It involves something else: I do not believe that we can yet close the books of twentieth-century history, certainly not as long as any of us remains alive who can remember the days of the mass murder. The wounds have not healed, and for some they never will. That is why the time has not come when Ezra Pound should be honored by his fellow writers. For it is not at all a matter of forgiving; it is a matter of remembering.

DOWN AND OUT IN NEW YORK AND CHICAGO

Saul Bellow, Professor Herzog and Mr. Sammler

WHERE SHALL A CONTEMPORARY NOVEL begin? Perhaps unavoidably: with the busted hero reeling from a messy divorce and moaning in a malodorous furnished room; picking at his psyche's wounds like a boy at knee scabs; rehearsing the mighty shambles of ambition ("how I rose from humble origins to complete disaster"); cursing the heart-and-ball breakers, both wives and volunteers, who have, he claims, laid him low; snarling contempt at his own self-pity with a Johnsonian epigram, "Grief, Sir, is a species of idleness"; and yet, amidst all this woe, bubbling with intellectual hope, as also with intellectual gas, and consoling himself with the truth that indeed "there were worse cripples around."

This is Moses Herzog, Saul Bellow's hero-patsy. Herzog is a representative man of the sixties, eaten away by those "personal relations" which form the glory and the foolishness of a post-political intelligentsia. He is a good scholar, but cannot complete his books. He rips off imaginary letters to great men, finessing their wisdom and patronizing their mistakes. He is a lady-killer, "aging" at 47 and worried about his potency. He is a loving father twice-divorced, who each time has left behind him a child as token of good will. He is a true-blue Jewish groaner, and perversely, groans against fashionable despair. Inside or outside our skins, we all know Herzog: *Hypocrite lecteur–mon semblable –mein schlemiehl.* Hungering for a life of large significance, eager for "a politics in the Aristotelian sense," he nevertheless keeps melting into the mercies of women, each of whom, in sequence, really understands him.

All of Bellow's books—whether melancholy realism, moral fable or picaresque fantasia—represent for him a new departure, a chosen risk in form and perception. Bellow has the most powerful mind among contemporary American novelists, or at least, he is the American novelist who best assimilates his intelligence to creative purpose. This might have been foreseen at the beginning of his career, for he has always been able to turn out a first-rate piece of discursive prose; what could not have been foreseen was that he would also become a virtuoso of fictional technique and language.

Behind Bellow's writing there is always a serious intention, but as he grows older he becomes increasingly devoted to the idea of the novel as sheer spectacle. His last few books comprise a hectic and at times ghastly bazaar of contemporary experience; they ring with the noise of struggle; characters dash in and out, glistening with bravura; adventures pile up merrily, as if the decline of the West had not been definitely proclaimed; the male characters plunge and rise, mad for transcendence; the women (a little tiresomely) are all very beautiful and mostly very damaging. And the language spins.

Before and, I hope, after everything else has been said, *Herzog* should be praised as a marvelously animated performance. The minor figures are drawn as sharp caricature, without the distraction of psychological probe or nuance, and sometimes, when Bellow's zest becomes compulsive, a little overfocused. There are foul-mouth lawyers, boiling with drug-store wisdom and "potato love"; a sadly ineffectual father fumbling at bootleggery; a professor who loves, solely but purely, his monkey. There are Herzog's ladies of the season: Sono, a Japanese doll who soothes the spirit and, Oriental-style, washes the back of Master Moses in an Upper West Side bathtub, while cooing at him in baby French, "mon professeur d'amour," and Ramona, bravely marching into middle age with an overload of "understanding"

and graduate credentials in sex, who "entered a room provoca-
tively . . . one hand touching her thigh, as though she carried
a knife in her garter belt."

And then the demons, the evil spirits: Madeleine, the wife
who betrays; Valentine Gersbach, the best friend with whom
she does it.

A talentless buffoon-double of the talented hero, Valentine
Gersbach (what a name!) booms out the latest highbrow cant in
his great bearish voice and ends by lecturing to Hadassah clubs
on Martin Buber. Toward Valentine Bellow is merciless, yet
one is seldom troubled by this open display of aggression; for
there is no pretense in this novel that we are being shown a
world which exists, self-sufficient, apart from the neurotic inflam-
mations of the central figure. Gersbach is a clown, a windbag,
a traitor, the kind of man who makes intellectuals wish they
were dead when they hear him parroting their words; yet he
is utterly alive, one waits for him to reappear on the page, and
finally even he wins a moment of humane redemption: secretly,
angrily, Herzog watches Gersbach bathing his (Herzog's) little
girl and must admit to himself that the act, though done by
a betrayer, is yet done with tenderness.

Madeleine is drawn with pure venom, a sentiment capable
of generating in writers, as in other men, great quantities of
energy. She is, naturally, a beauty; she piddles in Russian intellectual history and Catholic conversion; she outmaneuvers the
slumping Herzog not merely at sexual games (where she has,
after all, the advantage of youth) but also in intellectual competition. When Herzog complains about her extravagance, her arrogance, her paranoia, she replies with the great modern rationale:
"Anyway, it'll never be boring." A moony schoolgirl meets
Madeleine, and describes her in a phrase embodying the great
modern cant: "She gives a sense of significant encounter." With
her postures of depth, screeches of enthusiasm, learned references
and distinguished airs, Madeleine is the female pseudo-
intellectual done, and done in, once and for all. The portrait
is unjust, an utter libel, but a classic of male retaliation.

Herzog himself is not, in the traditional sense, a novelistic
character at all. He is observed neither from a cool distance
nor through intimate psychological penetration. We experience

him intensely, entering his very bones; yet, trapped as we are in his inner turmoil, we cannot be certain that finally we know him. For Bellow has not provided a critical check: there is no way of learning what any of the other characters, by way of Jamesian correction, might think or feel about Herzog. Bellow offers not a full-scale characterization but a full-length exposure of a state of being. We do not see Herzog acting in the world, we are made captive in the world of Herzog. The final picture is that of Herzog in cross-section, bleeding from the cut.

In one sense, then, there is a complete identification between Bellow and Herzog: the consciousness of the character forms the enclosing medium of the novel. But in a more important respect Bellow manages skillfully to avoid the kind of identification which might lead one to conclude that he "favors" his central character or fails to see through his weaknesses and falsities—a fault that could radically distort the line of vision by which everything is to be considered. That Herzog cannot accurately perceive the other figures in the novel and that we are closely confined to his sense of them, is true and in ways I shall later suggest, a limitation. But not a crippling limitation. For it soon becomes clear that, while totally committed to Herzog's experience, Bellow is not nearly so committed to his estimate of that experience.

Things, to be sure, do not always work out neatly. There are sections in which the malice toward Madeleine gets out of hand, so much so that one suspects Bellow of settling private scores. And while the device of having Herzog compose imaginary letters is often amusing—

> Dear Doktor Professor Heidigger, I should like to know what you mean by the expression "the fall into the quotidian." When did this fall occur? Where were we standing when it happened?

—one becomes somewhat irked at being unable, at times, to grasp which of the letters are serious, that is, Bellow's opinions, and which are not, that is, Herzog's conniptions. Ambiguity? No doubt. We all know about this prime blessing of modern literature; but there are occasions when the uses of ambiguity can themselves be ambiguous, shading off into confusion or evasiveness.

For the most part, however, *Herzog* marks a notable advance in technique over Bellow's previous books. He has become a master of something that is rarely discussed in criticism because it is hard to do more than point toward it: the art of timing, which concerns the massing, centering and disposition of the characters and creates a sense of delight in the sheer motion of the narrative.

Bellow has also found a good solution to a technical problem which keeps arising in the contemporary novel. Most readers, I imagine, groan a little when they see a novelist wheeling into position one of those lengthy and leaden flashbacks in which, we know in advance, the trauma will be unveiled that is to explain the troubles of time-present. These flashbacks, by now one of the dreariest conventions of the novel, result in a lumpiness of narrative surface and blockage of narrative flow. But Bellow has managed to work out a form in which the illusion of simultaneity of time—a blend of past with the present-moving-into-future—is nicely maintained. Instead of the full-scale flashback, which often rests on the mistaken premise that a novelist needs to provide a psychiatric or sociological casebook on his characters, Bellow allows the consciousness of his narrator to flit about in time, restlessly, nervously, thereby capturing essential fragments of the past as they break into the awareness of the present. Through these interlockings of time—brief, dramatic and made to appear simultaneous—he creates the impression of a sustained rush of experience.

Bellow began his career as a novelist of somber intellectuality: his impressive early book *The Victim* asks almost to be read as a fable concerning the difficulties of attempting a secure moral judgment in our day. With *Augie March* he made a sharp turn, casting aside the urban contemplativeness and melancholy of his previous work, and deciding to regard American life as wonderfully "open," a great big shapeless orange bursting with the juices of vitality. Though in some ways his most virtuoso performance, *Augie March* suffers from a programmatic exuberance: it is fun to watch the turns and tricks the suddenly acrobatic Bellow can execute, yet hard to suppress a touch of anxiety concerning his heartbeat.

With *Augie March* Bellow also began to work out a new fictional style, for which there may be some predecessors—possibly Daniel Fuchs and Nathanael West—but which in the main is an original achievement. By now it has come to be imitated by many American Jewish novelists as well as by a few gentiles trying wistfully to pass, but none of these manages it nearly so well as Bellow himself.

What Bellow did was to leave behind him the bleak neutrality of naturalistic prose and the quavering sensibility of the Jamesian novel: the first, he seemed to feel, was too lifeless and the second insufficiently masculine. Beginning with *Augie March*—but none of this applies to his masterful novella, *Seize the Day*—Bellow's prose becomes strongly anti-literary, a roughing up of diction and breaking down of syntax in order to avoid familiar patterns and expectations. The prose now consists of a rich, thick impasto of verbal color in which a splatter of sidewalk eloquence is mixed with erudite by-play. Together with this planned coarsening of texture, there is a great emphasis on speed, a violent wrenching and even forcing of images, all the consequence of his wish to break away from the stateliness of the literary sentence. Analytic refinement is sacrificed to sensuous vigor, careful psychological notation to the brawling of energy, syntactical qualification to kinesthetic thrust. (One is reminded a bit of action painting.) Psychology is out, absolutely out: for to psychologize means to reflect, to hesitate, to qualify, to modulate, to analyze. By contrast, the aim of Bellow's neo-baroque style is to communicate sensations of immediacy and intensity, even when dealing with abstract intellectual topics—to communicate, above all, the sense that men are still alive. Toward this end he is prepared to yield niceties of phrasing, surface finish, sometimes even coherence of structure.

It is a style admirably suited to the flaming set piece, the rapid vignette, the picaresque excursion. But it is not so well suited to a sustained and complex action, or a lengthy flow of experience, or a tragic plot, or what George Moore, in discussing the nature of fiction, called the "rhythmic sequence of events." In *Augie March* there is a run of action but hardly a plot; in *Herzog* a superbly realized situation but hardly a developing action; and in both of these novels, as well as in *Henderson*, not much of a "rhythmic sequence of events." That is why, I think, none of them has a fully satisfying denouement, an organic fulfillment of the action. In principle these books could continue forever, and that is one reason Bellow finds it hard to end them. He simply stops, much against one's will.

Finally, Bellow's style draws heavily from the Yiddish, not so much in borrowed diction as in underlying intonation and rhythm. Bellow's relation to Yiddish is much more easy and authoritative than that of most other American Jewish writers. The jabbing interplay of ironies, the intimate vulgarities, the strange blend of sentimental and sardonic which characterizes Yiddish speech are lassoed into Bellow's English: so that what we get is not a sick exploitation of folk memory but a vibrant linguistic and cultural transmutation. (Precisely at the moment when Yiddish is dying off as an independent language, it has experienced an astonishing, and not always happy, migration into American culture. In two or three decades students of American literature may have to study Yiddish for reasons no worse than those for which students of English literature study Anglo-Saxon.)

One of the most pleasing aspects of *Herzog* is that Bellow has brought together his two earlier manners: the melancholy and the bouncy, the "Russian" and the "American," *Seize the Day* and *Augie March*. *Herzog* is almost free of the gratuitous verbalism which marred *Augie March*, yet retains its vividness and richness of texture.

There is a similar marshaling of Bellow's earlier themes. For some years now he has been obsessed with that fatigue of spirit which hangs so dismally over contemporary life. *Seize the Day* shows a man utterly exhausted, unable so much as to feel his despair until the wrenching final page. *Augie March* shows a man composing a self out of a belief in life's possibilities. Of the two books *Seize the Day* seems to me the more convincing and authentic, perhaps because despair is easier to portray than joy, perhaps because the experience of our time, as well as its literature, predisposes us to associate truth with gloom. In any case, what seems notable about *Herzog* is that nothing is here blinked or evaded, rhetoric does not black out reality (Herzog declares himself "aging, vain, terribly narcissistic, suffering without proper dignity"); yet the will to struggle, the insistence upon human possibility, is maintained and not as a mere flourish but as the award of agony. Herzog learns that

> . . . To look for fulfillment in another . . . was a feminine game. And the man who shops from woman to woman, though his heart aches with idealism, with the desire for pure love, has entered the female realm.

Not, perhaps, a very remarkable lesson, but worth learning when the cost comes high. More importantly, Herzog says about himself, wryly but truthfully, that he is a man who "thought and cared about belief." That is the first step toward salvation.

For all its vividness as performance, *Herzog* is a novel driven by an idea. It is a serious idea, though, in my judgment, neither worked out with sufficient care nor worked into the grain of the book with sufficient depth. Herzog, he tells us, means to write something that will deal "with a new angle on the modern condition, showing how life could be lived by renewing universal connections, overturning the last of the Romantic errors about the uniqueness of the Self, revising the old Western, Faustian ideology. . . . " This time clearly speaking for Bellow, Herzog declares himself opposed to

> The canned sauerkraut of Spengler's "Prussian Socialism," the commonplaces of the Wasteland outlook, the cheap mental stimulants of Alienation, the cant and rant of pipsqueaks about Inauthenticity and Forlornness. I can't accept this foolish dreariness. We are talking about the whole life of mankind. The subject is too great, too deep for such weakness, cowardice. . . .

And in the magazine *Location* Bellow has written a sharp attack on "the 'doom of the West' [which] is the Established Church in modern literature." It is a Church, he says, which asserts the individual to be helpless among the impersonal mechanisms and sterilities of modern life; it cultivates self-pity and surrender; and it is wrong.

Bellow has touched on something real. Talk about "the decline of the West" can be elitist rubbish. The posture of alienation, like any other, can collapse into social accommodation. Cries of despair can become mere notes of fashion. Where the motif of alienation in the literature of modernism during the late 19th and early 20th centuries signified an act of truth, courage and sometimes rebellion too, now it can easily become the occasion for a mixture of private snobbism and public passivity. Yet may not all ideas suffer this sort of outcome in a culture which seems endlessly capable of assimilating and devitalizing everything? Suppose Bellow's assault upon alienation becomes fashionable: will it not then suffer a public fate similar to that of the ideas he attacks?

Bellow is being just a little too cavalier in so readily disposing of a central theme of modernist literature. Surely, as it was manifested in the work of writers like Joyce, Flaubert, Eliot and Baudelaire, the sense of alienation expressed a profound and even exhilarating response to the reality of industrial society. (An imagining of despair can be as bracing as a demand for joy can be ruthless.) And does not the sense of alienation, if treated not as a mere literary convenience but as a galling social fact—does this not continue to speak truthfully to significant conditions in our life?

I raise these matters because Bellow, as a serious writer, must want his readers to consider them not merely in but also beyond the setting of his novel. When, however, one does consider them strictly in the context of *Herzog*, certain critical issues present themselves. There is a discrepancy between what the book actually is—brilliant but narrow in situation and scope—and the sweeping intentions that lie behind it; or in other words, between the dramatic texture and the thematic purpose. In the end one feels that *Herzog* is too hermetic a work, the result of a technique which encloses us rigidly in the troubles of a man during his phase of withdrawal from the world. The material is absorbing in its own right; it is handled with great skill; but in relation to the intended theme, it all seems a little puny.

Bellow has conceived of the book as a stroke against the glorification of the sick self, but the novel we have—as picture, image, honest exposure—remains largely caught up with the thrashings of the sick self. One wants from Bellow a novel that will not be confined to a single besieged consciousness but instead will negotiate the kind of leap into the world which he proclaims, to savor the world's freshness and struggle against its recalcitrance, perhaps even to enter "politics in the Aristotelian sense."

II

From book to book, ornament and variations apart, Saul Bellow has really had one commanding subject: the derangements of the soul in the clutter of our cities, the poverty of a life deprived of order and measure. His work has in part continued the line of sensibility established by T.S. Eliot in *The Waste Land*, for in Chicago and New York one can ask as urgently as in London, "what branches grow out of this stony rubbish?" But Bellow has also diverged, in the more original portions of his work, from the Eliot line of sensibility, for he has come to feel that the once-liberating perceptions embodied in Eliot's great poem have, through the erosion of popularity, become clichés. Bellow now writes from a conviction that even today men can establish a self-ordering discipline which rests on a tentative-sardonic faith in the value of life without faith. As he remarks in his brilliant novel *Mr. Sammler's Planet:*

> . . . *people exaggerated the tragic accents of their condition. They stressed too hard the disintegrated assurances; what formerly was believed, trusted, was now bitterly circled in black irony. The rejected bourgeois black of stability thus translated. That too was improper, incorrect. People justifying idleness, silliness, shallowness, distemper, lust—turning former respectability inside out.*

There is always a danger in the work of an urban novelist like Bellow that his books will turn into still another tiresome afterword to the literary talk about Angst and Alienation; but what has saved Bellow from that fate has been his fierce insistence that, no matter how heavy the cloud of despair hanging over this (or any other) time, we can still find some pleasure in sociability and our bodies, or, at the least, still experience that root sense of obligation which the mere fact of being human imposes on us.

More and more, in recent years, Bellow has found himself cast as an adversary—not always openly, sometimes too cagily—of the dominant styles of our culture. Growing older, entering those hard years when one realizes that the middle of the journey is past, Bellow has not only become a master of his own special idiom, that verbal impasto which mixes demotic richness with mandarin eloquence; he has also found his place, no longer a dangling man, as person and writer, and set forth on a stubborn, uncertain quest for the cup of wisdom, that cup, if it exists at all, in which the veteran artist hopes to squeeze some essence of contemplation out of the wastes of experience.

For putting it so bluntly Bellow isn't likely to thank me, and indeed his characteristic strategy, at least until this book, has been to protect his flanks through smoke screens of elaborate comic rhetoric. He has maintained two narrative voices signifying two world-outlooks, the first sententious and the second sardonic, yet with the declamations of the sententious voice never quite undone, and sometimes even slyly reinforced, by the thrusts of the sardonic voice. This has kept the reader on his toes, precisely where he belongs.

Mr. Sammler's Planet is set in a milieu that has become Bellow's own, a created province of the imagination quite as much as Wessex is Hardy's and Yoknapatawpha Faulkner's. New York's Upper West Side is a grimy place, at once unfit for human habitation and the scene of what must, I suppose, be called an advanced civilization. It is ugly, filthy, dangerous; it reeks with dog shit; its streets are crammed with the flotsam of society: winos, junkies, pushers, whores, grifters; yet here too are stately refugees, stuffy reformers, literary intellectuals, eager Puerto Ricans, and elderly Jews haunted by memories of sweatshops and concentration camps and no longer able to take life as incessant struggle. In this menagerie of integration, anomie, and good feeling, people still manage to live.

Bellow first immortalized this neighborhood in *Seize the Day*, but the Upper West Side in that great novella was mainly a bright-colored backdrop to a personal drama. In *Mr. Sammler's Planet*, however, the Upper West Side is more than setting, it becomes a tangible sign of the nature of our time. In the Upper West Side, as Bellow sees it, the continuities of ordinary living, by no means always a triumph but never to be sneered at, manage somehow to coexist with the raspy notional foolishness our culture casts off like smoke. The Upper West Side becomes transformed in Bellow's fiction into a principle of sorts, a mixture of health and sickness exemplifying our condition, and not merely through his gift for evoking every street, every figure, every shade of light and dark, but still more through the saturation of his characters with the spirit of the place. On a smaller scale,

Bellow does for the Upper West Side what Lawrence has done for the Midlands and Hardy for Dorset: a linkage of setting and figure so close that the two come to seem inseparable parts in a tradition of shared experience.

Mr. Sammler is a Polish Jew in his seventies. In his early years he had worked as a correspondent in London, which accounts for his old-fashioned liberal courtliness and values; later he escaped miraculously from a death convoy in the Nazi camps. Sated with experiences beyond absorption and reflections forever conjectural, Artur Sammler looks out upon America in the sixties: its violence, its coarseness, its jabbery mindlessness, its sexual cult. He is not surprised, having lived in Europe after the First World War; he is alarmed, knowing that history can repeat itself. Yet Sammler is not a polemicist, he is too canny for easy visions of apocalypse. Preparing for death, he knows the world is no longer his.

Sammlen means "to collect" in Yiddish, and Sammler, like all those compulsive talkers, half-clown and half-philosopher, in Bellow's novels, is a collector of experience, sometimes a tentative sorter of conclusions. First of all his *Sammlung* consists of relatives, mostly female. Shula, Sammler's daughter, was saved by a Polish convent during the holocaust and now is "almost always at Easter" a "week-long Catholic." Mercilessly devoted to the higher things in life, this amiable loon believes her father is writing an inspired memoir of H.G. Wells. The complications of the plot, if there is a plot, devolve partly around Shula stealing an Indian scholar's manuscript because she thinks it will help her daddy. Any day on Broadway, our garbaged Mortality Row, you can see Shula between 72nd and 86th Streets:

> *She turned up in a miniskirt of billiard-table green, revealing legs sensual in outline but without inner sensuality; at the waist a broad leather belt; over shoulders, bust, a coarse strong Guatemalan embroidered shirt; on her head a wig such as a female impersonator might put on at a convention of salesmen.*

Next, Sammler's niece Margotte, also mad for culture but in a more *gemütlich* Weimar way: a dumpy lady prepared to discuss Hannah Arendt's theory of evil (or anyone else's theory about anything) all day long, while looking helplessly for a piece of salami with which to make a sandwich. And last, Angela, "one of those handsome, passionate, rich girls . . . always an important social and human category," who is driving herself crazy through sheer sexual concentration. The derangements of the first two women are of earlier decades, Angela's of this very moment.

This cast, with several supporting players, is more than a bit mad yet not at all insufferable. Human all too human, it is presented by Bellow with an affectionate sardonic detail, and the incidents that pile up with seeming casualness bring them into quick changes of relationship, all calculated to set off Sammler's dilemmas and reflections. He detects a black pickpocket, superbly elegant and powerful, working the Riverside bus; the pickpocket, aware that he has been seen but not frightened, follows Sammler into an apartment lobby; and there, as evidence of his superiority of being—quite as if he'd been reading certain reviews—he exposes to Sammler his formidable penis. It is an act of symbolism Sammler is prepared to understand, if not quite appreciate.

In another episode, again shot through with the fevers of our moment, Sammler accepts an invitation to lecture at Columbia about England during the thirties:

> *"Old Man! You quoted Orwell before."*
> *"Yes?"*
> *"You quoted him to say that British radicals were all protected by the Royal Navy? . . . "*
> *"Yes, I believe he did say that."*
> *"That's a lot of shit."*
> *Sammler could not speak.*
> *"Orwell was a fink. He was a sick counterrevolutionary. It's good he died when he did. And what you are saying is shit." Turning to the audience, extending violent arms and raising his palms like a Greek dancer, he said, "Why do you listen to this effete old shit? What has he got to tell you? His balls are dry. He's dead. He can't come."*

Lively-odd figures, brilliantly managed incidents—but what does it all come to? That, until the very last paragraph, is the question one keeps asking about *Mr. Sammler's Planet.*

Perhaps there's an answer of sorts in the lectures and speeches, more in the style of *Herzog* than *Seize the Day*, that Bellow scatters through his pages? For whole sections the book moves into a genre somewhat like those conversations Thomas Love Peacock wrote in the nineteenth century, in which voices of varying refinement representing disembodied but fixed opinions are set up in an interplay of friction. There are readers who have always felt these portions of Bellow's novels to be digressive or pretentious, in any case lessening the immediate emotional impact of his work. I think such criticisms mainly—not always—ill-conceived, first because Bellow is a man of high intelligence so that his generalized commentary is intrinsically absorbing, and second because he has the rare gift of transforming dialectic into drama, casuistry into comedy, so that one is steadily aware of the close relationship between his discursive passages and the central narrative. Here is Sammler-Bellow ruminating about the culture of the sixties:

> The labor of Puritanism now was ending. The dark satanic mills changing into light satanic mills. The reprobates converted into children of joy, the sexual ways of the seraglio and of the Congo bush adopted by the emancipated masses of New York. . . . Old Sammler with his screwy visions! He saw the increasing triumph of Enlightenment—Liberty, Fraternity, Equality, Adultery! . . . Dark romanticism now took hold. As old at least as the strange Orientalism of the Knights Templar, and since then filled up with Lady Stanhopes, Baudelaires, de Nervals, Stevensons, and Gauguins—those South-loving barbarians. Oh yes, the Templars. They had adored the Muslims. One hair from the head of a Saracen was more precious than the whole body of a Christian. Such crazy fervor! And now all the racism, all the strange erotic persuasions, the tourism and local color, the exotics of it had broken up but the mental masses, inheriting everything in a debased state, had formed an idea of the corrupting disease of being white and of the healing power of black. The dreams of nineteenth-century poets polluted the psychic atmosphere of the great boroughs and suburbs of New York. Add to this the dangerous lunging staggering crazy violence of fanatics, and the trouble was very deep. Like many people who had seen the world collapse once, Mr. Sammler entertained the possibility it might collapse twice. He did not agree with refugee friends that this doom was inevitable, but liberal beliefs did not seem capable of self-defense, and you could smell decay. You could see the suicidal impulses of civilization pushing strongly.

Yet we are still dealing with fragments, episodes, set pieces: our most gifted novelist turning somersaults and negotiating leaps like Villella on a spree. Is that all? Are we not bound to expect some ultimate unity of feeling and theme, no matter how slyly achieved?

It is there, but so risky in execution that many readers, I suspect, will deny its presence. Throughout the book Sammler keeps returning to the hospital room of a friend, Dr. Arnold Elya Gruner, a rich and crafty man, sometime Mafia abortionist, soured father of Angela the handsome nymph, and yet, as we come to see, a decent man in quite commonplace ways. Elya had rescued Sammler and Shula after the war, had given them money with which to live: a not very costly, and if you wish, a *bourgeois* gesture. Sammler knows his faults, but knows too that in this ordinary man there are strengths and resources of a kind we must have if we are not to perish on this earth.

An old man implicated, despite his wish for detachment, in the lunacies of his daughter, the gabble of his niece, the suicidal thrust of Angela, the brutalities of the Columbia heckler, the threat of the pickpocket, and a host of other menacing fantasies and realities that rise out of the very pavements of the Upper West Side, Sammler all the while keeps yielding himself to the most fundamental themes of gravity: a man is dying, a man who has been good to me. He has shown himself responsible to me, I must be responsible to him. Gradually all the foolishness of Sammler's days, all the absurdity and ugliness of his encounters, all the brittleness and bravura of his thought, give way. There remains only the imperative of the human obligation. Standing over the dead body of his quite unremarkable friend, Sammler speaks the final words of the book:

> *He was aware that he must meet, and he did meet—through all the confusion and degraded clowning of this life through which we are speeding—he did meet the terms of his contract. The terms which, in his inmost heart, each man knows. As I know mine. As all know. For that is the truth of it—that we all know, God that we know, that we know, we know, we know.*

These lines, like most of Bellow's endings, constitute an overwhelming stroke. Carrying its truth as a precious cargo I yet find myself wondering whether Eliot, a writer of different persuasion, might not ask, "Yes, in our inmost hearts we know, or at least remember, but *how* do we know? Is it not through the memory of traditions lapsed and beliefs denied?" What Bellow might say in reply I would not presume to guess, but the strength of the position from which he would speak seems very clear to me. Of all the "American Jewish writers" of the last few decades Bellow is not merely the most gifted by far, but the most serious—and the most Jewish in his seriousness. In him alone, or almost alone, the tradition of immigrant Jewishness, minus the *Schmaltz* and *Schmutz* the decades have stuccoed onto it, survives with a stern dignity. Sammler speaking at the end is something like a resurrected voice: experience fades, explanations deceive, but the iron law of life is the obligation we owe one another. The *Sammlung* is complete.

PHILIP ROTH RECONSIDERED

. . . the will takes pleasures in begetting its own image.

—J. V. CUNNINGHAM

WHEN PHILIP ROTH published his collection of stories, *Goodbye, Columbus*, in 1959, the book was generously praised and I was among the reviewers who praised it. Whatever modulations of judgment one might want now to propose, it is not hard to see why Roth should have won approval. The work of a newcomer still in his twenties, *Goodbye, Columbus* bristled with a literary self-confidence such as few writers two or three decades older than Roth could command. His stories were immediately recognizable as his own, distinctive in voice, attitude, and subject; they possessed the lucidities of definition, though I would now add, lucidities harsh and grimacing in their over-focus. None of the fiction Roth has since published approaches this first collection in literary interest; yet, by no very surprising turn of events, his reputation has steadily grown these past few years. He now stands close to the center of our culture (if that is anything for him to be pleased about), and he is accorded serious attention both by a number of literary critics and those rabbis and Jewish communal leaders who can hardly wait to repay the animus he has lavished upon them. At least for a moment or two, until the next fashion appears, we are in the presence not only of an interesting writer but also a cultural "case."

I

The stories in *Goodbye, Columbus* are of a special kind. They are neither probings through strategic incident to reach the inner folds of character nor affectionate renderings of regional, class, or ethnic behavior. They are not the work of a writer absorbed in human experience as it is, mirroring his time with self-effacing objectivity. Nor is Roth the kind of writer who takes pleasure in discovering the world's body, yielding himself to the richness of its surfaces and the mysteries of its ultimate course. If one recalls some of the motives that have moved our novelists—a hunger to absorb and render varieties of social experience, a respect for the plenitude of the mind, a sense of awe induced by contemplation of the curve of heroic fate, a passion for moral scrutiny—none of these seems crucially to operate in Roth's work. It is, in fact, a little comic to invoke such high motifs in discussing that work, and not because Roth is a minor writer but because he is a writer who has programmatically denied himself the vision of major possibilities.

What one senses nevertheless in the stories of *Goodbye, Columbus* is an enormous thrust of personal and ideological assertiveness. In the clash which, like Jacob with his angel, the writer must undertake with the world around him—and, unlike Jacob, must learn when and how to lose—there can be little doubt that Roth will steadily pin his opponent to the ground. His great need is for a stance of superiority, the pleasure, as Madison Avenue says, of always being "on top of it." (Perhaps he should have been a literary critic.) Only rarely do his fictions risk the uncharted regions of imaginative discovery; almost all his work drives a narrative toward cognitive ends fixed in advance. Roth appears indifferent to the Keatsian persuasion that a writer should be "capable of being in uncertainties, mysteries, doubts," since that would require a discipline of patience; nor does he pay much heed to the Coleridgean persuasion that "tragedy depends on a sense of the mind's greatness," since that would mean to acknowledge the powers of *another* mind, to soften his clattering voice, and to ease himself into that receptivity to experience which is one mark of the creative imagination.

For good or bad, both in the stories that succeed and those that fail, *Goodbye, Columbus* rests in the grip of an imperious will prepared to wrench, twist, and claw at its materials in order to leave upon them the scar of its presence—as if the work of fiction were a package that needed constantly to be stamped with a signature of self. With expectations of being misunderstood I am tempted to add that, despite their severe and even notorious criticisms of Jewish life in America, Roth's stories are marked by a quintessentially "Jewish will," the kind that first makes its historical appearance in the autobiography of Solomon Maimon, where the intellectual aspirant sees himself as a solitary antagonist to the world of culture which, in consequence, he must conquer and reduce to acknowledgment.

The will dominating *Goodbye, Columbus* clamors to impose itself—in part through an exclusion of inconvenient perceptions— upon whatever portions of imagined life are being presented. And that is one reason these stories become a little tiresome upon rereading: one grows weary of a writer who keeps nagging and prodding and beating us over the head with the poker of his intentions. What is almost always central in Roth's stories is their "point," their hammering of idea, and once that "point" is clear, usually well before a story's end, the portrayal starts to pale, for not enough autonomous life remains and too much of the matter seems a mere reflex of the will's "begetting."

Even in regard to details of milieu and manners, for which Roth has frequently been praised, the will takes over and distorts. In his title novella, "Goodbye, Columbus," there are some keen notations—the basement refrigerator bulging with fruit, the turgidities of the wedding—which help to characterize the newly-rich Patimkins in their suburban home. And there are moments of tenderness—a quality not abundant in Roth's work—during the romance between Neil Klugman, the poor Newark boy, and Brenda Patimkin, the self-assured Radcliffe girl (though nothing she says or does could persuade one that she would ever have been admitted to Radcliffe). Yet if the novella is read with any care at all, it becomes clear that Roth is not precise and certainly not scrupulous enough in his use of social evidence. The Patimkins are easily placed—what could be easier for a Jewish writer than to elicit disdain for middle-class Jews?—but the elements of what is new in their experience are grossly manipulated. Their history is invoked for the passing of adverse judgment, at least part of which seems to me warranted, but their history is not allowed to emerge so as to make them understandable as human beings. Their vulgarity is put on blazing display but little or nothing that might locate or complicate that vulgarity is shown: little of the weight of their past, whether sustaining or sentimental; nothing of the Jewish mania for culture, whether honorable or foolish; nothing of that fearful self-consciousness which the events of the mid-20th century thrust upon the Patimkins of this world. Ripped out of the historical context that might help to define them, the Patimkins are vivid enough, but as lampoon or caricature in a novella that clearly aims for more than lampoon or caricature. (There is, for example, a placing reference to Mrs. Patimkin's membership in Hadassah, employed as a cue for easy laughs in the way watermelons once were for Southern blacks—it is an instance of how a thrust against vulgarity can itself become vulgar, and by no means the only one in Roth's work.)

On the other side of the social spectrum Roth places Aunt Gladys, still poor, fretting absurdly over her nephew's health and, quite as if she were a stand-in for the Mrs. Portnoy yet to come, rattling off one-liners about the fruit in her icebox. Aunt Gladys, we learn, is preparing for a Workmen's Circle picnic; and for a reader with even a little knowledge of Jewish immigrant life, that raises certain expectations, since the Workmen's Circle signifies a socialist and Yiddishist commitment which time, no doubt, has dimmed but which still has left some impact on the sensibility of people like Aunt Gladys. But while named, as if to signal familiarity with her background, this aspect of Aunt Gladys's experience is never allowed to color Roth's portrait, never allowed to affect either the ridicule to which she is subjected nor the simplistic fable—so self-serving in its essential softness—of a poor but honorable Jewish boy withstanding suburban-Jewish vulgarity and thereupon left without any moral option in his world.

The price Roth pays for immobilizing the Patimkins into lampoon and Aunt Gladys into vaudeville is that none of the social or moral forces supposedly acting upon Neil Klugman can be dramatically marshalled. And Neil Klugman himself—poor cipher that he is—can never engage himself in the risks and temptations that are supposed to constitute his dilemma, if only because Roth is out there running interference, straight-arming all the other characters in behalf of this vapid alter ego. Even so extreme an admirer of Roth's work as Theodore Solotaroff acknowledges the "abstractness that Neil takes on. He . . . is too far along the path he is supposed to be traveling in the story. One could wish that he were more his aunt's nephew, more troubled and attracted by the life of the Patimkins, and more willing to test it and himself."

Now the issue is not, I had better emphasize, whether newly-rich suburban Jews are vulgar—a certain number, perhaps many, surely are—nor whether they are proper targets of satire—everyone is. What I am saying is that in its prefabricated counterpositions "Goodbye, Columbus" draws not upon a fresh encounter with the postwar experience of suburban Jews but upon literary hand-me-downs of American-Jewish fiction, popularizing styles of rebellion from an earlier moment and thereby draining them of their rebellious content.

I doubt, in any case, that Roth is really interested in a close and scrupulous observance of social life. He came to the literary scene at a moment when the dominant kind of critical talk was to dismiss "mere realism," as if that were a commodity so easily come by, and to praise "the imagination," as if that were a faculty which could operate apart from a bruising involvement with social existence. And this critical ideology served to reinforce Roth's own temperament as a writer, which is inclined to be impatient, snappish, and dismissive, all qualities hardly disposing him to strive for an objective (objective: to see the object as it is) perception of contemporary life.

Defending himself several years ago against the rather feckless attacks of outraged rabbis, some of whom complained that he did not provide a "balanced portrayal" of Jewish life, Roth wrote that "to confuse a 'balanced portrayal' with a novel is . . . to be led into absurdities." Absurdities, he continued, like supposing a group of 19th-century Russian students sending off a complaint to Dostoevsky that Raskolnikov is not a "typical student." Well, that's amusing, though I think it would be quite possible to show that, in some sense, Dostoevsky *does* present a "balanced portrayal" of Russian life. In any case, Roth in his defense, as in his fiction, makes things a little too easy for himself. For the critical issue is not whether he has given a "balanced portrayal" of the Jews as a whole or even the surburban Jews, but whether his portrayal of the Patimkins as the kind of people they are is marked by fullness and precision. After all, no fictional portrait is merely idiosyncratic, every novel or story aspires to some element of representativeness or at least reverberation—and indeed, at a crucial point in "Goodbye, Columbus," when Neil Klugman is reflecting upon what his fate would be if he were to marry Brenda, he at least takes the Patimkins to be representative of a way of life. It will not do to say that the Patimkins are "unique," for if they were they could have no interest other than as an oddity. What is at stake here is Roth's faithfulness to *his own materials*, the justice and largesse of his imaginative treatment.

There remains another line of defense against such criticism, which Roth's admirers frequently man: that he writes satire and therefore cannot be expected to hew closely to realistic detail. This is a defense that quite fails to apprehend what the nature of good satire is. To compose a satire is not at all to free oneself from the obligation to social accuracy; it is only to order that accuracy in a particular way. If it can be shown that the targets of the satirist are imprecisely located or that he is shooting wild, the consequences may be more damaging than if the same were shown for a conventional realist. And if it can be shown that the satire is self-serving—poor Neil, poor Alex . . . —then it becomes—well, imagine how absurd *Gulliver's Travels* would seem if we became persuaded that the satiric barrage against mankind allows for one little exception, a young hero troubled by the burdens of being English and resembling Jonathan Swift.

Roth's stories begin, characteristically, with a spectacular array of details in the representation of milieu, speech, and manners and thereby we are led to expect a kind of fiction strong in verisimilitude. But then, at crucial points in the stories, there follows a series of substitutions, elements of incident or speech inserted not because they follow from the logic of the narrative but because they underscore the point Roth wishes to extract from the narrative. In "The Conversion of the Jews" a bright if obnoxious Jewish boy becomes so enraged with the sniffling pieties of his Hebrew-school teacher, Rabbi Bender, that he races out of the classroom and up to the roof, threatening to jump unless the rabbi admits that "God can do anything" and "can make a child without intercourse." The plot may seem a bit fanciful and the story, as Mr. Solotaroff justly remarks, "inflated to get in the message"—but no matter, at least our attention is being held. Then, however, comes the breaking point, when the writer's will crushes his fiction: Ozzie "made them all say they believed in Jesus Christ—first one at a time, then all together." Given the sort of tough-grained Jewish urchin Ozzie is shown to be, this declamation strains our credence; it is Roth who has taken over, shouldering aside his characters and performing on his own, just as it is Roth who ends the story with the maudlin touch of Ozzie crying out, "Mamma. You should never hit anybody about God. . . . " Scratch an Ozzie, and you find a Rabbi Bender.

A richer and more ambitious story, "Eli the Fanatic" suffers from the same kind of flaws. An exotic yeshivah sponsored by a Hasidic sect settles in Woodenton, a comfortable suburb. The local Jews feel hostile, tension follows, and Eli Peck, a vulnerable Woodenton Jew, undergoes a kind of moral conversion in which he identifies or hallucinates himself as a victim in kaftan. It is difficult, if one bears in mind Roth's entire work, to take at face value this solemn espousal of yeshivah Orthodoxy as the positive force in the story; I cannot believe that the yeshivah and all it represents has been brought into play for any reason other than as a stick with which to beat Woodenton. Tzuref, the yeshivah principal, is well-drawn and allowed to speak for his outlook, as Aunt Gladys in "Goodbye, Columbus" is not: which is one reason this story builds up a certain dramatic tension. But again Roth feels obliged to drop a heavy thumb on the scales by making his suburbanites so benighted, indeed, so merely stupid, that the story finally comes apart. Here is a Woodenton Jew speaking:

Look, I don't even know about this Sunday school business. Sundays I drive my oldest kid all the way to Scarsdale to learn Bible stories . . . and you know what she comes up with? This Abraham in the Bible was going to kill his own *kid* for a sacrifice. She gets nightmares from it, for God's sake. You call that religion? Today a guy like that they'd lock him up.

Now, even a philistine character has certain rights, if not as a philistine then at least as a character in whose "reality" we are being asked to believe. To write as if this middle-class Jewish suburbanite were unfamiliar with "this Abraham" or shocked by the story of the near-sacrifice of Isaac, is simply preposterous. Roth is putting into the character's mouth, not what he could plausibly say, but what Roth thinks his "real" sentiments are. He is not revealing the character, he is "exposing" him. It is a crucial failure in literary tact, one of several in the story that rouse the suspicion Roth is not behaving with good faith toward the objects of his assault.

This kind of tendentiousness mars a number of Roth's fictions, especially those in which a first-person narrator—Neil Klugman, Alex Portnoy—swarms all over the turf of his imaginary world, blotting out the possibility of multiple perspective. It is a weakness of fictions told in the first person that the limits of the narrator's perception tend to become the limits of the work itself. Through an "unreliable" first-person narrator it is, of course, possible to plant bits of crucial evidence that call his version of things into question, but that requires a good deal of technical sophistication and still more, a portion of self-doubt such as our culture has not greatly encouraged these past two decades. There usually follows in such first-person narratives a spilling-out of the narrator which it becomes hard to suppose is not also the spilling-out of the author. Such literary narcissism is especially notable among minor satirists, with whom it frequently takes the form of self-exemptive attacks on the shamefulness of humanity. In some of Mary McCarthy's novels, for example, all the characters are shown as deceitful and venomous, all but a heroine pure in heart and close to the heart of the author. Neither Klugman nor Portnoy is exactly pure in heart, but as a man at ease with our moment, Portnoy has learned that "sincerity" can pay substantial dividends by soliciting admiration for the candor with which it proclaims impurities. And as for those of Roth's stories that avoid the looseness of the first-person narrative, his own authorial voice quickly takes over, becoming all but indistinguishable from a first-person narrator, raucous, self-aggrandizing, and damned sure that the denouement of his story will not escape the grip of his will.

To these strictures I would offer one exception, the Roth story that, oddly, was most attacked by his rabbinical critics: "Defender of the Faith." This seems to me a distinguished performance, the example of what Roth might have made of his talent had he been stricter in his demands upon himself. Roth's description of the story is acute: "It is about one man who uses his own religion, and another's uncertain conscience, for selfish ends; but mostly it is about this other man, the narrator, who because of the ambiguities of being a member of a particular religion, is involved in a taxing, if mistaken, conflict of loyalties." This conflict is at once urgent for those caught up in it and serious in its larger moral implications. Nathan Marx, back from combat duty in Germany, is made First Sergeant of a training company in Missouri; he is a decent, thoughtful fellow whose sense of being Jewish, important though it is to him, he cannot articulate clearly. A few recruits in his company, led by Sheldon Grossbart, attach themselves to Marx, presumably out of common feeling toward the problem of being Jews in an alien setting, but actually because Grossbart means to exploit this sense of solidarity in behalf of private ends—he looks forward to the crucial favor of not being sent overseas to combat. As Roth comments, Grossbart is "a man whose lapses of integrity seem to him so necessary to his survival as to convince him that such lapses are actually committed in the name of integrity." At the end of the story, Sergeant Marx, incensed at the manipulation to which he has been subjected, makes certain that Grossbart is indeed shipped overseas, while he, Marx, braces himself to face the consequences of an act he admits to be "vindictive."

The power of this story derives from presenting a moral entanglement so as to draw out, yet not easily resolve, its inherent difficulties. Unattractive as Grossbart may be, his cunning use of whatever weapons come to hand in order to protect his skin seems entirely real; one would have to be thoroughly locked into self-righteousness not to be drawn a little, however shamefacedly, to Grossbart's urgency. The willingness of Marx to bend the rules in behalf of the Jewish recruits is plausible, perhaps even admirable; after all, he shares their loneliness and vulnerability. Established thereby as a figure of humaneness, Marx commits an act that seems shocking, even to himself, so that he must then try to resist "with all my will an impulse to turn back and seek pardon for my vindictiveness." If it is right to punish Grossbart, Marx also knows the punishment is cruel, a result, perhaps, of the same Jewish uneasiness that had first made him susceptible to Grossbart's designs.

The story does not allow any blunt distribution of moral sympathies, nor can the reader yield his heart to one character. Before the painfulness of the situation, Roth's usual habit of rapid dismissal must melt away. We are left with the texture of reality as, once in a while, a writer can summon it.

Neither before nor after "Defender of the Faith" has Roth written anything approaching it in compositional rigor and moral seriousness. It may, however, have been the presence of this story in *Goodbye, Columbus* that led reviewers, including myself, to assume that this gifted new writer was working in the tradition of Jewish self-criticism and satire—a substantial tradition extending in Yiddish from Mendele to Isaac Bashevis Singer and in English from Abraham Cahan to Malamud and Bellow. In these kinds of writing, the assault upon Jewish philistinism and the mockery of Jewish social pretension are both familiar and unrelenting. Beside Mendele, Roth seems soft; beside Cahan, imprecise. But now, from the vantage point of additional years, I think it clear that Roth, despite his concentration on Jewish settings and his acerbity of tone, has not really been involved in this tradition. For he is one of the first American-Jewish writers who finds that it yields him no sustenance, no norms or values from which to launch his attacks on middle-class complacence.

This deficiency, if deficiency it be, need not be a fatal one for a Jewish writer, provided he can find sustenance elsewhere, in other cultures, other traditions. But I do not see that Roth has—his relation to the mainstream of American culture, in its great sweep of democratic idealism and romanticism, is decidedly meager. There is no lack of critical attitude, or attitudinizing, in Roth's stories, but much of it consists of the frayed remnants of cultural modernism, once revolutionary in significance but now reduced to little more than the commonplace "shock" of middlebrow culture. And there is a parasitic relation to the embattled sentiments and postures of older Jewish writers in America—though without any recognition that, by now, simply to launch attacks on middle-class suburbia is to put oneself at the head of the suburban parade, just as to mock the uptightness of immigrant Jews is to become the darling of their "liberated" suburban children.

One reason Roth's stories are unsatisfactory is that they come out of a thin personal culture. That he can quote Yeats and Rilke is hardly to the point. When we speak of a writer's personal culture we have in mind the ways in which a tradition, if absorbed into his work, can both release and control his creative energies. A vital culture can yield a writer those details of manners, customs, and morals which give the illusion of reality to his work. More important, *a vital culture talks back, so to say, within the writer's work*, holding in check his eccentricities, notions, and egocentrisms, providing a dialectic between what he has received and what he has willed—one can see this in novelists as various as Tolstoy, Hawthorne, Verga, and Sholem Aleichem.

When we say, consequently, that a writer betrays a thin personal culture we mean, among other possibilities, that he comes at the end of a tradition which can no longer nourish his imagination or that he has, through an act of fiat, chosen to tear himself away from that tradition. Many American writers of the late 19th and early 20th centuries, for example, could no longer continue with firm conviction in the line of transcendental idealism which had been so liberating fifty or sixty years earlier. It is, of course, a severe predicament for a writer to find himself in this situation; it forces him into self-consciousness, improvisation, and false starts; but if he is serious, he will try, like a farmer determined to get what he can from poor soil, to make a usable theme of his dilemmas.

Perhaps this thinness of culture has some connection with that tone of *ressentiment*, that free-floating contempt and animus, which begins to appear in Roth's early stories and grows more noticeable in his later work. Unfocused hostility often derives from unexamined depression, and the latter, which I take to be the ground-note of Roth's sensibility, fully emerges only in the two novels he wrote after *Goodbye, Columbus*. But even in the early stories one begins to hear a grind of exasperation, an assault without precise object, an irritable wish to pull down the creatures of his own imagination which can hardly be explained by anything happening within the stories themselves. If sentimentality is defined as emotion in excess of what a given situation warrants, what are we to say about irritability in excess? As one of Roth's critics, Baruch Hochman, has sharply noticed:

> The energy informing [Roth's] stories is scarcely more than the energy of irritation, an irritation so great that it makes the exposure of inanity seem a meaningful moral act. For Roth does not seem really to be concerned with the substance of the values he shows being eroded. It is not at all clear how Neil Klugman, who is so offended at the Patimkins, stands for anything substantially different from what they stand for—setting aside the fact that he is poorer than they, which he cannot help. His differences with them lie elsewhere than in the moral realm. . . .

At times the note of disgust is sounded in full, as in "Epstein," a nasty joke about a middle-aged man's hapless effort to revive his sexuality. Reading the last paragraphs of this story, arranged as a pratfall for the poor slob Epstein (and how pleasurable it is for "us," the cultivated ones, to sneer at those slobs, with their little box houses, their spreading wives, their mucky kids, their uncreative jobs), one is reminded of D. H. Lawrence's jibe about writers who "do dirt" to their characters.

II

The standard opinion of Roth's critics has been that his two novels, *Letting Go* and *When She Was Good*, add slight luster to his reputation, and there is not much use in arguing against this view. Yet it should be noticed that there are patches of genuine achievement in both books, sometimes a stumbling, gasping honesty. They are not novels that yield much pleasure or grip one despite its absence, but both are marked by tokens of struggle with the materials of American life. And there are moments that come off well—the persistence of the battered divorcee, Martha Reganhart *(Letting Go)*, in raising her children decently, the precocious eeriness of little Cynthia Reganhart, the struggle of Lucy *(When She Was Good)* to raise herself above the maudlin stupor of her family. Conventional achievements all of these are, and of a kind novelists have often managed in the past—of a kind, also, they will have to manage in the future if the novel is to survive. But right now, in our present cultural situation, this is hardly the sort of achievement likely to win much attention, as Roth evidently came to see.

Roth is not a "natural" novelist at all, the kind who loves to tell stories, chronicle social life, pile on characters, and if in his early fiction he seems willfully bent on scoring "points," in the novels his will exhausts itself from the sheer need to get on with things. He is an exceedingly joyless writer, even when being very funny. The reviewers of his novels, many of them sympathetic, noticed his need to rub our noses in the muck of squalid daily existence, his mania for annotating at punitive length the bickerings of his characters. Good clean hatred that might burn through, naturalistic determinism with a grandeur of design if not detail, the fury of social rebellion—any of these would be more *interesting* than the vindictive bleakness of Roth's novels.

What, one wonders, does he really have against these unhappy creatures of his? Why does he keep pecking away at them? I think the answer might furnish a key to Roth's work. Perhaps as a leftover from the culture of modernism and perhaps as a consequence of personal temperament, Roth's two novels betray a swelling nausea before the ordinariness of human existence, its seepage of spirit and rotting of flesh. This is a response that any sensitive or even insensitive person is likely to share at some point and to some extent, but it simply does not allow a writer to sustain or provide internal complications of tone in a large-scale work. It starts as a fastidious hesitation before the unseemliness of our minds and unsightliness of our bodies; it ends as a vibration of horror before the sewage of the quotidian. Men grow paunches, women's breasts sag, the breath of the aged reeks, varicose veins bulge. It all seems insufferable, an affront to our most cherished images of self, so much so that ordinary life must be pushed away, a disorder to be despised and assaulted. It is as if, in nagging at his characters, Roth were venting some deep and unmanageable frustration with our common fate.

III

The cruelest thing anyone can do with *Portnoy's Complaint* is to read it twice. An assemblage of gags strung onto the outcry of an analytic patient, the book thrives best on casual responses; it demands little more from the reader than what a nightclub performer does: a rapid exchange of laugh for punchline, a breath or two of rest, some variations on the first response, and a quick exit. Such might be the most generous way of discussing *Portnoy's Complaint* were it not for the solemn ecstasies the book has elicited, in line with Roth's own feeling that it constitutes a liberating act for himself, his generation, and maybe the whole culture.

The basic structural unit of *Portnoy's Complaint* is the skit, the stand-up comedian's shuffle and patter that come to climax with a smashing one-liner—indeed, it is worth noticing that a good many of our more "advanced" writers during the last two decades have found themselves turning to the skit as a form well-suited to the requirements of "swinging" and their rejection of sustained coherence of form. The controlling tone of the book is a shriek of excess, the jokester's manic wail, although, because it must slide from skit to skit with some pretense of continuity, this tone declines now and again into a whine of self-exculpation or sententiousness. And the controlling sensibility of the book derives from a well-grounded tradition of feeling within immigrant Jewish life: the coarse provincial "worldliness" flourishing in corner candy-stores and garment centers, at cafeterias and pinochle games, a sort of hard, cynical mockery of ideal claims and pretensions, all that remains to people scraped raw by the struggle for success. (This sensibility finds a "sophisticated" analogue in the smart-aleck nastiness of Jules Feiffer's film, *Carnal Knowledge*, which cannot really be understood without some reference to the undersides of Jewish immigrant life, as these have affected not the subject-matter of the film but the vision of the people who made it.)

Much of what is funny in Roth's book—the Monkey's monologues, some rhetorical flourishes accompanying Alex's masturbation, Sophie Portnoy's amusement at chancing upon her son's sexual beginnings—rests on the fragile structure of the skit. All the skit requires or can manage is a single broad stroke: shrewd, gross, recognizable, playing on the audience's embarrassment yet not hurting it too much, so that finally its aggression can be passed off as good-fellowship. (We all have Jewish mamas, we're all henpecked husbands, we all pretend to greater sexual prowess than. . . .) The skit stakes everything on brashness and energy, both of which Roth has or simulates in abundance. Among writers of the past Dickens and Céline have used the skit brilliantly, but Dickens always and Céline sometimes understood that in a book of any length the skit—as well as its sole legitimate issue, the caricature—must be put to the service of situations, themes, stories allowing for complication and development. (A lovely example can be seen in the skits that Peter Sellers performs in the movie version of *Lolita.*)

It is on the problem of continuity that Portnoy—or, actually, Roth himself—trips up. For once we are persuaded to see his complaints as more than the stuff of a few minutes of entertainment, once we are led to suppose that they derive from some serious idea or coherent view of existence, the book quickly falls to pieces and its much-admired energy (praised by some critics as if energy were a value regardless of the ends to which it is put) serves mainly to blur its flimsiness. Technically this means that, brief as it is, the book seems half again too long, since there can be very little surprise or development in the second half, only a recapitulation of motifs already torn to shreds in the first.

It is worth looking at a few of the book's incoherences, venial for a skit, fatal for a novel. Alex is allowed the human attribute of a history within the narrative space of the book, presumably so that he can undergo change and growth, but none of the characters set up as his foils, except perhaps the Monkey, is granted a similar privilege. Alex speaks for imposed-upon, vulnerable, twisted, yet self-liberating humanity; the other characters, reduced to a function of his need, an echo of his cry, cannot speak or speak back as autonomous voices but simply go through their paces like straight-men mechanically feeding lines to a comic. Even more than in Roth's earlier work, the result is claustrophobia of voice and vision: *he never shuts up*, this darling Alex, nor does Roth detach himself sufficiently to gain some ironic distance. The psychic afflictions of his character Roth would surely want to pass up, but who can doubt that Portnoy's cry from the heart—enough of Jewish guilt, enough of the burdens of history, enough of inhibition and repression, it is time to "let go" and soar to the horizons of pleasure—speaks in some sense for Roth?

The difficulty that follows from this claustrophobic vision is not whether Mrs. Portnoy can be judged a true rendering, even as caricature, of Jewish mothers—only chuckleheads can suppose that to be a serious question!—but whether characters like Mr. and Mrs. Portnoy have much reality or persuasiveness within the fictional boundaries set by Roth himself. Sophie Portnoy has a little, because there are moments when Alex, or Roth, can't help liking her, and because the conventional lampoon of the Jewish mother is by now so well established in our folklore it has almost become an object of realistic portraiture in its own right. As for Mr. Portnoy, a comparison suggests itself between this constipated *nudnik* whom Alex would pass off as his father and "Mr. Fumfotch" in Daniel Fuchs's novel *Homage to Blenholt*. Fuchs's character is also a henpecked husband, also worn down by the struggle for bread, but he is drawn with an ironic compassion that rises to something better than itself: to an objectivity that transcends either affection or derision. In his last novel Fuchs remarks, while writing about figures somewhat like those in Roth's work, "It was not enough to call them low company and pass on"—and if this can be said about Depression Jews in Brighton Beach, why not also about more or less affluent ones in the Jersey suburbs?

We notice, again, that Portnoy attributes his sexual troubles to the guilt-soaked Jewish tradition as it has been carried down to him by his mother. Perhaps; who knows? But if we are to accept this simplistic determinism, why does it never occur to him, our Assistant Commissioner of Human Opportunity who once supped with John Lindsay in the flesh, that by the same token the intelligence on which he preens himself must also be attributed to the tradition he finds so repugnant—so that his yowl of revulsion against "my people," that they should "stick your suffering heritage up your suffering ass," becomes, let us say, a little ungenerous, even a little dopey.

And we notice, again, that while Portnoy knows that his sexual difficulties stem from his Jewishness, the patrician New England girl with whom he has an affair also turns out to be something of a sexual failure: she will not deliver him from the coils of Jewish guilt through the magic of fellatio. But if both Jewishness and Protestantism have deeply inhibiting effects on sexual perfor- mance—and as for Catholicism, well, we know those Irish girls! —what then happens to this crucial flake of Portnoy's wisdom, which the book invites us to take with some seriousness? As for other possible beliefs, from Ethical Culture to Hare Krishna, there can surely be little reason to suppose they will deliver us from the troubles of life which, for all we know, may be lodged in the very nature of things or, at the least, in those constraints of civilization which hardly encircle Jewish loins exclusively.

There is something suspect about Portnoy's complaining. From what he tells us one might reasonably conclude that, in a far from perfect world, he is not making out so badly; the boys on his block, sexual realists that they are, would put it more pungently. Only in Israel does he have serious difficulties, and for that there are geographical solutions. What seems really to be bothering Portnoy is a wish to sever his sexuality from his moral sensibilities, to cut it away from his self as historical crea- ture. It's as if he really supposed the super-ego, or *post coitum triste*, were a Jewish invention. This wish—Norman O. Brown as a *yingele*—strikes one as rather foolish, an adolescent fantasy carrying within itself an inherent negation; but it is a fantasy that has accumulated a great deal of power in contemporary culture. And it helps explain Roth's true feelings about, or relation to, Jewishness. *Portnoy's Complaint* is not, as enraged critics have charged, an anti-Semitic book, though it contains plenty of con- tempt for Jewish life. Nor does Roth write out of traditional Jewish self-hatred, for the true agent of such self-hatred is always indissolubly linked with Jewish past and present, quite as closely as those who find in Jewishness moral or transcendent sanctions. What the book speaks for is a yearning to undo the fate of birth; there is no wish to do the Jews any harm (a little nastiness is something else), nor any desire to engage with them as a fevered antagonist; Portnoy is simply crying out to be left alone, to be released from the claims of distinctiveness and the burdens of the past, so that, out of his own nothingness, he may create himself as a "human being." Who, born a Jew in the 20th century, has been so lofty in spirit never to have shared his fantasy?

But who, born a Jew in the 20th century, has been so foolish in mind as to dally with it for more than a moment?

What, in any case, *is Portnoy's Complaint*—a case-history burlesqued, which we are invited to laugh at, or a struggle of an afflicted man to achieve his liberation, which we are invited to cheer on? Bruno Bettelheim has written a straight-faced essay purporting to be the case notes of Alex's psychoanalyst, Dr. O. Spielvogel, who can barely restrain his impatience with Alex's effort to mask his true problems with "all the clichés of a spoiled Jewish childhood."

> A few times I [Dr. Spielvogel] indicated the wish to say something, but he only talked on the more furiously. . . . This extremely intelligent young Jew does not recognize that what he is trying to do, by reversing the Oedipal situation, is to make fun of me, as he does of everyone, thus asserting his superiority. . . . His overpowering love for his mother is turned into a negative projection, so that what becomes overpowering is the mother's love for him. . . . While consciously he experienced everything she did as destructive, behind it is an incredible wish for more, more, more. . . .

Now this is amusing, though not as amusing as the fact that it often constitutes the line of defense to which Roth's admirers fall back when the book's incoherence is revealed ("after all, it's a patient on the couch, everyone knows you can't take what he says at face value . . ."). But to see the book in this light, as the mere comic record of a very sick man, is radically to undercut its claims for expressing new truths. Roth, never unwary, anticipates the problem by having Portnoy say, "Is this truth I'm delivering up, or is it just plain *kvetching?* Or is *kvetching* for people like me a *form* of truth?" Well, there's *kvetching* and *kvetching.* At times it can be a form of truth, but when the gap is so enormous between manifest content and what Dr. Spielvogel *cum* Bettelheim takes to be its inner meaning, then *kvetching* becomes at best an untruth from which the truth must be violently wrenched.

It seems hard to believe that Roth would accept the view that his book consists merely of comic griping; certainly the many readers who saw it as a banner behind which to rally would not accept that view. For, in a curious way, *Portnoy's Complaint* has become a cultural document of some importance. Younger Jews, weary or bored with all the talk about their heritage, have taken the book as a signal for "letting go" of both their past and perhaps themselves, a guide to swinging in good conscience or better yet, without troubling about conscience. For some Gentile readers the book seems to have played an even more important role. After the Second World War, as a consequence of certain unpleasantnesses that occurred during the war, a wave of philo-Semitism swept through our culture. This wave lasted for all of two decades, in the course of which books by Jewish writers were often overpraised and a fuss made about Jewish intellectuals, critics, etc. Some literary people found this hard to bear, but they did. Once *Portnoy's Complaint* arrived, however, they could almost be heard breathing a sigh of relief, for it signaled an end to philo-Semitism in American culture, one no longer had to listen to all that talk about Jewish morality, Jewish endurance, Jewish wisdom, Jewish families. Here was Philip Roth himself, a writer who even seemed to know Yiddish, confirming what had always been suspected about those immigrant Jews but had recently not been tactful to say.

The talent that went into *Portnoy's Complaint* and portions of *Goodbye, Columbus* is real enough, but it has been put to the service of a creative vision deeply marred by vulgarity. It is very hard to be explicit about the concept of vulgarity: people either know what one is referring to, as part of the tacit knowledge that goes to make up a coherent culture, or the effort to explain is probably doomed in advance. Nevertheless, let me try. By vulgarity in a work of literature I am not here talking about the presence of certain kinds of words or the rendering of certain kinds of actions. I have in mind, rather, the impulse to submit the rich substance of human experience, sentiment, value, and aspiration to a radically reductive leveling or simplification; the urge to assault the validity of sustained gradings and discriminations of value, so that in some extreme instances the very concept of vulgarity is dismissed as up-tight or a mere mask for repressiveness; the wish to pull down the reader in common with the characters of the work, so that he will not be tempted to suppose that any inclinations he has toward the good, the beautiful, or the ideal merit anything more than a Bronx cheer; and finally, a refusal of that disinterestedness of spirit in the depiction and judgment of other people which seems to me the writer's ultimate resource.

That I have here provided an adequate definition of vulgarity in literature I do not for a moment suppose—though I don't know of a better one. It ought, however, to serve our present purposes by helping to make clear the ways in which a book like *Portnoy's Complaint,* for all its scrim of sophistication, is spiritually linked with the usual sentimental treatment of Jewish life in the work of popular and middlebrow writers. Between *Portnoy's Complaint* and *Two Cents Plain* there is finally no great difference of sensibility.

Perhaps the matter can be clarified by a comparison. Hubert Selby's novel, *Last Exit to Brooklyn,* portrays a segment of urban life—lumpen violence, gang-bangs, rape, sheer debasement —that is utterly appalling, and the language it must record is of a kind that makes Roth seem reticent; yet as I read Selby's book there is no vulgarity in it whatever, for he takes toward his barely human figures a stance of dispassionate objectivity, writing not with "warmth" or "concern" but with a disciplined wish to see things as they are. He does not wrench, he does not patronize, he does not aggrandize. Repugnant as it often is, *Last Exit to Brooklyn* seems to me a pure-spirited book; amusing as it often is, *Portnoy's Complaint* a vulgar book.

IV

About the remainder of Roth's work I have little to say.

Our Gang, purporting to be a satire on Richard Nixon, is a coarse-grained replica of its subject. A flaccid performance, it has some interest through embodying an impulse in our culture to revert not so much to the pleasures of infantilism as to the silliness of the high-school humor column. About this book I would repeat what Henry James once said of a Trollope novel: "Our great objection . . . is that we seem to be reading a work written for children, a work prepared for minds unable to think, a work below the apprehension of the average man or woman."

The Breast, extravagantly praised by my literary betters, is a work to which, as students would say, "I cannot relate." Well-enough written and reasonably ingenious, it is finally boring—tame, neither shocking nor outrageous, and tasteless in both senses of the word. Discussions will no doubt persist as to its "meaning," but first it might be better to ask whether, as a work of literature, it exists. For simply on the plane of narrative it cannot, or ought not, hold the interest of a reasonably mature reader.

Flaubert once said that a writer must choose between an audience and readers. Evidently Roth has made his choice.

P.S. Since the above essay was written, there have appeared both a new fiction by Philip Roth, *The Great American Novel*, and a refutation of my essay by Wilfred Sheed in the *New York Times Book Review*. Neither prompts me to change anything I have written.

THE PLATH CELEBRATION

A Partial Dissent

A GLAMOUR OF FATALITY hangs over the name of Sylvia Plath, the glamour that has made her a darling of our culture. Extremely gifted, her will clenched into a fist of ambition, several times driven to suicide by a suffering so absolute as to seem almost impersonal, yet in her last months composing poems in which pathology and clairvoyance triumphantly fuse—these are the materials of her legend. It is a legend that solicits our desires for a heroism of sickness that can serve as emblem of the age, and many young readers take in Sylvia Plath's vibrations of despair as if they were the soul's own oxygen. For reasons good and bad, the spokesmen for the sensibility of extreme gesture—all the blackness, confession, denial, and laceration that are warranted by modern experience but are also the moral bromides of our moment—see in Sylvia Plath an authentic priestess. Because she is authentic, the role would surely displease her; dead now for a decade, she can offer no defense.

Quantities of adoring criticism pile up around her, composed in a semi-mimetic frenzy designed to be equivalent in tone to its subject. The result is poor criticism, worse prose. In a collection of essays devoted to Sylvia Plath, the editor writes—almost as if he too were tempted by an oven: "The courting of experience that kills is characteristic of major poets."[1] Is it? Virgil, Petrarch, Goethe, Pope, Hugo, Wordsworth, Bialik, Yeats, Stevens, Auden, Frost?

In dissenting a little from the Plath celebration, one has the sense not so much of disagreeing about the merits of certain poems as of plunging into a harsh *kulturkampf.* For one party in this struggle Sylvia Plath has become an icon, and the dangers for those in the other party are also considerable, since it would be unjust to allow one's irritation with her devotees to spill over into one's response to her work. So let us move quickly to the facts about her career and then to the poems she wrote toward the end of her life, crucial for any judgment of her work.

Her father, a professor of biology and (it's important to note) a man of German descent, died when she was nine. The reverberations of this event are heavy in the poems, though its precise significance for Sylvia Plath as either person or poet is very hard to grasp. She then lived with her mother in Wellesley, Massachusetts; she went to Smith, an ardent student who swept up all the prizes; she suffered from psychic disorders; she won a Fullbright to Cambridge University, then met and married a gifted English poet, Ted Hughes. In 1960 she published her first book of poems, *The Colossus*—it rings with distinguished echoes, proclaims unripe gifts, contains more quotable passages than successful poems (true for all her work). She had two children, in 1960 and 1962, to whom she seems to have been fiercely attached and about whom she wrote some of her better poems. She was separated from her husband, lived one freezing winter in London with her children, and, experiencing an onslaught of energy at once overwhelming and frightening, wrote her best-known poems during the last weeks of her life. On February 11, 1963, she killed herself.

Crossing the Water contains some of the poems she wrote between the early work of *The Colossus* and the final outburst that would appear posthumously in 1965 as *Ariel*. There are graphic lines in *Crossing the Water*, but few poems fully achieved. "The desert is white as a blind man's eye,/ Comfortless as salt . . ." we read in a poem not otherwise notable. The drive to self-

[1] *The Art of Sylvia Plath*, edited by Charles Newman (Indiana University Press).

destruction that would tyrannize the last poems is already at work in these "middle" ones:

> If I pay the roots of the heather
> Too close attention, they will invite me
> To whiten my bones among them.

The poems in *Crossing the Water* are, nevertheless, more open in voice and variable in theme than those for which Sylvia Plath has become famous; they have less power but also less pathology. She writes well, in snatches and stanzas, about the impersonal moments of personal experience, when the sense of everything beyond one's selfhood dominates the mind. She writes well, that is, precisely about the portion of human experience that is most absent in the *Ariel* poems; such poems as "Parliament Hill Fields," "Small Hours," and a few others in *Crossing the Water*, unheroic in temper and unforced in pitch, can yield familiar pleasures. The flaws in her work she describes charmingly in "Stillborn," though it's characteristic that, after the vivid opening stanza, the poem should itself seem stillborn:

> These poems do not live: it's a sad diagnosis.
> They grew their toes and fingers well enough,
> Their little foreheads bulged with concentration.
> If they missed out on walking about like people
> It wasn't for any lack of mother love.

II

At a crucial point in her career Sylvia Plath came under the influence of Robert Lowell's *Life Studies,* and it is this relationship that has led many admirers to speak of her late work as "confessional poetry." The category is interesting but dubious, both in general and when applied to Sylvia Plath.

In *Life Studies* Lowell broke into a new style. He abandoned the complex interlacings of idea and image, the metaphysical notations and ironic turnings of his earlier work, and instead wrote poems that were to deal immediately with his own experience: his time as CO, his nervous breakdowns, his relations with his wife. When he wrote "I" it was clear he really did mean his private self, not a *persona* created for the poem's occasion. To the small number of people who read poetry at all, *Life*

Studies came as a valued, perhaps overvalued, shock—a harsh abandonment of the Eliotian impersonality that had previously dominated American poetry. Inevitably, this new style was widely imitated and its inherent difficulty frequently ignored. The readiness with which Lowell exposed his own life caused people to admire his courage rather than scrutinize his poems. Candor was raised to an absolute value, such as it need not often be in either morals or literature. Our culture was then starting to place an enormous stress on self-exposure, self-assault, self-revelation—as if spontaneity were a sure warrant of authenticity, and spilling out a sure road to comprehension. The bared breast replaced the active head.

Insofar as a poem depends mainly on the substance of its confession, as blow or shock revealing some hidden shame in the writer's experience, it will rarely be a first-rate piece of work. It will lack the final composure that even the most excited composition requires. Insofar as it makes the confessional element into something integral to the poem, it ceases, to that extent, to be confessional. It becomes a self-sufficient poem, not dependent for its value on whatever experience may have evoked it. Perhaps the greatest achievement of this kind in English is the group of poems Thomas Hardy wrote in 1912-13 after the death of his first wife: they are full of the regrets of wasted life, missed opportunities, shamed quarrels, but they take on an autonomous life, beyond the rawness of confession.

Now, this is dogma and, as such, suspect—even by those who may agree with it. For obviously there are cases where residues of personal confession can be detected, yet the poem constitutes more than a mere notation of incident or memory. I would also add that the short lyric is a form likely to resist confessional writing, since it does not allow for the sustained moral complication, the full design of social or historical setting, that can transform confession from local act to larger meaning. The confessions of Augustine and Rousseau are long works, and they are in prose.

A flaw in confessional poetry, even the best of it, is one that characterizes much other American poetry in the twentieth century. It is the notion that a careful behavioral notation of an event or object is in itself sufficient basis for composing a satisfactory poem: the description of an orange, a wheelbarrow, a woman's gait. What such poems depend on, for their very life, is the hope of creating an aura, a network of implication, that will enlarge the scope of their references. Sometimes, as in Frost's "Spring Pools," this feat is managed; too often, what we get is a mere verbal snapshot, a discrete instance, that has little reverberation. And this holds true even if the snapshot records an event that rouses our curiosity or dismay.

Robert Lowell's poem, "Man and Wife," shook many readers when it first appeared in 1952. When you read a poem that begins—

> Tamed by Miltown, we lie on Mother's bed;
> the rising sun in war paint dyes us red;
> in broad daylight her gilded bedposts shine,
> abandoned, almost Dionysian.

—some feeling of involvement, even pain, is likely to be invoked through the very announcement of its subject. There is the compressed suggestibility of "Mother's bed," the vividness of the "war paint" in the second line. But the poem as a whole no longer seems quite so remarkable as I once thought. In the middle—and the middle is where confessional poems get into trouble, once the subject has been declared and something must now be *done* with it—Lowell declines into a recollection about the time he "outdrank the Rahvs in the heat/ Of Greenwich Village." Most readers do not know "the Rahvs," and the reference is therefore lost upon them; those few who do may find it possible to resist the poet's intention. Here the poem has slipped into self-indulgence. At the end, Lowell does achieve a recovery with several lines describing his wife's invective after a quarrel, presumably before Miltown "tamed" them both:

> your old-fashioned tirade—
> loving, rapid, merciless—
> breaks like the Atlantic Ocean on my head.

These lines move the center of the poem away from the confessing, preening self of the poet and reveal a counteraction: that's not just a prop lying there in bed with him, it's another human being. True, the reference remains local and thereby, perhaps, open to the kind of criticism I made earlier of confessional poetry as a whole. But through severe detail Lowell has managed to

suggest reverberations that move the poem beyond the edges
of his personal wound.

At times Sylvia Plath also wrote confessional poetry, as in
the much-praised "Lady Lazarus," a poem about her recurrent
suicide attempts. Its opening lines, like almost all her opening
lines, come at one like a driven hammer:

> I have done it again.
> One year in every ten
> I manage it—
>
> A sort of walking miracle, my skin
> Bright as a Nazi lampshade,
> My right foot
>
> A paperweight,
> My face a featureless, fine
> Jew linen.

The tone is jeeringly tough, but at least partly directed against
herself. There is a strain of self-irony ("a sort of walking miracle")
such as poetry of this kind can never have enough of. Still,
one must be infatuated with the Plath legend to ignore the poet's
need for enlarging the magnitude of her act through illegitimate
comparisons with the Holocaust (a point to which I will return
later).

Sylvia Plath's most notable gift as a writer—a gift for the
single, isolate image—comes through later in the poem when,
recalling an earlier suicide attempt, she writes that they had
to "pick the worms off me like sticky pearls." But then, after
patching together some fragments of recollection, she collapses
into an archness about her suicide attempts that is shocking in
a way she could not have intended:

> I do it so it feels like hell.
> I do it so it feels real.
> I guess you could say I've a call.
>
> It's easy enough to do it in a cell,
> It's easy enough to do it and stay put.

As if uneasy about the tone of such lines, she then drives

toward what I can only see as a willed hysteric tone, the forcing of language to make up for an inability to develop the matter. The result is sentimental violence:

> A cake of soap,
> A wedding ring,
> A gold filling. . . .

> Out of the ash
> I rise with my red hair
> And I eat men like air.

In the end, the several remarkable lines in this poem serve only to intensify its badness, for in their isolation, without the support of a rational structure, they leave the author with no possibility of development other than violent wrenchings in tone. And this is a kind of badness that seems a constant temptation in confessional poetry, the temptation to reveal all with one eye nervously measuring the effect of revelation.

There's another famous poem by Sylvia Plath entitled, "Cut," in which she shows the same mixture of strong phrasing and structural incoherence. "Cut" opens on a sensational note, or touch:

> What a thrill—
> My thumb instead of an onion.
> The top quite gone
> Except for a sort of hinge

> Of skin,
> A flap like a hat,
> Dead white.
> Then that red plush.

This is vivid, no denying it. Morbid too. The question is whether the morbidity is an experience the writer struggles with or yields to, examines dispassionately or caresses indulgently.

There is a saving wit in the opening lines ("My thumb instead of an onion") and this provides some necessary distance between invoked experience and invoking speaker. But the poem collapses through Sylvia Plath's inability to do more with her theme than thrust it against our eyes, displaying her wound in all its red plushy woundedness.

> The stain on your

> Gauze Ku Klux Klan
> Babushka
> Darkens and tarnishes . . .

The bandage is seen as a babushka, an old lady's scarf. All right. But the Ku Klux Klan? And still more dubious, the "Ku Klux Klan Babushka?" One supposes the KKK is being used here because it is whitely repressive, the Babushka-bandage is "repressing" the blood, and in the poem's graphic pathology, the flow of blood from the cut is attractive, fruitful, perhaps healthy ("a celebration, this is," runs one line). But even if my reading is accurate, does that help us very much with the stanza? Isn't it an example of weakness through excess?

Sylvia Plath's most famous poem, adored by many sons and daughters, is "Daddy." It is a poem with an affecting theme, the feelings of the speaker as she regathers the pain of her father's premature death and her persuasion that he has betrayed her by dying:

> I was ten when they buried you.
> At twenty I tried to die
> And get back, back, back to you.

In the poem Sylvia Plath identifies the father (we recall his German birth) with the Nazis ("Panzer-man, panzer-man, O You") and flares out with assaults for which nothing in the poem (nor, so far as we know, in Sylvia Plath's own life) offers any warrant: "A cleft in your chin instead of your foot/ But no less a devil for that . . ." Nor does anything in the poem offer warrant, other than the free-flowing hysteria of the speaker, for the assault of such lines as, "There's a stake in your fat black heart/ And the villagers never liked you." Or for the snappy violence of

> Every woman adores a Fascist,
> The boot in the face, the brute
> Brute heart of a brute like you.

What we have here is a revenge fantasy, feeding upon filial love-hatred, and thereby mostly of clinical interest. But seemingly aware that the merely clinical can't provide the materials for a satisfying poem, Sylvia Plath tries to enlarge upon the personal plight, give meaning to the personal outcry, by fancying the girl as victim of a Nazi father:

> An engine, an engine
> Chuffing me off like a Jew.
> A Jew to Dachau, Auschwitz, Belsen.
> I began to talk like a Jew,
> I think I may well be a Jew.

The more sophisticated admirers of this poem may say that I fail to see it as a dramatic presentation, a monologue spoken by a disturbed girl not necessarily to be identified with Sylvia Plath, despite the similarities of detail between the events of the poem and the events of her life. I cannot accept this view. The personal-confessional element, strident and undisciplined, is simply too obtrusive to suppose the poem no more than a dramatic picture of a certain style of disturbance. If, however, we did accept such a reading of "Daddy," we would fatally narrow its claims to emotional or moral significance, for we would be confining it to a mere vivid imagining of a pathological state. That, surely, is not how its admirers really take the poem.

It is clearly not how the critic George Steiner takes the poem when he calls it "the 'Guernica' of modern poetry." But then, in an astonishing turn, he asks: "In what sense does anyone, himself uninvolved and long after the event, commit a subtle larceny when he invokes the echoes and trappings of Auschwitz and appropriates an enormity of ready emotion to his own private design?" The question is devastating to his early comparison with "Guernica." Picasso's painting objectifies the horrors of Guernica, through the distancing of art; no one can suppose that he shares or participates in them. Plath's poem aggrandizes on the "enormity of ready emotion" invoked by references to the concentration camps, in behalf of an ill-controlled if occasionally brilliant outburst. There is something monstrous, utterly disproportionate, when tangled emotions about one's father are deliberately compared with the historical fate of the European Jews; something sad, if the comparison is made spontaneously. "Daddy" persuades one again, through the force of negative example, of how accurate T. S. Eliot was in saying, "The more perfect the artist, the more completely separate in him will be the man who suffers and the mind which creates."

III

The most interesting poems in *Ariel* are not confessional at all. A confessional poem would seem to be one in which the writer speaks *to* the reader, telling him, without the mediating presence of imagined event or *persona*, something about his life: I had a nervous breakdown, my wife and I sometimes lie in bed, sterile of heart, through sterile nights. The sense of direct speech addressed to an audience is central to confessional writing. But the most striking poems Sylvia Plath wrote are quite different. They are poems written out of an extreme condition, a state of being in which the speaker, for all practical purposes Sylvia Plath herself, has abandoned the sense of audience and cares nothing about—indeed, is hardly aware of—the presence of anyone but herself. She writes with a hallucinatory, self-contained fervor. She addresses herself to the air, to the walls. She speaks not as a daylight self, with its familiar internal struggles and doubts, its familiar hesitations before the needs and pressures of others. There is something utterly monolithic, fixated about the voice that emerges in these poems, a voice unmodulated and asocial.

It's as if we are overhearing the rasps of a mind that has found its own habitation and need not measure its distance from, even consider its relation to, other minds. And the stakes are far higher than can ever be involved in mere confession. She exists in some mediate province between living and dying, and she appears to be balancing coolly the claims of the two, drawn almost equally to both yet oddly comfortable with the perils of where she is. This is not the by-now worn romanticism of *Liebestod*. It is something very strange, very fearful: a different kind of existence, at ease at the gate of dying. The poems Sylvia Plath wrote in this state of being are not "great" poems, but one can hardly doubt that they are remarkable. For they do bring into poetry an element of experience that, so far as I know, is new, and thereby they advance the thrust of literary modernism by another inch or so. A poem like "Kindness" is set squarely in what I have called the mediate province between living and dying:

> What is so real as the cry of a child?
> A rabbit's cry may be wilder
> But it has no soul.

And then, a few lines later:

> The blood jet is poetry,
> There is no stopping it.

The poems written out of this strange equilibrium—"Fever 103," "Totem," "Edge"—are notable, and the best of them seems to me "Edge":

> The woman is perfected.
> Her dead
>
> Body wears the smile of accomplishment,
> The illusion of a Greek necessity
>
> Flows in the scrolls of her toga,
> Her bare
>
> Feet seem to be saying:
> We have come so far, it is over.
>
> Each dead child coiled, a white serpent,
> One at each little
>
> Pitcher of milk, now empty.
> She has folded
>
> Them back into her body as petals
> Of a rose close when the garden
>
> Stiffens and odours bleed
> From the sweet, deep throats of the night flower.
>
> The moon has nothing to be sad about,
> Staring from her hood of bone.
>
> She is used to this sort of thing.
> Her blacks crackle and drag.

The vision of death as composure, a work done well, is beautifully realized in the first four stanzas. The next several, with "Each dead child coiled, a white serpent," seem to me to drop into a kind of sensationalism—not the kind one finds in the confessional poems, with their alternating archness and violence, but one that invokes the completion that may come once death is done and finished. The penultimate stanza is very fine; the last lines again seem forced.

Even in this kind of poetry, which does strike an original note, there are many limitations. The poems often shock; they seldom surprise. They are deficient in plasticity of feeling, the modulation of voice that a poet writing out of a controlled maturity of consciousness can muster. Even the best of Sylvia Plath's poems, as her admirer Stephen Spender admits, "have little principle of beginning or ending, but seem fragments, not so much of one long poem, as of an outpouring which could not stop with the lapsing of the poet's hysteria."

Perhaps the hardest critical question remains. Given the fact that in a few poems Sylvia Plath illustrates an extreme state of existence, one at the very boundary of nonexistence, what illumination—moral, psychological, social—can be provided of either this state or the general human condition by a writer so deeply rooted in the extremity of her plight? Suicide is an eternal possibility of our life and therefore always interesting; but what is the relation between a sensibility so deeply captive to the idea of suicide and the claims and possibilities of human existence in general? That her story is intensely moving, that her talent was notable, that her final breakthrough rouses admiration—of course! Yet in none of the essays devoted to praising Sylvia Plath have I found a coherent statement as to the nature, let alone the value, of her vision. Perhaps it is assumed that to enter the state of mind in which she found herself at the end of her life is its own ground for high valuation; but what will her admirers say to those who reply that precisely this assumption is what needs to be questioned?

After the noise abates and judgment returns, Sylvia Plath will be regarded as an interesting minor poet whose personal story was poignant. A few of her poems will find a place in anthologies—and when you consider the common fate of talent, that, after all, will not be a small acknowledgment.

THE LITERATURE
OF SUICIDE

ABOUT THE MOST IMPORTANT THINGS in life we know almost nothing. The problem of suicide has always perplexed intelligent men, and as far as we can tell, the possibility of taking one's own life has tempted all kinds of men, intelligent or not. Suicide has seemed to some the conclusive thrust of their freedom, for what greater freedom can a man have than to overcome his fear of death and then dispose of himself? To others it has seemed the culminating moment of their bondage, for what greater proof could there be of the unrelieved tyranny of the flesh?

In some eras, such as the one now coming to an end, suicide has been regarded with a kind of uncanny dread—I confess, so that the reader will know my bias, to feelings of this sort. In other eras, it has been regarded as a quite rational way of concluding one's affairs on earth. But despite the massive contributions of sociology and psychology, we know almost nothing about the unique experience, or even whether it is a unique experience, that enables a man to kill himself—since whatever reports we have about the states of mind flourishing immediately before self-destruction come from failed suicides who, at least in regard to the completed act, must be judged as unreliable witnesses.

This profoundly absorbing subject is treated in two recent books, each very good in its way. Jacques Choron's *Suicide* is a compact, lucid summary of whatever is known about the matter, and A. Alvarez's *The Savage God* is a wonderfully readable, though frequently irritating, work in which this English poet-critic, himself a failed suicide, tries to approach the subject intimately and directly, as a kind of experience open to dramatic portrayal.

A criticism of Alvarez at the outset: he does not distinguish sufficiently between suicide as a literary theme or element in the life of literary men and suicide as a problem affecting humanity as a whole. Like many literary people, he tends to forget that the "evidence" of the extreme instance, while crucial in modernist literature, is by no means convincing for general statements about humanity; what seems pertinent to the work of avant-garde artists may have only a tenuous connection with the daily experience of ordinary people. I am not saying there is no connection between the two, since that would have chilling consequences for those of us who believe in the centrality of literature; I am only saying that we can't be at all certain as to what the connections are.

II

The evidence from the past is at once fascinating and utterly inconclusive, except insofar as it is reassuring to know that with regard to the most important puzzles of existence we are still likely to think and say what people did thousands of years ago. At least formally, our cultural attitudes toward suicide derive mainly from the doctrines advanced in the sixth century by the Church, which at the instigation of St. Augustine declared that since life is the gift of God and each body the home of an immortal soul, the destruction of one's body is a rejection of God's will. Provided one accepts the Christian premises, this argument is a strong one and its impact decidedly moral; yet, as Alvarez remarks, "what began as moral tenderness and enlightenment finished as the legalized and sanctified atrocities by which the body of the suicide was degraded, his memory defamed, his family persecuted. So, although the idea of suicide as a crime was a late, relatively sophisticated invention of Christianity . . .

it spread like a fog across Europe because its strength came from primitive fears . . ." Nor is this, of course, the first or last time that moral scruple led to social cruelty.

Before the Church had codified this view, which drew upon a sense of dread toward self-destruction that may be intrinsic to our consciousness, there had existed a bewilderingly wide range of attitudes. When the Jewish Zealots defending Massada against Roman troops in 73 A.D. concluded that their situation was hopeless, they decided upon mass suicide, and their commander, Eleazar, quite as if he had just read Camus, declared that "death affords our souls their liberty and sends them to their own place of purity, where they are to be insensible to all sorts of miseries." Yet a few years earlier Josephus, also leading Jewish troops against the Romans, argued, quite as if he had just read St. Augustine, that it was "a wicked and perfidious act to cast out of one's body the soul which God had committed to it."

Choron and Alvarez find this same duality among the Greek philosophers. Aristotle regarded suicide as "an offense against the state"; he judged the moral value and social utility of behavior by its impact on the community and could not have anticipated the modern devotion to the absolutism of individual will. Alvarez, totally caught up with this modern view, objects that Aristotle's "style of argument [is not] likely to impinge on the state of mind of a man about to take his own life." Probably not; but that was the main interest of neither Aristotle nor the classical Christian thinkers deriving from him. They cared more about social prophylaxis than personal crisis.

Plato, while opposed in principle to suicide, felt that when life did become insupportable it was rational to consider ending it. This view of things, to be elaborated and refined by such later writers as John Donne and David Hume, reached a kind of chilling apogee in those Greek cities that kept a supply of poison for citizens wishing to die. Alvarez quotes an ancient writer:

> Whoever no longer wishes to live shall state his reasons to the Senate, and after having received permission shall abandon life. If your existence is hateful to you, die; if you are overwhelmed by fate, drink the hemlock.

Hard as it may be to argue against this view, it is equally

hard to avoid some revulsion against its frigid rationalism. But even the cool-minded Greeks must also have felt some dread before the idea of self-destruction, since they required the corpse of a suicide to be interred outside the city, its hand cut off and buried separately.

The primitive Christians, in their disgust with this world and yearning for a rapid shuttle to heaven, took a radically different view. For the primitive Church, life was intolerable whatever its conditions. Why, then, live unredeemed when heavenly bliss is only a knife stroke away? No wonder, comments Alvarez, that Christian teaching was at first a powerful incitement to suicide. Some of the early Church Fathers, like Tertullian and Origen, even suggested that the death of Jesus must be seen as a kind of suicide, for it was unthinkable that He should have had no choice when giving up the ghost. In its turbulent emotional life, primitive Christianity broke past some taboos, including the one against self-destruction, but it also reinstated such tribal attitudes as the notion that a violent death, if the result of a courageous action, could become a passport to paradise.

One can see why the sixth-century bishops had to condemn suicide as a crime. Yet Alvarez is also right in saying that the consequences of their position have been terribly inhumane. He quotes a contemporary account of the punishment of an early seventeenth-century English suicide: the victim is "drawn by a horse to the place of punishment and shame, where he is hanged on a gibbet, and none may take the body down but by the authority of a magistrate." Nor is there any difficulty at all in agreeing with Alvarez's prescription that suicide should be regarded with compassion and that all legal and social punishment should be removed from those who undertake it. That is easy enough—but what remains is the problem of suicide itself and, first of all, trying to figure out exactly what we mean by the problem of suicide. Here we find ourselves not much wiser than the commentators of two thousand years ago: the centuries do not help.

III

Both Choron and Alvarez offer cogent reports on the enormous amount of scholarly literature about suicide. What has often characterized these studies is an indifference to, or avoidance of, the immediate life-situation leading to suicide, perhaps because that seems beyond the reach of sociological or even psychological investigation. Instead, the sociologists, and to a lesser extent the psychologists, have tried to find aggregate trends or statistical patterns concerning suicide as a public phenomenon. Alvarez, in that tiresome way some literary men affect, tends to look down his nose at sociological studies, mostly because he is not interested in getting answers to the questions they ask. But he is quite wrong. It seems, for example, of great interest to know that in the U.S. the suicide rate for men has been three times larger than that for women, or that many more women try and fail to kill themselves than do men, or that the rate for physicians is three times as great as that for the general population. From such pieces of hard evidence, even if they can't yet be put to much practical use, it becomes possible to develop useful hypotheses and propositions. They can't, to be sure, satisfy Alvarez's hunger, which I share, for insight into the immediate emotional dynamics that precede the taking of one's life, but surely they are of help to the various social agencies that act to prevent the spread of suicide.

Quoting statistics from Sweden to show that even an enlightened welfare state "makes more or less no difference to the suicide rate," Alvarez writes:

> It seems to me that even the most elegant and convincing sociological theories are short-circuited by this simple observation that suicide is a human characteristic, like sex, which not even the most perfect society will erase.

Now, the comparison with sex is, for most people, very much open to question; were Alvarez accurate in making it, the race would literally be in danger of extinction. More important, he should also know that the question sociologists try to cope with is not whether suicide can be "erased" in a "perfect society"—no one in his right mind supposes that—but whether, as with other human troubles, it can be significantly reduced, at least by removing those of its causes that may be designated as social.

It is really a valuable piece of information, at least insofar as it confirms statistically what might otherwise be a mere impression, that the young attempt suicide far more often than do the old, but that the old succeed in killing themselves far more often than do the young. Such information helps establish distinctions among kinds of suicides, one of the most difficult tasks facing students of the subject. Clearly, many young people who engage in suicide attempts are uttering "cries for help," intent upon forcing attention and compliance through the most extreme gesture they can imagine, while people in their sixties are simply signing off, through a decision they may have considered carefully and rationally.

On all these matters Choron is more objective than Alvarez, for Choron recognizes that in regard to so recalcitrant a matter, the accumulation of small bits of information can be as useful as the accumulation of large theories. Choron is very careful on the touchy matter of whether suicides are to be regarded as generic among the mentally ill, a view many psychiatrists accept but which Alvarez, with his desire to domesticate the act, strongly resists. Choron distinguishes between motives and causes—between, that is, the reasons suicidal people give or believe and the factors that actually precipitate their actions; and, of course, this distinction tends to support the views of those who think that, as a rule, mental illness is the crucial cause of suicide. Yet he is realistic enough to see that there are situations in which some people who are "mentally normal" can decide sensibly in favor of suicide.

Choron is also very lucid in discussing the Freudian approach to suicide, which is to regard it as a breakthrough of "the death instinct" induced by some pathological condition. Apart from the uncertain status of this "instinct," which by now even many psychoanalysts treat gingerly, the invocation of a pervasive human drive toward death does not help us very much in understanding suicide. For, as Choron remarks, the problem remains "of why it manifests itself with such force only in a few cases." Toward such an understanding, the classification of suicides into a number of different kinds—those emitting "a cry for help," those making a warranted decision, those engaged in a public gesture, those suffering from mental illness, etc.—seems a useful preliminary for therapeutic and preventive action. For the central problem, in Choron's words, follows from the fact that "the overwhelming majority of people in similar situations [to those of suicides] do not commit suicide. The question then is why these particular people do kill themselves." And the truth is, we hardly know.

IV

Throughout *The Savage God* there are intimations—perhaps not always fully intended—that suicide is to be seen not merely as evidence of a psychic predicament, or even as an act that may properly conclude a normal existence, but also as a token of a superior or more sensitive state of consciousness. Whoever has fully exposed himself to the horror of our time, it is suggested, must accept the risks of crack-up, breakdown, and suicide; it is the great writers, bearing the pain of modern awareness, who have taken upon themselves this heroism. Writes Alvarez:

> *Before the 20th century it is possible to discuss cases individually, since the artists who killed themselves or were even seriously suicidal were rare exceptions. In the 20th century the balance suddenly shifts; the better the artist the more vulnerable he seems to be. Obviously, this is in no way a firm rule.*

Not only isn't this "a firm rule," but if one remembers the long line of modern masters who lived to a ripe age, their faces still turned toward life, then Alvarez's generalization seems weak. One thinks of Yeats, Stevens, Joyce, Eliot, Forster, Gide, Mann, Marianne Moore, Williams, many others: all responsive to the terrors of our time but not really "vulnerable" in that special sense Alvarez intends. He has burdened himself with a view of modern literature that forces him to overvalue its ordealist side, everything tormented, high-pitched, violent, and drawn toward annihilation.

That there is a side to modern literature that does seem deeply absorbed with death it would be idle to deny. About such writing, and what it represents aesthetically and morally, Alvarez is painfully divided. He can write:

> *Twentieth century art may start with nothing but it flourishes by virtue of its belief in itself, in the possibility of control over what seems essentially uncontrollable . . . and in its ability to create its own values.*

But then he can also write:

> *In a sense, the whole of 20th century art has been dedicated to*

the service of this earthbound Savage God [suicide] who like the rest of his kind has thrived on blood sacrifice. As with modern warfare, enormous sophistication of theory and technique has gone into producing an art which is more extreme, more violent and finally more self-destructive than ever before.

In the first of these passages Alvarez is describing modernist sensibility at its severe best, and in the second its decadent or nihilist decline; in the first he speaks with the voice of critical balance and in the second with the voice of a distraught passion. As the book proceeds, the latter voice takes over, to the point where suicide gradually ceases to be treated as a problem at all.

It is at this point that we arrive at the blank wall of ultimate difference, where people can no longer argue opinions but must content themselves with accepting a polarity of life-attitudes. Let us try to look at these deeply contrasting attitudes, not to assert a claim of moral superiority either way, but simply to lay out a division among human beings that is perhaps "given" in our natures and perhaps a result of varying experiences in childhood and adult life.

Alvarez, in a strongly felt passage, speaks of "the closed world of suicide. For [people inclined to it], the act is neither rash nor operatic nor, in any obvious way, unbalanced. Instead it is, insidiously, a vocation. Once inside the closed world, there seems never to have been a time when one was not suicidal."

Now, what can it mean to speak of suicide as a vocation? If I understand him rightly, Alvarez is saying that there are people who must keep returning to suicide, precisely because they fail to complete the act and perhaps until they do complete it—quite in the way that writers must write, painters paint, and women, or at least some, be mothers. Suicide thus becomes, in a gruesome turn of phrase, *a way of life*, though a way of life that depends on a steadily eroding commitment to life.

But there are a great many people, no doubt the vast majority, for whom it is life itself that is their vocation, people imbued with the Tolstoyan feeling that life is an absolute value in its own right. It is easy to sneer at such people by saying they live an unexamined life without confronting the problematic elements of our nature; but even those of us to whom consciousness has come to be a supreme value must also acknowledge, a little ruefully, the power and the rightness of such a rootedness in quotidian existence.

Suppose a group of ordinary people were asked under what conditions they could imagine committing suicide. My guess is that they'd answer: if I were being tortured in a concentration camp or were suffering horribly from an incurable illness. But to feel that these are the only possibilities for so much as imagining suicide is clearly not to look upon it as a "vocation." It is to announce—with what degree of honesty is another matter—the hold that life continues to have, not necessarily a good or happy life, nor a fulfilled or successful life, but life itself, in its brute irreducibility and essential unsatisfactoriness.

Is it, furthermore, inconceivable that among the people holding to this view there could be a literary man as talented and sensitive as Alvarez, and with a past more or less as happy or unhappy as that of Alvarez? Obviously, this is by no means inconceivable, for the problem of suicide, as Choron says, is to explain why among people "in similar situations" some do and most do not take their own lives.

Someone might, of course, reply that such a person did not experience emptiness and despair as deeply as did those writers cited by Alvarez who have indeed committed suicide, the proof being that our hypothetical literary man did not attempt it. But that seems to me both a tautological and a trivial argument, since there is neither a way nor a reason to refute it. The problem is interesting, the problem is really a problem, only if one grants the possibility that X, sensitive and distinguished, may respond to his despair by taking his life, while Y, sensitive and distinguished, may respond to his despair by clinging to life. And here occurs the great divide, one of the most significant among human beings, between those who can see suicide as a "vocation" and those who cannot see it as any kind of "solution" to the normal course of their lives.

Why this divide? No one seems really to know, and I can only offer a tautology, but not, I think, a trivial one. Those to whom suicide is inconceivable in all but the most extreme circumstances of torture—that is, those who cannot see it as a way out of the despair that *all* human beings encounter—are people in whom the life-force, that elemental energy for survival, remains dominant.

But is this attachment to life no more than an instinctive response or does it also rest, however slenderly, on some elements of belief? If the former, there is nothing more to say: we are as we are. If, however, there are some elements of belief that affect the nature and intensity of our attachment to life, then these elements may constitute precisely the area where men do have a measure of freedom in determining their fate.

The argument used to justify a distinctively modern predilection toward suicide was first and most brilliantly advanced by Kirillov in Dostoevsky's *The Possessed*. Kirillov is a rationalistic atheist, warm-hearted and morally upright, who wishes once and for all to shake off the fear of God, which he sees as the fear of death, that has oppressed humanity through the ages. Kirillov commits suicide, to show that he no longer fears a God who is nothing but "the pain of the fear of death," and thereby he registers, as it seems to him, the supreme expression of his free will.

But there is a possible answer to Kirillov, and it has been given by the poet Mayakovsky: "In this life it is not difficult to die/It is more difficult to live." I would gloss these lines as suggesting that if man does feel bereft after the loss of God and if he does wish to shake off the fear of death that has always been deeply intertwined with the power of faith, then it is through the discipline of life that we show our freedom, while suicide is a sign of continued dependence on the fallen gods.

At least for some people, it is precisely the loss of faith, with its dimming vision of an afterlife, that makes suicide seem a less plausible way out of conditions that can be quite as wretched as Alvarez says. For if what faces us inexorably is the prospect of eternal dissolution, then the little bit of life allowed us becomes all the more precious—even in its failure and despair. Intellectually, Alvarez grasps this point very well, when he writes that secular man "chooses life because he has no alternative, because he knows that after death there is nothing at all . . . When neither high purpose nor the categorical imperatives of religion will do, the only argument against suicide is life itself." It is a sufficient argument.

Alvarez offers a harvest of literary testimony—at these points his book is completely fascinating—but there is one citation that he neglects. The Russian-Jewish writer Isaac Babel has a story, "In the Basement," about a thirteen-year-old boy who in momentary despair tries to drown himself in a water barrel. His Jewish grandfather pulls him out:

> *"Grandson," he said, pronouncing the word with scornful distinctness. "Grandson, I am going to take a dose of castor oil, so as to have something to lay on your grave."*

What the grandfather says here may seem coarse, barbaric. But wait. The story ends as the boy comes to himself in bed, his "Aunt Bobka . . . warming my hands on her bosom," and saying. "How he trembles, our blessed ninny! Where can the child find the strength to tremble so?' " while "Grandfather was stalking about the room whistling."

That whistle signifies a melody of gratification. The grandfather has won a triumph for life, and his shocking, vulgar speech about defecating on the boy's grave is a way of enforcing the urgency of the commandment to life. There is a rich tradition here, expressed tragically by another Russian-Jewish writer, Osip Mandelstam, who said, when his wife proposed that they commit suicide before Stalin's police would come to arrest them, "Life is a gift that nobody should renounce."

AUSCHWITZ AND
HIGH MANDARIN

A PHALANX OF CRUCIAL TOPICS, a tone of high-church gravity, a light sprinkle of multilingual erudition, a genteel stab at prophecy—it's easy to imagine the strong impression Mr. George Steiner's lectures must have made when first delivered for the T.S. Eliot Memorial Foundation at the University of Kent.[1] And now, when we read his first sentence announcing that his book is written "in memoration" of T.S. Eliot, we are prepared for some decidedly high-class prose.

Western culture, Mr. Steiner says, is irremediably shattered, all our certainties destroyed and axioms bent; yet not for a moment does this cause him to strain his syntax, lose his cool, or breathe an ill-mannered rasp. His style, in all its mincing equanimity, can assimilate equally a few paragraphs on Milton's verse and a few on the slaughter of six million Jews. His prose remains creamy and mellifluous, a high Mandarin patter that reads at times as if it were a parody by Lucky Jim. Here is a glorious passage:

> At every knot, from the voices of public men to the vocabulary

---

[1] Published as In Bluebeard's Castle: Some Notes Toward the Redefinition of Culture. (New Haven: Yale University Press. 1971)

of dreams, language is close-woven with lies. Falsehood is inseparable from its generative life. Music can boast, it can sentimentalize,
it can release springs of cruelty. But it does not lie. (Is there
a lie, anywhere in Mozart?)

Smiles of appreciative concord flit through the auditorium—
and who would be so rude as to remark that the reason there
is no "lie," anywhere, in Mozart's music is precisely the same
reason that there is no "truth"? In short, that Mr. Steiner isn't
making sense?

In his first chapter, concerned to bound our cultural crisis,
Mr. Steiner looks back to the 19th century and finds that "certain
specific origins of the inhuman . . . are to be found in [its]
long peace. . . ." He is right. The point has been made frequently, but is surely worth repeating, that in the century of
melioristic progress "we can find a counterstatement of nervous
fatigue." It consists of ennui, signs of which Mr. Steiner traces
in European culture during the second half of the century, and
this ennui gives rise to "a longing for violent dissolution."

But, we might remember, this is the time in which the cultural
phenomenon we call "modernism"—in all its brilliance and force,
all its truth and deception—was coming to the forefront. For
a moralist of culture, a historian of sensibility, it would, at this
point, seem necessary to struggle with the painful questions: What
is the relation between the problematic genius of the modernist
outburst and the historical catastrophe that soon followed it? Are
they, in some way or to some extent, causally linked? Are they
polar opposites, enemies in a struggle to the death? Is it
methodologically appropriate, or merely vulgar, to search for
some of the roots of 20th-century social disaster in the cultural
upheavals preceding it? By no means sure of the answers, I
can hardly expect anyone else to be; but it seems inconceivable
that, in a book discussing both the nature of cultural modernism
and the subsequent convulsions of Europe, Mr. Steiner should
not even ask such questions. Anyone, to be sure, who did ask
them would be obliged to confront some major literary reputa-
tions and would have to expect, no matter which line of attack
he took, some bitter and passionate replies. Why not?

Mr. Steiner's skittishness deepens in the second part of the
book. He sees the triumph of Nazism as the last in a series
of impulsive rebellions by natural man against the noble tyranny

of monotheism, that dubious and unwanted blessing the Jews lowered upon the world:

> By killing the Jew, Western culture would eradicate those who had "invented" God, who had, however imperfectly, however restively, been the declarers of his unbearable Absence. The holocaust is a reflex, the more complete for being long-inhibited, of natural sensory consciousness, of instinctual polytheistic and animist needs.

This notion, too, is rather well-worn, though the claim that polytheism constitutes or stems from an "instinct" may be novel. If at first glance it seems flattering to the Jews to be told that they have been the "bad conscience" of Western history, bringing with them "the blackmail of transcendence," a moment's reflection ought to reveal that it is empty talk, at once grandiose and trivial. As an explanation for the rise of totalitarianism, it suffers from a characteristic fault of *Geistesgeschichte:* the encapsulation of an extremely complex group of historical events by a theory so nebulously inclusive that it leaves no possibility for refutation. And a theory that can't be refuted can't be demonstrated. If I say, Nazism arose because of certain nameable failures of German capitalism in the 1920's, or because there occurred a severe historical dislocation of the lumpen intelligentsia which could then exploit uglier elements of the Germanic and Christian traditions, or because of the vengeful consequences of the Versailles Treaty, or because the Stalinists and/or Social Democrats pursued disastrous policies, then whoever disagrees can bring evidence to bear. But how can anyone verify or argue against Mr. Steiner's notion? Of what use is it, therefore, to remark that "Western culture" can hardly be said to have killed the Jews, it was the Nazis who killed them, and indeed, it might be a little more plausible to say that "Western culture" destroyed the Nazis? Or that at least in some cultures the "instinctual" pressures of polytheism seem very slight (perhaps because of a difference in climate or geography)? Or that Stalinism, the second major form of European totalitarianism, even though sharing some essential traits of cataclysmic inhumaneness with Nazism, could not possibly be explained by a conflict between regnant monotheism and rebellious polytheistic impulses?

To persons of Mr. Steiner's cast of mind, such matters constitute evidence of a "lower" order, mere historical phenomena, which cannot possibly compete with the convolutions of *Geist*. Surely, when Mr. Steiner writes, "The abruptness of the Mosaic revelation, the finality of the creed at Sinai, tore up the human psyche by its most ancient roots," he is not making a statement open to historical scrutiny. How abrupt was this Mosaic revelation? Where, in which discoverable instances, was "the human psyche" torn up by "its most ancient roots"? And what does Mr. Steiner make of those cultures that continued to live in benighted comfort, unaware of the "Mosaic revelation"?

Now it will be said that statements such as those I have quoted are not proposed for verification, they are a kind of "historical poetry" to be valued for their suggestiveness. Very well. Any student of Nazism would probably agree that it was freighted with elements of the irrational and demonic, and that these played a significant role in its history—for reasons, however, that had less to do with the psychic damage inherited from Moses than with the strongly visible Germanic and Christian traditions, as well as the specific historical experiences of the last century. But to start considering such elements of Nazism is already to submit oneself to the cautions of partial answers and multiple causation—which means to abandon the lordly tone of humanistic declamation which literary men (all of us) assume when pronouncing on the state of the world.

Mr. Steiner's theory has the immediate effect of releasing major institutions from their moral responsibilities. For if it is "natural sensory consciousness" that was at work in promoting the Holocaust, how much weight can we then give to Rolf Hochhuth's denunciation of the Papacy or Leon Trotsky's of the Stalinists? And if "instinctual polytheistic. . . needs" lie behind the horrors of Auschwitz, then the Christian churches, with their frequently disgraceful records in regard to anti-Semitism in Germany, may partly be let off the hook. Indeed, if such overpowering instincts are at work, instincts that have kept breaking out through the entire course of human history, how then can anyone be held morally responsible for the Nazi murders?

But what interests Mr. Steiner most is not the cause of the Holocaust, it is the consequences that follow. He is deeply shaken, as any sensitive person must be, by the systematic inhumanity of the camps, "the transference of Hell from below the earth to its surfaces." In scrutinizing Western culture he concludes that things can never be the same again: we have entered a phase of "post-culture." Precisely what "post-culture" can mean I have tried to make out, and failed. If someone says, we are entering a time of "post-modernist" or "post-bourgeois" or "post-rational" culture, then we may be able to muster some sense of what he means: he is trying to suggest that Western culture has abandoned the norms and securities of the liberal enlightenment, or that it is finished with the need to experiment and transvalue. But I cannot imagine that Mr. Steiner wishes to say anything so limited. He seems to be toying with the notion that we will soon be living in a world that has left behind or gone beyond the institutions, traditions, activities, and values—especially as these adhere to the Word—which we associate with culture in general. Whether this is even possible, he does not ask.

Having stimulated himself with high Germanic notions about culture, Mr. Steiner now seems to be suffering from a bad letdown. "What good did high humanism do the oppressed mass of the community? What use was it when barbarism came? What immortal poem has ever stopped or mitigated political terror?" These questions, in their hopeless mixture of innocence and corruption, are precisely the questions that can be heard in any freshman class. What's the good of Plato if he "came out of" a slave society? How can I enjoy Chaucer if he contains anti-Semitic passages? Why study physics if scientists made the atom bomb? Several times, in this spirit, Mr. Steiner remarks that Beethoven concerts were held in Munich while people were being tortured in nearby Dachau.

To both our freshmen and Mr. Steiner, though with varying degrees of patience, one must give a number of familiar answers: that culture is by no means the only value, nor always the highest value, of human existence; that the kind of questions he asks are likely to be put by those who had mistakenly supposed that culture *is* the highest value of human existence; that the cultural achievements of the past must be seen not only as conditioned and thereby contaminated by historical exigencies, but also as "transhistorical" or "potential" works which survive those exigencies; that great works of culture are radically defenseless, being available to use and misuse by persons of all kinds, from saints to butchers; and that there is always likely to be an inherent conflict between the domain of culture and the demands of morality.

In the fate of the Jews during the Holocaust Mr. Steiner finds the turning point of Western culture. One feels that there must be merit in this view, though exactly what it means is very hard to say. What, after all, *can* it mean? Are we to abandon, as hopelessly besmirched, the heritage of Western culture? Are we to cease engaging in those activities by means of which, well or badly, we maintain that heritage? One can hardly suppose that Mr. Steiner means anything so extreme. Does he then propose that we take a more skeptical attitude toward ideologists of culture, those aristocrats of the Word who dominated European literary life for a good many decades before the Holocaust and who often proved less than heroic when it came? Here one would quickly agree.

Again one suspects Mr. Steiner has more in mind, as witness his fashionable references to the Third World and to the fact, or supposed fact, that young people no longer take for granted "the image of Western culture as self-evidently superior." Yet the very values Mr. Steiner would like to advance—where do they come from but Western culture? And those Jews who survived the camps, Jews who one presumes are precious to his imagination—what are they to live by if not the heritage that somehow they have kept?

The claim that after the Holocaust nothing can again be as once it was in our cultural and intellectual experience must strike some deep chords in our being, just as does the repeated verbal injunction by some writers that the only authentic response to the Holocaust is silence. But there are elemental continuities in our existence which, even if they make us uncomfortable, cannot be denied. People continue to live; living, they develop a culture; and at this moment it would seem just as well that it be grounded, with whatever modulations, in the Western tradition. This means to accept—as if we had a choice!—the bone in our throats: the knowledge of the possible misuses of culture, the memory of the topographical, and spiritual, juxtaposition of Weimar and Buchenwald. Speaking of that juxtaposition, the

Times Literary Supplement reviewer of Mr. Steiner's book aptly remarked: "There are facts that the mind can do nothing with, and this seems to be one of them: by itself it offers neither condemnation nor vindication of Western liberal culture."

Even those Jewish writers who employ Yiddish and Hebrew find themselves obliged to live by some such view. Mr. Steiner, though notably distraught over the fate of the Jews in general, pays very little attention to Jews in particular. Surely, no one is under the slightest obligation to know a Jewish language or be familiar with the writings of Yiddish and Hebrew poets and novelists; but a cultural critic who has become distinguished for his concern with the fate of the Jews—*he*, one would think, might trouble to find out what they have been saying in the post-Holocaust years. He might look into Jacob Glatstein's poems about the Holocaust, or into Aaron Zeitlin's "I Believe," a long Yiddish poem that deals with some of the matters troubling Mr. Steiner:

> *Can I then choose not to believe*
> *in that living God whose purposes*
> *when He destroys, seeming to forsake me,*
> *I cannot conceive;*
> *choose not to believe in Him*
> *Who having turned my body to fine ash*
> *begins once more to wake me?*
> (translated by Robert Friend)

Among the survivors themselves—actual, bodied Jews and not mere tokens of literary gesture—a dominant motif is not that of discarding or declaring obsolete the traditions of either the Jews themselves or Western culture but rather of reasserting them in defiance of Gentile history. Mr. Steiner would be at liberty, if he wished, to regard such assertions as parochial or ritualistic or inconsequent, but given the concerns that dominate his book, it would be appropriate if he knew something about them.

There is, however, one respect in which Mr. Steiner's claim that the Holocaust is the great turning-point in modern life ought to be insistently affirmed, and that is in our politics, a low order of affairs with which he will apparently have little commerce. If someone were to write that after Hitler and Stalin, intellectuals

must never, no matter what the occasion or pretext, allow themselves to provide ideological rationales for the suppression of
liberty, he would be saying something profoundly important.
If he were so unmannerly as to name a few of the intellectuals
who, in behalf of the Revolution or the Third World, do provide
such rationales, he would be performing a double service. But
about such mundane matters not a word enters *In Bluebeard's
Castle.*

Mr. Steiner, in a final chapter called "Tomorrow," proposes
to "offer conjectures as to what may be synapses worth watching."
The conjectures have to do with the familiar problem of the
relation between high culture and mass literacy, the
"musicalization of our culture," and the growing dominance of
mathematics and science, all of which threaten to destroy the
power of the Word. About this threat Mr. Steiner is either unclear
in his mind or so ambivalent as to seem unclear. Part of what
he says is commonplace and thereby acceptable, part an effort
to hop onto the disintegrating bandwagon of the "counterculture." At times Mr. Steiner sounds like a humanist in mourning. At other times he can write, "Personally, I feel most drawn
to the conviction, irrational, even tactless as it may be, that
it is enormously interesting to be alive at this cruel, late stage
in Western affairs." Perhaps; but as a conclusion to so darkly
portentous a book or as a statement of cultural diagnosis, this
Saturday Review-like sentence, chin up and best foot forward,
seems absurd.

There is, however, no reason to get angry, no reason until
one remembers the central point of the book: the gas ovens and
the collapse of Western culture, the juxtaposition of Weimar
and Buchenwald. And then it is hard to remain calm. After
all those rumblings of apocalypse, is *this* to be the conclusion?
The critic declaring the death of Western culture in the ovens
of Auschwitz—he can then, a few pages later, content himself
with the journalistic fatuity of "it is enormously interesting to
be alive" etc. etc.? One minute Western culture is dying, and
the next we are to be charmed by new developments in linguistics
and long-playing records?

There is something strange and tasteless in so extreme an
incongruence. One fails to understand, one looks for complex

explanations. But perhaps the truth is really simple, perhaps his book is just an old-fashioned case of teakettle chopping (cf. Uriel Weinreich, *Modern English-Yiddish Yiddish-English Dictionary*, p. 202, col. 1, entry 15).

GANDHI AND
PSYCHOANALYSIS

How do you remember Gandhi?

"He was like a good night's sleep," answered Ambalal the industrialist. "He was my mother!" declared Anasuya, the sister of Ambalal. "He was a consummate politician," said a political opponent Indulak Yagnik.

The question came from the American psychoanalyst, Erik Erikson, during a visit to India, and once he had elicited this lovely triad of memories everything could follow in his lovely book on Gandhi.[1] Ambalal was a millowner in the city of Ahmedabad, against whom Gandhi led a strike of textile workers in 1918, perfecting his method of *Satyagraha*, usually mistranslated as "passive resistance." For Ambalal, Gandhi signified the force of conscience, and only through its assuagement could he gain "a good night's sleep." Anasuya had become a labor leader even before the strike, pitting her faith and will against a beloved brother. To her, Gandhi evoked the gratification she had found in caring for workers, and more deeply, that maternal bisexuality, at once comforting and claustrophobic, which seems pervasive in Hindu religious culture. And for Yagnik, Gandhi figured not as saint but as strategist, a shrewd actor in the struggle

[1] *Gandhi's Truth* by Erik Erikson (New York, Norton, 1970).

190

for power. If it were possible to structure these replies into a coherent vision of Gandhi, we might have the foundations of a great man's greatness.

The story opens with Gandhi's childhood: he is the youngest son, clever but a bit spoiled, never playing with other children except as a peacemaker in their disputes, teasing his way into adult favor but also suffering a series of tests that begin to establish his distinctiveness. The book ends in 1930, twelve years after the Ahmedabad victory, with the Mahatma launching his great March to the Sea in protest against the British Salt Act. Thousands of disciplined followers act out the peaceful aggression of *Satyagraha;* the rule of British imperialism is shaken beyond repair; Gandhi pays a triumphant visit to the Viceroy, where —saintly rascal—he pours a pinch of the forbidden salt into his tea in order, he smiles, "to remind us of the famous Boston Tea Party."

Gandhi's Truth is extraordinary: an almost-great book that yields intellectual pleasure from start to finish. If I add the judgment that in demonstrating its essential thesis the book is also a failure, you will understand that I am applying to Erik Erikson standards he must suppose it flattering to fall short of (though only by an inch or two, he's not the kind of man who'd care to fall *very* short). What I propose to question is the link Erikson claims to establish in his books on Luther and Gandhi between psychoanalysis and history—so let us look, schematically, at each book in turn.

II

Less disciplined in central exposition but more fecund in local detail, *Gandhi's Truth* follows the pattern of Erikson's earlier book, *Young Man Luther.* In the life of a great man there occurs a moment when he suffers a crisis of definition. He is young, he separates himself from others and himself, he comes apart, he struggles for a new self and a new conception of his place in the world. Erikson calls this an "identity crisis," that crucial moment which occurs in all men of some self-awareness and with a special force in great ones. Erikson has seized upon this concept with a fascination that cannot be explained simply by his clinical concerns. My guess is that it has something to do with a gradual and unacknowledged movement away from a strict psychoanalytic role: the concept of "identity crisis" lures him into speculations about the psychic attributes of greatness, it enables him to attempt a new biographical genre resting on a fusion of psychoanalysis and history, and it satisfies his strong taste for the dramatics of character.

In writing about Luther, he rests an elaborate portrait on a single incident, one not even fully authenticated as history: the "fit in the choir," a seizure during Luther's early twenties in the Erfurt monastery. From that point on, Luther torments himself into a new self and a new historical command. So persuasive is Erikson's portrait of this gradual struggle for self-transformation that one comes to feel it barely matters whether the "fit in the choir" actually occurred or was as crucial as Erikson supposes. At worst, it is a dramatic fiction skillfully employed.

What Erikson then does, through a refined use of psychoanalytic categories, is to show how the neurotic strains in Luther's character contributed—both as spur and brake—to his towering achievement as voice of the Reformation. Here, as in the later book on Gandhi, Erikson avoids the sin of Freudian reductionism or what he calls *originology*, "the habitual effort to find the 'causes' of a man's whole development in his childhood conflict." How much then remains of Freudianism is something of a question.

With Gandhi the case is more difficult, and that may explain why Erikson's new book is more self-consciously elaborate than the one on Luther. Psychoanalysis, no matter what its claims to universality, employs a language drawn from Western culture, and Western too is the more conventional language of historical study and moral experience Erikson necessarily uses. But where Luther stands at the very center of Western experience, accessible to us through perceptions by which we have lived for centuries, Gandhi is very far away—and the more one learns about him, the greater does his cultural distance seem. Even in Erikson's sympathetic account, Indian religion and culture are hard for a Westerner to grasp; the very terms we employ in translating such Hindu concepts as *dharma*, *ahimsa*, and *brahmacharya* must involve distortion. Very shrewdly, Erikson tries to penetrate beneath his own psychoanalytic premises and Gandhi's religious-cultural premises in order to find universal modes of experience that hold for men of all cultures. Such universal modes must surely exist, but the immediate consequence of looking for them is, paradoxically, to become aware of the distance, the "strangeness" of Hindu styles of life. Erikson must therefore keep providing exegesis, "translation" from culture to culture—and the possibilities for error, both by author and reader, become alarming.

Even in his tactful pages on Gandhi's boyhood—you'd suppose infantile traumas as decisive in the East as in the West—Erikson continually struggles with the problem of cultural distance. Consider a passage such as this:

> *Gandhi's protestations of motherliness [are] more than an emotional inversion: the primary power of motherliness (symbolized in the cow) is an ancient and all-pervasive ingredient of Indian tradition. When this boy appointed himself his father's nurse, there was a drive in it which later could suffice for the care of all India as well as of Untouchables and lepers. . . .*

An Indian, however, might be startled at the suggestion that Gandhi's "motherliness" needs to be protected from the charge of "emotional inversion"—what, he might wonder, is the matter with those Westerners? And even we can ask whether, or to what extent, the religious-cultural tradition of Hinduism calls into question the force of Erikson's psychoanalytic categories when these are applied to a man like Gandhi.

Or consider the painful story of Gandhi's marriage in early adolescence, not at all unusual in late-nineteenth-century India, with all the troubles it brought a boy who felt not only guilty toward a father he supposed himself to be neglecting but also guilty toward himself because of what he took to be his "lustfulness":

> *The nursing care of the father is pictured as the one endeavour superior to all other purpose: was this a parable in which the son not only atones for his own sins but also forgives the father for his too? . . . Gandhi's sexuality, by omission or commission, became permanently marred by what to him was juvenile excess, depleting his power of spiritual concentration.*

What strikes one here is the utter *Westernness* of Erikson's analysis, the distance between the life described and the values that Erikson, for all his charming tolerance, cannot help bringing to it. And the troubles that follow are most striking in two areas of experience, that of social role and that of sexual relations.

Erikson relies a good deal on an Indian concept called *dharma*, almost untranslatable but roughly signifying a mixture of social task, caste position, and moral obligation. People of certain castes and perhaps certain natures have distinctive *dharmas*. By this is apparently meant something at once less improvisatory than what we would mean by personal destiny (a Napoleon says, "it's my destiny," but makes sure to determine its content himself) and a good deal more flexible in practice than our revulsion against the Indian caste system would allow us to believe. For the mission of *dharma* is complicated, and humanized, by the Hindu vision of the life-cycle, according to which all men must go through a series of stages in their experience, with each stage offering unique responsibilities and occasions. The ritualized life-cycle is seen as a kind of spiral, first a movement toward involvement with the world and then a gradual withdrawal. Presumably —I am not clear on this and Erikson isn't much help either—one's distinctive *dharma* "intersects" with one's stage in the life-cycle to create the terms of personality.

Perhaps because he sees in them strong analogies with his own sense of human experience, Erikson is attracted to both *dharma* and the life-cycle. *Dharma* he relates to our views of role and obligation; the Hindu life-cycle to his own notions concerning psychic growth, tension, and the conquest of identity. The young Gandhi is pictured as being harassed by all the embarrassments, awkwardnesses, self-confrontations, and ultimatistic demands we associate with youth; but he experiences these within a sequence of expectation and limitation that allows him to locate his personal needs within traditional ways. Thereby, the "identity crisis" of the young Luther is transferred to the young Indian barrister who journeys to England and fancies himself a bit of a swell; to the apprentice leader in South Africa who rallies the mistreated Indians behind the still-formative tactics of civil disobedience; and to the emerging spokesman-saint who travels throughout India in third-class coaches rallying both a moral elite and the inexperienced masses to the struggle for national revival.

In his section on the young Gandhi, Erikson keeps in delicate balance the Hindu vision of the life-cycle and his own neo-Freudian sense of human experience. He grants the reality of Hindu wisdom, which, all cultural embarrassment apart, seems to me a sign of his own wisdom. He keeps steadily trying to relate the patterns of Indian culture to his own faith in the generative capacities of mankind. What I am not convinced of is that he has shown Gandhi to have lived through an "identity crisis" during or shortly before the Admedabad strike.

For we must remember that this strike occurred when Gandhi was forty-eight years old, the Indian equivalent, I would guess, of being a decade older in our culture. Gandhi was by then a seasoned veteran of social struggle, a man who had worked out his commanding vision of life, if not yet all the strategies by which to realize it. The very concept of "identity crisis" as formulated by Erikson seems distinctive to youth, and especially youth in cultures where entry into adulthood is abrupt and painful. Obviously, Gandhi, like any other sensitive (or even insensitive) middle-aged man, went through a range of personal troubles that may in sum have constituted a crisis. He must have asked himself during the strike: what do I do next? will I be able to fulfill my task? have I undertaken a campaign for which I do not yet have the resources? But I don't see any evidence in Erikson's book that he asked the kinds of questions one associates with an "identity crisis." By then Gandhi knew exactly who he was, even if not quite yet the magnitude of the public role he would create; his friends and opponents certainly knew who he was, and that is a good part of what comprises a public man's identity. True, he was not yet the national leader of India, but in part that was because India was not yet a coherent nation; he would become a national leader precisely through the struggle to achieve a rebirth for India.

The traditional culture in which Gandhi was raised, whatever moral discomfort it may evoke in us, was so organized as to provide young men with a range of opportunities for experiment and contemplation, assertion and withdrawal; it gave them fixed terms of self-definition but left the organization of those terms to the young themselves; and thereby it tended, as traditional societies can, to smooth out and ease up the inevitable bumps of psychic growth. Reading *Gandhi's Truth* I became convinced by Erikson's scrupulously assembled evidence that his essential scheme of analysis just doesn't work—the book is better than its thesis. For if Gandhi went through a crisis at Ahmedabad it was the crisis that comes to men at the middle of their journey, when they ask themselves whether their expectations have been vain, their struggle worthwhile, and their ambitions delusionary; and that kind of crisis, though, God knows, it can be severe enough, doesn't involve problems of identity.

When Erikson comes to discuss Gandhi's principled refusal of sexuality in his mature years, there are even greater difficulties. He struggles bravely and gallantly with this problem, if sometimes also a bit comically. Gandhi, he tells us, believed that "higher brain power is enhanced by the physical sexual substance which is lost in ejaculation but can be saved in continence and pumped up to the brain—that seems to be a traditional Indian model of a theory of sublimation." Now Erik Erikson is a very sophisticated man; he lives in Cambridge, Massachusetts; and if we can believe the jacket of his book, he is a handsome fellow too. What then can he make of these weird, if not archaic, notions about sexuality, so embarrassingly reminiscent of *Dr. Strangelove*, and furthermore so downright unhealthy? How is he to cope with the Hindu doctrine of *brahmacharya*, defined by Gandhi as "control of the senses in word, thought and deed," and in effect advocating a program of celibacy? An historian can content himself with description; an anthropologist can note the diversity of man's ways; but a psychoanalyst—isn't this a challenge for him to start performing like mad?

How ingenious he is in trying to bridge the gap between the norms by which Gandhi lived and the premises by which he writes! "It is of importance here," he reminds us, "that Gandhi gave up sexual intimacy for a wider communal intimacy and *not just* because sexuality seemed immoral in any Calvinist sense." Fine, but don't the two words I have italicized evade the issue? For, Calvinism or not, Gandhi did seem to feel that except in behalf of procreation, sexuality was immoral; and Erikson must therefore try to explain to himself, as an enlightened psychoanalyst, how it can be that a man whose sexuality was "permanently marred" (no small hurt, one would think) could yet be so marvelously unmarred, so creative and gay and inspiring, throughout his life?

Some years back, in a brilliant essay on Gandhi, the American writer Isaac Rosenfeld put the matter sharply: "Gandhi emerged uncrippled from the crippling inner life he made himself lead. . . ." And the explanation Rosenfeld gave, as it relied upon the cushioning traditionalism of Indian culture, wasn't very different from that of Erikson. Now, as long as we persist in holding to our own frame of reference—even if it's a hoop through which our subject won't jump—then this seems clever and perhaps satisfying. But suppose, just suppose Gandhi's inner life wasn't "permanently marred" or "crippled" at all? And in any case, what sense does it make to speak of a crippled life if a man of Gandhi's stature is said to have had one?

I raise these questions not because I have answers to them— obviously I do not—but because they enable me to underscore the dangers in Erikson's method of "translating" from culture to culture.

While I am plunging into these uncomfortable regions, let me ask a few more questions. Erikson's concept of "identity crisis" has a strong relevance for problems we encounter in America today; its methodological value depends, I would think, largely on the extent to which it remains abstract and formal, that is, the extent to which it gives the clinician a flexible mode of perception for dealing with specific disorders and difficulties. Insofar as it remains abstract and formal, it must make some claims—even if only within the boundaries of our culture— for universality of application: it describes a generic pattern of maturation, a common potential for conflict. What, however, can it contribute to a psychological analysis of "greatness"? In the case of Luther, Erikson shows how his neurotic energies not merely impeded but also helped release his ambitions. About the historical figure Martin Luther we may not know very much more than before reading Erikson, but we do gain a keener sense of the relation between that figure and the private person of the same name. There is profit in this, for it shows what great men share with the rest of us. But what can it contribute to illuminating their differences from the rest of us?

Very little, I think. My impudent surmise is that Erikson has turned to writing about great men because in part he senses the limitations of psychoanalysis once an effort is made to apply it beyond the therapeutic setting. In both the Luther and Gandhi books he keeps warning against *originology*, but insofar as he heeds the warning he tends to move from psychoanalysis into psychology, that is, from a system of concepts concerning unconscious springs of behavior to a complex of insights drawn partly from his own clinical experience and partly from a very supple intelligence. (As he jokingly warns—himself?—in *Young Man Luther:* "This sounds dangerously like common sense.") And in moving from psychoanalysis to psychology, he is also, I think, moving from both into history, for by now psychology has become part of history, assimilated into our consciousness of the past. The link between psychoanalysis and history never being fully achieved, Erikson tends to replace the idea of fusion with the reality of replacement. As two of his recent admirer-critics, Daniel Yankelovich and William Barrett, remark in their book *Ego and Instinct:*

> To the basic Freudian insistence on the development of the infant out of frustration of preemptory instinctual demands within the family setting, there are added the later struggles of the individual . . . for self-validity and meaning in a larger setting. . . . Yet the two parts of the synthesis still stand in unstable equilibrium. . . . For, if we trace Luther's life as a structure of meaning, certain "explanations" having to do with unknown infantile experiences become merely gratuitous and unexplanatory relapses into another form of reductionism that would seek to derive the whole person from the psycho-social phenomena of infancy and adolescence. The truth is that Erikson has thought beyond Freud to a degree that, in his reticence and loyalty to the psychoanalytic movement, he does not stress. . . .

A distinction should be made here between Erikson the writer and Erikson the clinician. It is quite possible that in his work as an analyst he can still rest more securely on the Freudian tradition than he can in his work as an historian. By now psychoanalysis has accumulated a store of insights and experiences concerning the problems of mental disorder which seem likely to survive, and which probably are not dependent on Freudianism as an intellectual system. It is even possible that a break-up of Freudian ideology could lead to a strengthening of psychoanalysis as a distinctive therapeutic method.

And one more question. In the hands of an Erikson, psychoanalysis can beautifully describe the pattern of "identity crisis." But what can it tell us about the content of this crisis? I will be told this is a naïve question, but that is precisely the reason to ask it. Christianity, like other religions, has had a theory about the content of such crises. Luther would not have regarded his "fit in the choir" as a *psychological* event, he would have insisted he was an instrument in the hands of superior powers. Dostoevsky would have said that young people reach a point where they must decide whether to admit or expel the presence of Christ, whether to open themselves to transcendent suffering or, in behalf of entering the world, suppress their religious possibilities. Now it hardly matters whether one accepts the religious view—I do not. The point is that seen in this or some parallel way, "identity crisis" takes on more than an internal character, it acquires a large ethical and historical value. So, I think, would Gandhi have seen the matter. But insofar as the psychoanalyst remains a psychoanalyst, he can tell us little about the significance and magnitude of any given "identity crisis," and if he is not as supple as Erikson he is almost certain to deprecate its moral and intellectual substance in favor of its inner dynamic. Perhaps it was some such realization that led Erikson into his new field of study; if so, it led him farther than he probably expected. For in plain fact, he has become a historian.

And a first-rate historian. In describing Gandhi's *Satygraha* campaigns in South Africa and India, Erikson writes with verve and authority. He destroys the common misconception of *Satyagraha* as an outcry of helplessness or as a refusal of masculine strength. In Hindu the term signifies "truth-force," a mode of militant nonviolence that draws upon Indian tradition but manifests itself as a secular strategy. As Erikson nicely remarks, Gandhi struck "the religious imagination of an angry people," and still more important, he tried to work out a politics that would not merely be effective but would retain at least some congruence with the ethical precepts of traditional Hinduism. Gandhi's own description of *Satyagraha* is that of a strenuous, manly, and even combative creed:

> *What am I to advise a man to do who wants to kill but is unable owing to his being maimed? Before I can make him feel the virtue of not killing, I must restore to him the arm he has lost. . . . A nation that is unfit to fight cannot from experience prove the virtue of not fighting. I do not infer from this that India must fight. But I do say that India must know how to fight.*

The strength of Erikson's historical narrative rests in part on his understanding of the way Gandhi mobilized traditional

resources for modern ends: "He had to call for a rapid moderniza-
tion of awareness and aspiration and yet also to acknowledge
and even preserve those aspects of the ancient social structure
which alone could provide irreplaceable elements of a traditional
identity." If, as his critics charge with some justice, Gandhi's
reliance on Indian traditionalism delayed solutions to some social
problems, it also helped India maintain a unity which, in turn,
enabled it to preserve democracy during and after its liberation.
Right now, this may not rouse much excitement among American
intellectuals, some of whom prefer to admire Mao's totalitarianism; but I believe that in a longer reckoning the ability
of the Indians to keep their democratic society afloat will be
regarded as one of the revolutionary achievements of the age.

When Erikson reaches the Ahmedabad strike, his analysis
becomes especially keen and his prose especially vibrant. He
reprints the leaflets Gandhi issued each day of the strike: they
are not only marvels of political shrewdness, but also models
of the art of speaking simply to uneducated workers while avoiding condescension. Erikson is strongest when he connects the
public struggle in Ahmedabad to Gandhi's inner life—it almost
convinces me that the ideal historian for the life of the spirit
is a genuinely worldly man. Only once does his critical intelligence fail him, and that is in sentimentalizing the responses of
Ambalal, the cultivated millowner against whom Gandhi led
the struggle. Erikson offers recondite explanations for Ambalal's
mixed responses to Gandhi, but neglects what must surely be
the fundamental one: that insofar as he was an Indian oppressed
by British imperialism Ambalal wished to follow Gandhi, but
insofar as he was a capitalist trying to maximize his profit, he
had to resist Gandhi. It's interesting to note that, after
Ahmedabad, Gandhi shied away from labor issues, apparently
persuaded that a too active prosecution of the class struggle would
endanger Indian national unity.

Let me put down a few notions about the Gandhian strategy,
and we will be done.

• *Satyagraha* is inherently elitist. It depends, as Erikson says,
on "a disciplined core of expert volunteers." It is a politics likely
to thrive when a unified national emotion can be mobilized,
as in India, or when the struggle is brief in time and with limited

stakes, as in the deep South during the early sixties. But it does not provide a stable basis for a long-range politics in a democratic country.

● Gandhi helped create a democratic society, but it is a question whether he could have been its leader after independence. His method depended on an appeal to the conscience of opponents, and any politics that puts conscience *in the forefront*—quite apart from majorities or minorities, parliamentary procedures or legal restraints—is peculiarly open to misuse by charismatic leaders and fanatic minorities. Gandhi knew this. He once urged that those "being fasted against" who considered the fast to be blackmail should "refuse to yield to it, even though the refusal may result in the death of the fasting person." Ideally, a democratic society rests upon a consensus of conscience, but in its daily operations it can survive only through a common acquiescence in formal rules.

● *Satyagraha* is most effective against opponents who fail to live up to standards they claim to accept. Its aim is reconciliation, not widening conflict; it proposes not the destruction of the enemy, but his conversion; and thereby it can succeed only within strictly limited circumstances.

● *Satyagraha* is not a strategy for revolution. Erikson shows that it aspires toward a ritualization of conflict in order to prevent violence; he even compares it with Konrad Lorenz's observations concerning the ritualization of conflict among animals as a way of minimizing violence. Along these lines Erikson keeps stressing that Gandhi urged the Ahmedabad workers to demand only what was "fair and right," and this seems to him evidence of Gandhi's reasonableness. Perhaps; but what if the workers had come to believe that "fair and right" required the expropriation and socialization of Ambalal's mill? Could Gandhi's approach have ritualized a conflict that was so deep-going in nature?

● In one of his resistance appeals Gandhi said: "Real suffering bravely borne melts even a heart of stone." Does it? Gandhi had not yet learned about the stones of our century. If he had tried to fast a Hitler or Stalin into submission, they would have been delighted to let him die—assuming they had not already killed him for his gesture of defiance. George Orwell's remarks seem to me incontrovertible:

> *The important point is not so much that the British treated Gandhi forbearingly as that he was always able to command publicity. . . . It is difficult to see how Gandhi's methods could be applied in a country where opponents of the regime disappear in the middle of the night and are never heard of again. Without a free press and the right of assembly, it is impossible not merely to appeal to outside opinion, but to bring a mass movement into being, or even to make your intentions known to your adversary.*

ON SEXUAL POLITICS
The Middle-Class Mind of Kate Millett

GOOD CAUSES ATTRACT poor advocates. The demands of the women's movements, at least those demands that can be brought to socioeconomic focus, are transparently just. So much so that to some people, including the more fanatical Women's Liberationists, they also seem a little dull. Equal pay for equal work, child-care centers for working mothers—these could become realities within a decade or two, and without bombs, guerrilla warfare, or even the razing of Western Civilization. But precisely because they don't lend themselves to ideological dramatics, such proposals gain little attention.

Our dominant economic classes and institutions seem to find this a satisfactory state of affairs. Just as they regard the rhetoric of black power as less troublesome than paying to build houses in black slums, so they are likely to find declamations against "sexism" less troublesome than having to raise the wages of women workers. And not only less troublesome, but also a good deal more entertaining. For at a time when boredom has become a crucial social fact, many people, especially in the professional classes, feel a need for new kinds of entertainment drawing upon ideologies of ultimate salvation and the rhetoric of desperate acts. Among segments of the intellectuals and the young there keeps growing a quasi-religious hunger for total system, total solution, total apocalypse; and soon enough ideologues appear with doctrines to match.

Kate Millett, author of *Sexual Politics*, is such an ideologue, and one would need a heart of stone not to be amused by the success she has won. Imagine the sheer comedy of it: a book declaring itself to be a "revolutionary" manifesto, presenting Jean Genet as a moral exemplum, and with the barest moral lilt of the eyebrow envisaging the abolition of the family, gains for its author a not-so-small fortune, selection by the Book-of-the-Month Club, and the cover of *Time*.

Miss Millett is a writer entirely of our moment, a figment of the *Zeitgeist*, bearing the rough and careless marks of what is called higher education and exhibiting a talent for the delivery of gross simplicities in tones of leaden complexity. Brilliant in an unserious way, she has learned at Columbia University how to "work up" a pastiche of scholarship that will impress those unable or disinclined to read with care. She has a mind of great energy but small regard for nuance. She ranges wildly over history, politics, psychology, and anthropology, but with little respect for these disciplines in their own right. She is the ideal highbrow popularizer for the politics and culture of the New Left.

In all the favorable reviews of *Sexual Politics* that I have seen, not one has so much as troubled to compare the book with Simone de Beauvoir's *The Second Sex*. Now it is true that de Beauvoir's book was published in this country all of seventeen years ago, for us roughly the equivalent of a millennium. Still, anyone comparing the two books would immediately recognize the extent to which Miss Millett has drawn upon de Beauvoir's famous work. The central ideas and sentiments of *Sexual Politics* are simply appropriated, in vulgarized form, from *The Second Sex*, and reviewers with some intellectual conscience might consequently have shown restraint in praising Miss Millett's originality of thought. Those inclined to rigor might also have remarked that she has yet to master the ethic of intellectual obligation: she cites de Beauvoir twice, in relatively minor contexts, thereby avoiding the *gaffe* of pretending the earlier book doesn't exist, but at no point does she make an adequate acknowledgment of her debt.

II

At the heart of *Sexual Politics*, in the key chapter, "Theory of Sexual Politics," lies a nightmare vision of endless female subordination to and suffering at the hands of men. "Sexual dominion [is] perhaps the most pervasive ideology of our culture and provides the most fundamental concept of power." The relations between the sexes are basically political, that is, relations of power. Everything else that happens to and between men and women—from sex to love to mutual responsibility in family life—is secondary. In these relationships the status of woman is that of a "chattel," a status accorded legal sanction through marriage: "an exchange of the female's domestic service and (sexual) consortium in return for financial support." The woman is exploited for her labor and/or used as a sexual object; and the exploiters are men.

Since sexual dominion is the very fundament, as also the *raison d'être*, of the patriarchal family and can't, indeed, be eradicated short of destroying the patriarchal family, we soon arrive at a terrifying impasse: an all-but-timeless and all-but-indestructible system of oppression, one in which "the entire culture supports masculine authority in all areas of life and—outside of the home—permits the female none at all." Why all-but-timeless and all-but-indestructible? Because the patriarchal family seems virtually coextensive with history itself; as Miss Millett must acknowledge, it has been "a basic form . . . within all societies."

This system of power, in which the woman "is customarily deprived of any but the most trivial sources of dignity or self-respect," rests primarily, in Miss Millett's judgment, on the social indoctrination of "sexual temperament," a learning process whereby little boys and girls are persuaded not merely of their differences but also of male superiority. Sometimes this process of indoctrination occurs through outright insistence upon male dominance, sometimes through rationales for confining women to home and children, and sometimes through "the chivalrous stance . . . a game the master group plays in elevating its subject to pedestal level."

Now what needs first to be noted about this theory is that, in any precise sense of the term, it isn't a theory at all. It is a cry of woe, partly justified; and it offers a description of sexual relationships said to hold pretty much for all of human history. But a cry of woe is not a theory, and neither is a description. For a group of statements to be given the status of a theory, good theory or bad, it must account for a complex of phenomena in respect to genesis, persistence, necessary characteristics, and relations to other phenomena. With the possible exception of the third item in this list, Miss Millett satisfies none of these requirements. To say "man is a beast" is not a theory about the nature of humanity, it is at best a statement of description; but to say "man is a beast because he is fallen in nature, or because he fails to obey the injunctions of Christianity, or because he has been brutalized by capitalist society"—that is to *begin* developing a theory. Miss Millett, however, makes no effort to account for the origins of male "sexual dominion," and more important, the reasons for its remarkable persistence and prevalence. Given her approach, she really cannot do so. She has no theory.

Miss Millett is determined to resist the view that biological and physical differences between the sexes may have determined or may still crucially determine a sequence of secondary and social differences, for she fears, rather naïvely, that any concession to biology must mean to accept as forever fixed the traditional patterns of male domination. The result is that she must fall back upon an unarticulated but strongly felt vision of conspiracy. And also upon a mode of reasoning utterly circular. Why does the patriarchal family persist through all recorded history? Because the social learning process trains us to accept it as a necessary given. But why does this learning process itself persist through history? Because it is needed for sustaining the patriarchal family. And what does Miss Millett spinning in circles illuminate here? Very little. Worse still, she presents a vision, misnamed a theory, which if taken seriously offers little hope of change or relief, for she cannot specify any historical factors, other than the "altered consciousness" of a "revolutionary" intellectual elite, which might enable us to end the dominion of patriarchy.

Let us approach the problem from a slightly different angle. Miss Millett argues that there "is no biological reason why the two central functions of the family (socialization and reproduction) need be inseparable from or even take place within it"; further, that we shouldn't take seriously the view that male physical endowment has been or remains a crucial factor in male social ascendancy. One must consequently ask: how then has so "basic a form [as] patriarchy" managed to arise and survive in just about every civilized society? If this "basic" form isn't even needed for socialization and reproduction, what is the secret of its hold? In what way can it even be considered "basic"? These questions, which follow inexorably from her assertions, seem never to trouble Miss Millett, since she writes with the thrust of the polemicist rather than the curiosity of the historian; and the punishment she thereby suffers is to create a picture, all but unknowingly, of endless female subordination from which, analytically, there seems hardly an escape. The root premise of her work, which naturally she does not care to express openly, is that women have been kept down because men have chosen to keep them down—which seems a more terrible tribute to the masculine will than any of its celebrants have ever dreamt of proposing. As a key to "the most pervasive ideology of our culture and . . . the most fundamental concept of power," this view of the life of the sexes is, let us say, a little inadequate.

Now, there have been other theories positing the centrality of social oppression in history. Marxism, for one, sees history thus far as a sequence of class struggles, though with the nature and relationships of the contending classes in constant change. Whatever one may think of this theory, the Marxist approach has one overwhelming advantage over Miss Millett's: it provides a principle of causation and change within society. Far from looking upon man's physical setting and conditions as an "enemy" of the hope for social change, as Miss Millett does, the Marxist view places social change within a natural context, or more precisely, it sees mankind as making its history through the materials and within the limits provided by nature. As men gain mastery over nature and thereby free themselves from the burdens of brute labor, the internal relationships of society are transformed and men begin *to be able* to determine their own destinies in a distinctly "human" way. (At the least, this avoids the simplistic either-or of biology/culture to which Miss Millett is addicted.) And while Marx believes all history to have been a history of class struggle, he is utterly scornful of those—precursors in economic terms of Miss Millett's sexual monism—who see history as a vista of undifferentiated oppression. He insists upon the crucial difference, say, between the master-slave relationship and the bourgeois-proletarian relationship: that is, he insists that historical change occurs and that historical change matters.

By contrast Miss Millett makes no concession to this central fact of history. Fixated upon the patriarchal family as if it were an all but supra-historical constant, and forced to acknowledge its omnipresence, she sketches out a grisly picture of the life of women. She makes no serious effort to differentiate among varous kinds of patriarchal family (after all, there may have been and of course were enormous differences in its endless manifestations) or to differentiate among the life-styles by which women have tried to fulfill themselves at different points in history. Her method here is exactly that of "vulgar Marxism," that caricature of Marxist thought which insists that the only reality is the economic and all else, being "superstructural," must be insignificant. Thus, with a reckless thrust of the phrase, Miss Millett can dismiss chivalry as "a game the master group plays. . . ." But such "games" crucially affected the lives of millions of men and women during the Middle Ages when the cult of Mariolatry became so powerful in the Church that a symbolic struggle between Mother and Son, female and male principles, was enacted among the faithful. Can one really explain such complex events as "a game the master group plays"? Isn't such historical reductionism a sign of an impoverishment of sensibility? It is striking that for all her far-ranging ambition of reference and passion of female defense, Miss Millett does not even list in her index, and only mentions two or three times in trivial contexts, the single most important woman in all Western history: the Virgin Mary.

A host of other questions press for consideration. The woman who worked sixteen hours a day in the Midland mines during the Industrial Revolution—was she really a "sexual object" up for "barter" to the "master group" (the wretched men who also worked sixteen hours a day in the same mines) quite in the same way as the bourgeois ladies of, say, Matisse's Paris? Does the "passivity" Miss Millett says patriarchal society induces in women characterize the American pioneer wife staking out a homestead in Oklahoma? Was the Jewish immigrant mother working in a sweatshop, often shoulder to shoulder with her equally exploited husband, "customarily deprived of any but the most trivial sources of dignity or self-respect"? Are the ladies of the Upper East Side of Manhattan simply "chattels" in the way the wives of California grape pickers are, and if so, are they "chattels" held by the same kinds of masters? Has the fact of being female been more important in the social history of most women than whether they were rich or poor, black or white, Christian or Jewish? Has the condition of women since the rise of the patriarchal family been so unvarying, so essentially the same endless story of oppression, that it can really be summoned through Miss Millett's one simple model? Have not human beings, men and women, found *some* paths to fulfillment and fraternity, *some* side alleys to decency of relationship and respect for sexual difference, even under the patriarchal curse? In short, does Miss Millett have any sense at all of the range and variety and complexity—and yes, even once in a while the humane achievements—of our history?

For what I am trying to suggest through the questions I have just asked is not only that Miss Millett flattens out all history into a tapestry of "sexual dominion," not only paints a picture of the past and present depriving women of any initiative, will, or capacity, but that she systematically ignores those crucial factors of class position which have the most far-reaching impact on the life of women. Most of the time, when she speaks of women she really has in mind middle-class American women during the last thirty years. About the experience of working-class women she knows next to nothing, as in this comic-pathetic remark: "The invention of labor-saving devices has had no appreciable effect on the duration, even if it has affected the quality, of their drudgery." Only a Columbia Ph.D. who has never had to learn the difference between scrubbing the family laundry on a washboard and putting it into an electric washing machine can write such nonsense. As with most New Left ideologues, male or female, Miss Millett suffers from middle-class parochialism.

And more: she suffers from a social outlook which, despite its "revolutionary" claims, is finally bourgeois in character. She writes that "nearly all that can be described as distinctly human rather than animal activity (in their own way animals also give birth and care for their young) is largely reserved for the male." And again: "Even the modern nuclear family, with its unchanged and traditional division of roles, necessitates male supremacy by preserving specifically human endeavor for the male alone, while confining the female to menial labor and compulsory child care."

These sentences indicate that Miss Millett is at heart an old-fashioned bourgeois feminist who supposes the height of satisfaction is to work in an office or factory and not be burdened with those brutes called men and those slops called children. For one must ask: why is the male's enforced labor at some mindless task in a factory "distinctly human," while the woman bringing up her child is reduced to an "animal" level? Isn't the husband a "chattel" too? Hasn't Miss Millett ever been told about the alienation of labor in an exploitative society? And is the poor bastard writing soap jingles in an ad agency performing a "human" task morally or psychologically superior to what his wife does at home, where she can at least reach toward an uncontaminated relationship with her own child? Why can't Miss Millett here remember the sentence, one of the best in her book, that appears in another context: "In conservative economies with an ethos of aggressive competition [and in other economies too!—I.H.], the 'home' seemed to offer the last vestiges of humane feeling, the only haven of communal emotion"? That animals also raise their young (in the same way? toward the same ends of socialization and ethical continuity?)—does this remarkable piece of information really deny the "distinctly human" character of women's experience in raising their children? In such remarks Miss Millett betrays a profound distortion of values, a deep if unconscious acquiescence not only to the corruptions of the bourgeois society against which she rails but to all those "masculine values" she supposes herself to be against.

What is lacking in Miss Millett's "theory of sexual politics," as throughout her book, is a felt sense of, a deep immersion in, the actualities of human experience which must always be the foundation of any useful theory. What is present in her "theory" is an imperious condescension toward all those complications of past and current experience that won't fit into her scheme, as toward all human beings who don't satisfy her categories.

In a remark worthy of that other leftist snob, Herbert Marcuse, she tells us that "many women do not recognize themselves as discriminated against; no better proof could be found of the totality of their conditioning." And those women who *do* recognize themselves as discriminated against—would not Miss Millett leap to declare that "no better proof could be found of the acuteness with which they recognize the reality"? Against the imperviousness of circularity, reason is helpless.

Now, it is true that the lot of women has frequently been that of a subordinate group—though not that alone. The relationship between men and women, like other relationships in our society, does often have a strand of ugly commercialism—though not that alone and often not that predominantly. (How many of Miss Millett's readers or admirers, one wonders, would be ready to apply her categories—"chattel," "barter," "sexual object" etc.—to themselves?) Women have been exploited throughout history, but most of the time in ways quite similar to those in which men have been, and more often than not, as members of oppressed or disadvantaged classes rather than as women alone. Yet it is also true that many women have suffered a kind of super-exploitation, though this can't be understood in the gross terms of "sexual politics" but must be studied as an element in the tortuous development of mankind from the penalties of scarcity to the possibilities of plenty. And at the risk of being charged with "playing the game of the master group," let me add that even in their conditions of disadvantage women have also been able to gain for themselves significant privileges and powers. Males may have been "masters" and females "chattels," but this is perhaps the only such relationship in human history where the "masters" sent themselves and their sons to die in wars while trying to spare their "chattels" that fate.

That the relations between men and women have had and still have an element of "power" similar to that characterizing the relations between social classes is true. But not the whole truth and very often not the most important truth. Indeed, the more closely one applies Miss Millett's "theory" to concrete instances both in history and immediate experience, the less adequate does it seem even as description. For the word "power" is very tricky in this context, and Miss Millett isn't the one to look carefully into its complexities. In any relationship of caring, people gain power over one another: the power to please, the power to hurt. Sexuality is a mode of power, and often, as history indicates (for Miss Millett, one gathers, no face ever did launch a thousand ships . . .), sexual power has been of a magnitude to overcome the effects of economic power. Sexuality gives us power at varying times of our lives, and often with radical inequities for which there seems to be no solution or even solace. That men have held power over women, in both the desirable and deplorable senses, is a truth that was noticed before the appearance of Miss Millett's book. That women have held power over men, usually in the more desirable but often enough in quite deplorable ways, is a thought with which Miss Millett will have no commerce. And it is even possible—indeed, if one clings to some sort of tragic view of life, it is likely—that the powers we hold over one another are both of the desirable and the deplorable kinds, the two fatally and forever mixed.

Yet it would be a sad mistake, and for the women's movements a strategic folly, to suppose that the relations between men and women, so entwined with the deepest and most mysterious elements of our psychic life, can ever be understood by the sexual monism, the historical reductionism of Miss Millett.

III

From "theory" to "history"—and with similar results. Miss Millett begins with a sketch of the "sexual revolution" in nineteenth-century England that reveals immediately the poverty of her historical imagination. With the ideologist's willfulness, she keeps grafting upon the past categories of analysis and standards of judgment drawn from the immediate present, so that, as you might expect, the past is forever found wanting. The very period she begins by praising she ends by berating, since the women's movements of the nineteenth century concentrated on such practical matters as suffrage, while Miss Millett, snug with hindsight, would have preferred that they devote themselves to exposing "patriarchal ideology." But if she is serious about her idea of what a "sexual revolution" is—"an end of traditional sexual inhibitions and taboos, particularly those that threaten patriarchal monogamous marriage: homosexuality, 'illegitimacy,' adolescent, pre- and extra-marital sexuality"—then it is hard to see how she can speak of a "sexual revolution" in nineteenth-century England and America at all.

She proceeds to examine some intellectual and literary texts of this period concerning women, and John Stuart Mill, because of his unambiguous advocacy of equal rights for the sexes, stands out as an heroic figure. I think he deserves all the praise Miss Millett gives him. But since she isn't one to rest with an advantage, she must scurry about in search of a villain, naturally a male villain. And she finds him in the sad person of John Ruskin, the critic of art and society who, between his major works, wrote an essay urging that women, as guardians of sensibility and moral purity, cultivate these values at home. Poor Ruskin—how could anyone suppose him a representative figure of Victorian patriarchalism, this man notoriously askew in his own sexual life and about as distant from standard masculine assertion as Miss Millett from standard feminine submission? Here too an historian with a sense of scruple would have added that Ruskin's paean to femininity wasn't merely Victorian bilge; as a bitter opponent of industrial society, he felt that the home was the last resort for suffering human beings, hardly, of course, an adequate view but not a view simply to be ridiculed.

As historian Miss Millett enters high gear in the next section of her book, where she discusses the "sexual counterrevolution" of the last four decades, her evidence for which is first the reactionary family policies of Nazi Germany and Stalinist Russia, second the theories of Freud and his followers, and third the fiction of D. H. Lawrence, Henry Miller, and Norman Mailer.

Now, as is typical with Miss Millett, her intelligence has not played her false in supposing that there has been a counterrevolution of some sort during the past several decades: she is, after all, talking about the age of totalitarianism. But once beyond this useful generalization, she betrays the sloppiness characteristic of her entire book. A few instances:

● The "sexual revolution" she had previously celebrated was located mainly in England and America. The "counterrevolution" she locates mainly in Germany and Russia. Is a causal or reactive or any other kind of relation being proposed between the nineteenth-century "sexual revolution" of England and America and the twentieth-century "sexual counterrevolution" of Germany and Russia? No answer from Miss Millett. While Hitler and Stalin were pontificating about motherhood, what was meanwhile happening to the relations between men and women in the original locale of Miss Millett's "sexual revolution"?

My own sense of what was happening in England and America is that the gradual process of sexual reform through the first three decades of this century came to be felt by cultivated and humane persons—they can hardly have all been "sexists"—as a social-cultural trend bringing with it serious and unforeseen difficulties. Women seemed often to feel that their liberation, whether partial or complete, had cast them adrift, without adequate personal or public security. Men felt disturbed by the growing uncertainty as to their social roles and sexual obligations. There was much talk, some of it cant but some very serious, about "inadequacy" and "crisis of identity," reflecting a system of anxieties created by changes in sexual relations. Even persons of advanced opinions came to feel, through the bitter prodding of experience, that certain kinds of liberation (for example, the childless marriages favored by some intellectuals in the twenties) had a strong element of sterility. As a result, there was an inclination among such people to reinforce the family structure, not by returning to the old-style Victorian patriarchy (it's a joke to imagine anyone thought that a genuine option) but by trying to establish distinctive sexual roles within a fraternal marriage. Sometimes it worked, sometimes it didn't.

Now Miss Millett can, if she wishes, dismiss all this as "sexual counterrevolution"—but only at the price of disdain for the experience of others.

• The "sexual counterrevolution" that did occur in Germany and Russia is placed by Miss Millett in an expository and, as it turns out, logical parallel to the rise of Freudianism and the writings of Lawrence, Miller, and Mailer. Intellectually, this is feckless; morally, shameful. Miss Millett never troubles to notice that the "reactionary" Freud was anathema to Hitler and Stalin, both of whom understood perfectly well that he threatened their despotism not because of one or another opinion but because of his fearlessness and skeptical openness of mind. Perhaps Miss Millett can explain the fact that Freud, whom she declares to be a theoretician of "counterrevolution," was banned in the very countries she designates as its central locale; if so, she is saving the explanation for another book.

• Equally squalid is Miss Millett's linkage of Lawrence, Miller, and Mailer ("The Literary Reflection") with the "Sexual Counter-revolution" of Nazi Germany and Stalinist Russia, and then with the alleged Freudian "Reaction in Ideology"—subtitles that promise connections which the text cannot establish. Of *precisely what* were Lawrence, Miller, and Mailer the "Literary Reflection"? The "sexual counterrevolution" in Germany and Russia? But Lawrence wrote his main books before the counterrevolution occurred. Henry Miller, a cracker-barrel American anarchist, was developing his sexual sentiments in the twenties, again before the counterrevolution. How can writings reflect something that hasn't yet happened? Mailer, who until recently supposed he was breaking past "the last frontier" of sexual repressiveness, has been strongly influenced by the Wilhelm Reich whom Miss Millett relies on so heavily for documenting what happened in the totalitarian countries. In short, we have here an intellectual goulash that could be taken seriously only in a moment when serious standards have collapsed.

But let us turn to the "sexual counterrevolution" itself. Miss Millett quotes the standard reactionary hymns of Nazi and Stalinist propagandists. Very good; except that she contents herself with remaining strictly on the level of their ideological claims. Had Miss Millett read carefully the scholarly authorities she cites, she would have learned what even such radical critics as Herbert Marcuse have acknowledged: that in every totalitarian society there is and must be a deep clash between state and family, simply because the state demands complete loyalty from each person and comes to regard the family as a major competitor for that loyalty. For both political and nonpolitical people, the family becomes the last refuge for humane values. The defense of the "conservative" institution of the family becomes under totalitarianism a profoundly subversive act.

Now the comedy of all this is that Miss Millett prints, at one point, a footnote quoting from a book by Joseph Folsom:

> *The Nazis have always wanted to strengthen the family* as an instrument of the state. State interest is always paramount. *Germany does not hesitate to turn a husband against a wife or children against parents when political disloyalty is involved. (Emphasis added.)*

Miss Millett prints this footnote but clearly does not understand it; otherwise she would recognize how completely it undermines her claim that in the totalitarian countries the "sexual counterrevolution" consisted in the reinforcement of the family.

Miss Millett seems especially ill-informed about what happened in Russia. She attacks Lenin for not finding "the sexual revolution . . . important enough to speak on," and then, with that sloppiness steadily characterizing the relation between her assertions in the text and her evidence in the footnotes, she quotes Lenin in a footnote as saying, "Perhaps one day I shall speak or write on these questions—but not now. Now all our time must be dedicated to other matters." That is, during the revolution and civil war, a time of hunger and death, Lenin felt he had more urgent obligations than to speculate on the end of the family. Similarly, Miss Millett notices that in *The Revolution Betrayed* Trotsky attacked the reactionary turn of Stalinist policy toward women, "but this," she adds, "is the hindsight of 1936." No, Trotsky was attacking the reversal of progressive state policies concerning divorce, abortion, nurseries, salaries, etc., that had been enacted by the Bolshevik regime during the early twenties. Does Miss Millett suppose these reforms were adopted behind Trotsky's back?

IV

It is upon Sigmund Freud that Miss Millett directs her heaviest fire. Freud has "generally been accepted as a prototype of the liberal urge toward sexual freedom," but this, we are now informed, was a delusion, since the effect of his work was to "rationalize the invidious relationship between the sexes." Yet, throughout the chapter attacking Freud, as throughout the book as a whole, Miss Millett keeps employing Freudian concepts as if they were the merest axioms and specifically notes her approval of the "theories of the unconscious and infant sexuality." (Apparently, as old Freud noticed once or twice, there are times when too great an awareness of what one is doing can be burdensome.) We must then ask: how could the Freudian theories of which Miss Millett approves have left their mark on modern thought and experience without also profoundly affecting for the better—as in fact they did—"the invidious relationship between the sexes"? Could the current concern about sexual roles even have begun without the contributions of Freud?

Miss Millett opens her attack by discussing Freud's treatment of his early patients, most of whom were women. He "did not accept his patients' symptoms as evidence of a justified dissatisfaction with the limiting circumstances imposed on them by society, but as symptomatic of an independent and universal feminine tendency." Now this won't do, if only because it sets up much too crude a disjunction between what is biological and what is cultural. It won't do, because Freud tried always to work with the observed dynamics of his patients' experience rather than with fixed categories borrowed from other disciplines (whether leaning toward the biological or cultural) which he rightly felt psychoanalysis could not handle. It won't do, because Freud did see in his patients' symptoms "evidence of a justified dissatisfaction," though not in the sense Miss Millett would like.

Many of Freud's early patients were women suffering from symptoms of "hysteria," often grossly somatic in nature; their troubles were related to the repressiveness of the upper-middle-class families in which they had grown up, especially to an excessive subordination to domineering fathers. What Freud tried to do was to enable them to accept their sexuality and thereby be freed from the symptoms. To the extent that he succeeded, Freud struck an oblique but powerful blow at the tyrannical aspects of the Victorian family. If anything can be described as militating against "the limiting conditions imposed . . . by society," it is precisely this therapy—even though Freud's investigations also led him to believe that there were indeed problems deriving from a "universal feminine tendency" which were not likely to be resolved through social measures.

All this, in a notably vulgar sentence, Miss Millett summarizes as follows: "Female patients consulted him in the hope of becoming more productive in their work; in return for their fees Freud did what he could to cause them to abandon their vocations as unnecessary aberrations." And as evidence for this charge Miss Millett offers a footnote quoting from Freud:

> . . . *at no point in one's analytic work does one suffer more from the oppressive feeling that one is "talking to the winds" than when one is*

> *trying to persuade a female patient to abandon her wish for a penis on
> the ground of its being unobtainable.*

Now if Freud is right in supposing penis envy to be a pervasive
fact of female experience, then what he is doing here—and in
a voice wryly, "philosophically" sympathetic—is not engaging
in vocational guidance but reflecting upon the sheer recalcitrance
of human desire, the difficulties we all have in reconciling ourselves to the limitations of our being.

The theory of penis envy comes in for a special barrage from
Miss Millett, and while I have no stake in this or any other
Freudian notion, the issue here is one of simple intellectual
responsibility. Freud writes:

> *As we learn from psychoanalytic work, women regard themselves as wronged
> from infancy, as undeservedly cut short and set back; and the embitterment
> of so many daughters against their mothers derives, in the last analysis,
> from the reproach against her of having brought them into the world
> as women instead of men.*

The crucial phrase is the opening one, "As we learn from
psychoanalytic work . . ." For a central problem in considering
Freudianism, or any other theory claiming to probe psychic life
at levels deeper than those of rational consciousness, is the problem of validation. The validation of Freudian concepts cannot
yet have, and perhaps can never have, the rigor to which scientific
propositions are subjected (as Freud knew well, and therefore
kept hoping that physiological bases might be found for his
psychological constructs). For the time being, validation must
depend on the accumulated and critically sorted observations
of analysts for whom a notion like penis envy[1] is not, I should
think, a fixed certainty but a usable lead by means of which

---

[1] Miss Millett offers an array of questions-and-assaults about penis envy, not
empirical in nature but rather concerned with internal consistency, and they
are worth looking at, together with possible Freudian replies. What matters
here, I would stress again, is not the "rightness" of the Freudian view, about
which I cannot form a qualified judgment, but her method of intellectual
discourse:

How does the little girl, discovering her lack of a penis, "make the logical
jump from the sight of bathing or urination [to] knowledge that the boy mastur-
bates with the novel article"? She makes the jump more experientially than

to form hypotheses about the material they gather during analytic sessions.

Freud's "entire psychology of women," writes Miss Millett, "is built upon an original tragic experience—born female." This is true enough in a way, and there is also a simplified truth in the claim that Freud sees women as defining their existence through their relations to men (though to say that isn't necessarily to *convict* him of a falsehood or bias). Finally, however, this is not so devastating a charge as Miss Millett supposes. For it is Freud's judgment that the psychology of men rests also on an original tragic experience—born male. Miss Millett manages to neglect the fact that in the Freudian system the theory of penis envy finds a polar equivalent and necessary balance in the theory of castration anxiety. The male is seen as being quite as heavily burdened by nature and circumstance as the female, and perhaps less well equipped to cope. *In Freud's view, nature lets no one off easily.* If women feel it "unjust" to be told they are conditioned by residues of their childhood envy for that "novel article"—Miss Millett's high-ironic parlance for

logically, these events occurring during the years between three and five, when there is a great deal of experimentation in infantile sexuality.

"Might she not just as easily, reasoning from the naïveté of childish narcissism, imagine the penis is an excrescence and take her own body as norm?" No; since the "novel article" clearly has the power of directed stream which she discovers herself to lack, and since this power becomes associated for her with other, greater ones.

"Surely the first thing all children must notice is that mother has breasts, while father has none." Does this not impress the child as evidence of female advantage? Yes, but the female child has no breasts and the possibility of their later growth, not very clear at this stage in her development, can hardly mean much to her; while the male child does have that "novel article," and he has it now.

"It is interesting that Freud should imagine the young female's fears center about castration rather than rape—a phenomenon which girls are in fact, and with reason, in dread of, since it happens to them and castration does not." Several answers, seemingly in contradiction but actually involving different layers of consciousness: (a) at this stage of infantile sexuality as Freud conceives it, female children aren't likely to have yet formed a strong idea as to rape; (b) in psychic life that which may not happen can be feared at least as much as that which does; (c) as Miss Millett has surely learned from her studies, reports of being raped by their fathers were so frequently proffered by Freud's early women patients that at first he took these literally and only later came to regard them as projective fantasies.

"penis"—then men may feel it quite as "unjust" that they must live out their lives in constant anxiety as to sexual performance. Freud does, however, envisage a possibility for at least a partial relief or transcendence of these troubles, and perhaps a shade more so for women than for men. Women are said by him to be able to emerge from the hold of penis envy, in part through a strong and positive identification with their mothers. Nor, by the way, are they the only ones in the Freudian outlook who experience envy; men are seen as at times quite envious of that very passivity which Miss Millett regards as so libelous an attribution to her sex.

Why should all this outrage Miss Millett so much? She really has, I would venture, only a slight intrinsic concern with Freudianism. A major reason for her passionate assault is that, by making a simplistic leap from one order of experience (psychological) to another (social policy), she sees the theory of penis envy as the basis for an alleged Freudian belief that "the intellectual superiority of the male, constitutionally linked with the penis, is close to an ascertainable fact. . . ." And again she provides a footnote from Freud supposedly buttressing this claim:

> *We often feel that when we have reached the penis wish and the masculine protest we have penetrated all the psychological strata and reached "bedrock" and that our task is completed. And this is probably correct, for in the psychic field the biological factor is really rock bottom. The repudiation of femininity must surely be biological fact, part of the great riddle of sex.*

Whatever the truth or falsity of what Freud says here, he is clearly not saying what Miss Millett claims he is saying. She simply will not read with care.

Yet, once her ideological assaults and manipulations are put aside, there does remain the fact that Freud's view of women, his analysis of their sexual natures and roles, doesn't happen to lend itself to the more extreme visions of the Women's Liberationists. Freud tended to believe, as Philip Rieff says, that "women are erotic hoarders in the male economy of culture. In the strife between sensuality and culture, women represent the senses." To someone like Miss Millett this immediately seems an invidious distinction, for she is completely identified with the values of the bourgeois activist male, the one who performs what she supposes to be "distinctly human" work. But in Freud's canny and ambiguous view, those who "represent the senses" are at times far more "distinctly human." For even while regarding women as the agents of racial survival and men as the culture-creators, Freud also fears, like many other nineteenth-century European thinkers, the death of spontaneous life at the hands of an increasingly tyrannical culture, the nightmare of a rationalistic self-destruction as "the world of the senses becomes gradually mastered by spirituality." No one is obliged to accept these views, but anyone wishing to attack Freud in a serious way ought to be able, at the least, to report the complexities, the inner sequence of change and doubt, and the frequently problematic tone which characterize his work.

What shall we say, however, if we are committed to equality between the sexes and yet continue to believe that Freud remains one of the great minds of our age? It is the kind of question that divides those who want everything neatly aligned, slogan stacked against slogan, from those prepared to accept conflict and contradiction.

We can say of course that Freud was a product of his age, and that while he did more than anyone else to overcome its prejudices, inevitably he still shared some of them. If there is a streak of patriarchalism in his writing, as I suppose there is, we must recognize that fifty or sixty years ago people could not possibly see things as they are seen today: that is known as historical perspective. In fairness, we must then add something Miss Millett fails to mention, that Freud greatly admired intellectual women and that the psychoanalytic movement was one of the first intellectual groups in this century to give a large number of gifted women the opportunity to fulfill themselves professionally. Still, to say this isn't enough.

We can add that Freud's views on women, especially those expressed in his more "philosophical" moments, must be separated from some clinically more cogent portions of his work. Freud would not be the first great thinker whose method can be used critically against portions of his writings. Still, to say that isn't enough.

We can then try to struggle with the fact that Freud advances conclusions as to the nature and consequence of sexual differences which rub against our progressive inclinations—but which can't, simply for that reason, be dismissed. For we must always recognize that analytically he may be right. Yet why should even this possibility create anxiety or anger? If the concepts of penis envy and castration anxiety prove, in some sense, to be valid for psychoanalysis, this surely doesn't at all affect the claims of women for socioeconomic justice—though it may affect some of the more nightmarishly utopian fantasies of writers like Miss Millett.[2]

Freud believed that the process of maturation for women presented certain special difficulties, and perhaps these would persist in the best of societies—though to say that such difficulties seem to be rooted in biology isn't at all to say that they can't be eased by social policy and education. To persuade a woman to like herself and to accept herself sexually, which was one of Freud's aims, isn't necessarily to persuade her to stay in the kitchen—though it may well be to tell her that if she does prefer to stay at home, this doesn't stamp her as inferior or brainwashed or a "chattel" of the "master group."

Freud seemed also to believe that the biological differences, or if you prefer disadvantages, of women inclined them toward the sphere of private values and experience. Even if we suppose

[2] The most egregious of these fantasies is Miss Millett's cavalier play with the notion of the abolition of the family. That the family, at once the most conservative of human institutions and endlessly open to social and psychological changes, has been coextensive with human culture itself and may therefore be supposed to have certain powers of endurance and to yield certain profound satisfactions to human beings other than merely satisfying the dominating impulses of the "master group," hardly causes Miss Millett to skip a phrase. Nor does the thought that in at least some of its aspects the family has protected the interests of women as against those of men.

In any case, one might suppose that Miss Millett would cast a glance at one of the very few contemporary social institutions—the Israeli *kibbutz*—where a serious effort has been made, if not to abolish the family, then at least significantly to modify its nature. Had she troubled to do so, and read the reports of, say, Stanley Diamond, an anthropologist of radical inclination, she would have had to recognize that at least in terms of psychological consequences [that is, the kind of children it brings forth], the evidence from the *kibbutz* isn't likely to persuade one that abolishing the family will greatly enrich the human race.

this to be true, why should it at all lessen our zeal—I mean the zeal of both women and men—for seeing to it that those women who enter upon careers be given every kind and equality of opportunity? I suspect, however, that what troubles Miss Millett is not merely the injustice of sexual discrimination but the very idea of sexual difference. For all that she is so passionate an advocate of the cause of women, she shows very little warmth of feeling toward actual women and very little awareness of their experience. Freud speaks in his essay on "Femininity" of the woman's "active pursuit of a passive function," and Miss Millett finds the phrase "somewhat paradoxical," thereby revealing a rather comic ignorance of essential experiences of her sex, such as the impulse toward the having of children. Indeed, the emotions of women toward children don't exactly form an overwhelming preoccupation in *Sexual Politics*.

V

For what seems to trouble Miss Millett isn't merely the injustices women have suffered or the discriminations to which they continue to be subject. What troubles her perhaps most of all—so one is inclined to say after immersing oneself in her book—is the sheer existence of women. Miss Millett dislikes the psychobiological distinctiveness of women, and she will go no further than to recognize—what choice is there, alas?—the inescapable differences of anatomy. She hates the perverse refusal of most women to recognize the magnitude of their humiliation, the shameful dependence they show in regard to (not very independent) men, the maddening pleasures they even take in cooking dinners for "the master group" and wiping the noses of their snotty brats. Raging against the notion that such roles and attitudes are biologically determined, since the very thought of the biological seems to her a way of forever reducing women to subordinate status, she nevertheless attributes to "culture" so staggering a range of customs, outrages, and evils that this "culture" comes to seem a force more immovable and ominous than biology itself.

Miss Millett lashes out against the Freudians not merely because some of them indulge in male chauvinism, but because they persist in seeing, within the common fate of humanity, a distinctive nature and role for women. Insofar as Miss Millett assaults the notion that current styles of perceiving "masculine" and "feminine" must be taken as eternal verities, I don't see that she can be faulted. Who would care to deny the attractiveness of historical variability, or the hope that men and women will be able to define themselves with greater freedom than they have in the past? But Miss Millett will not let it go at that, for she is driven by some ideological demon—the world as commune? the end of the nuclear family? the triumph of unisex? —which undermines what is sound in the cause of women's protest. In a remarkable sentence she writes:

> *Removed from their contexts of social behavior, where they function to maintain an order not only of differentiation but of dominance and subordinance, the words "masculine" and "feminine" mean nothing at all and might well be replaced with what is biologically or naturally verifiable–male and female.*

No longer is Miss Millett insisting on the probable truth that the claim for the biological determination of sexual roles has often been an excuse for reactionary laziness. She is now saying that the very idea of distinctive sexual psychologies, responses, and life patterns—in short, masculine and feminine as modes of behavior deriving from, but more extensive in consequence than the elemental differences between male and female—means "nothing at all." And here she betrays a rashness such as one rarely finds in scholars genuinely committed to their subject.

For what is obvious to anyone who even glances at the literature on this matter—and that is all I claim to have done—is the agreement among scholars (who may agree on nothing else) that they don't yet know enough to make the kind of absolutist declaration I've just quoted from Miss Millett. There appear to be three *kinds* of difference between the sexes: the quite obvious physical and physiological ones; the more shadowy and ambiguous ones in role, attitude, and potential that are sometimes called "secondary"; and those that are culturally derived or imposed. Just as few scholars would now deny the last two in favor of the hegemony of the first, so few would deny the first two in favor of the hegemony of the third. The most problematic is of course the second, that is, those differences pertaining to behavior yet seeming to derive mainly from the physical and physiological.[3]

Now there are moments when one is tempted to dismiss the whole matter by repeating Oscar Wilde's reply to a question about the differences between the sexes: "Madam, I can't conceive." For Wilde's remark points to a fundamental fact of our existence which ideologists forget at their peril and most other people, whatever their failings, do seem to remember. Together with the accumulated prejudice and mental junk of the centuries, there really is something we might call the experience, even the wisdom, of the race, and it is not to be disposed of simply by fiat or will (as many revolutionists find out too late). It tells us, through the historical pattern of a sexual division of labor universal in form but sharply varying in content, that for good or ill our natures shape our conduct.

We can perhaps say with some assurance that the "secondary" sexual differences have to do with:

1. the distinctive female experience of maternity (one supposes that the act of carrying another human creature in one's body for nine months would have the profoundest behavioral consequences, what the anthropologist Malinowski calls an "intimate and integral connection with the child . . . associated with physiological effects and strong emotions");

2. the hormonic components of our bodies as these vary not

[3] This tripartite division is similar to that which Freud applies in a valuable footnote to his book, *Three Contributions to the Theory of Sex,* in the section called "Differentiation Between Man and Woman." He writes here that the conceptions of "masculine" and "feminine" belong "to the most confused terms in science and can be cut up into at least three paths. One uses masculine and feminine at times in the sense of activity and passivity, again, in the biological sense, and then also in the sociological sense. The first of these three meanings is the essential one and the only one utilizable in psychoanalysis." A bit later, Freud continues: "Every individual person shows a mixture of his own sex characteristics with the biological traits of the other sex and a union of activity and passivity; this is the case whether these psychological characteristic features depend on the biological *or whether they are independent of it.*" (Emphasis added.)

How anyone reading this passage from Freud could suppose him guilty of unqualified biological determinism, or, as Miss Millett charges, of "a major and rather foolish confusion between biology and culture, anatomy and status," is hard to understand.

only between the sexes but at different ages within the sexes and lead to a range of behavioral results, some of them manipulable, that have not yet been fully grasped;

3. the varying possibilities for work created by varying amounts of musculature and physical controls;

· 4. the psychological consequences of different sexual postures and possibilities (Diana Trilling writes: "This fundamental distinction between the active and passive sexual roles is an irrefutable fact in nature—the most active sexual seduction or participation on the part of a woman cannot relieve the male partner of his primary responsibility in their sexual union. To put the matter at its crudest, the male can rape the female, the female cannot rape the male").

Can we go any further? Miss Millett cites with approval a study by Dr. Eleanor Maccoby on women's intelligence which calls into question the notion that women are inherently less capable of doing abstract intellectual work by "pointing out [I quote Miss Millett] that the independence and ego strength necessary for first-rate achievement in certain analytical fields is completely absent from the cultural experience of nearly every girl child." Again, if we turn back to the source we see Miss Millett handling citations with her customary care. Were one to take literally what she says in the above-quoted sentence, there would be no way of explaining the increasing number of women who do have to their credit "first-rate achievement in certain analytical fields." And while it is true that Dr. Maccoby does make out a strong case for the view that much of the deficiency of female performance in certain intellectual fields is due to cultural inhibition, she is also careful to add:

> I think it is quite possible that there are genetic factors that differentiate the two sexes and bear upon their intellectual performance other than what we have thought of as innate "intelligence." For example, there is good reason to believe that boys are innately more aggressive than girls—and I mean aggressive in the broader sense, not just as it implies fighting, but as it implies dominance and initiative as well—and if this quality is one which underlies the later growth of analytic thinking, then boys have an advantage which girls who are endowed with more passive qualities will find difficult to overcome.

In the same way, with the same admirable tentativeness, Dr.

Maccoby remarks: "We don't know what the biological under-pinnings of maternal behavior are, but if you try to divide child training among males and females, we might find out that females need to do it and males don't."

Now the real question is, why should any of this trouble Miss Millett? That there are sexual differences extending beyond anatomy and into behavior—why should this be supposed to endanger the case for equality, *unless Miss Millett tacitly or explicitly accepts the male chauvinist view that the mere evidence of difference is proof of superiority?* Why cannot intelligent and humane people look upon sexual difference as a source of pleasure, one of the givens with which nature compensates us for the miseries of existence? Why must differences be seen as necessarily invidious? And even if these differences suggest the possibility that fewer women will reach "first-rate achievement" than men, why should that keep anyone from being responsive and responsible to those women who will do valuable work outside the home? Any more, say, than we should feel dismay at the possibility that an adjust-ment in sexual roles might decrease the number of men reaching "first-rate achievement"?

The dominating obsession of Miss Millett's book—which is to insist that all but rudimentary sexual differences are cultural rather than biological in origin—is a token of her lack of intel-lectual sophistication. If you insist, as she in effect does, that the biological be regarded as somehow untouched by cultural alloy, then it becomes virtually impossible to offer any biological evidence, if only because man is a creature that always exists in a culture, so that whatever we can learn about him must always be through the prism of cultural perspective. Culture is, at least in part, that which we make of our biology. If certain patterns of existence, such as the family, are invariable through-out the development of human culture, then it seems reasonable to suppose, even if it may be difficult to prove, that they satisfy requirements of our biology as these have manifested themselves through culture.

But as Miss Millett uses "biology" and "culture," they become absolutist polarities ranged in an endless battle against one another. She begins by noting quite properly that in the past the case for biological determinism has been overstated, especially in popular writings, and ends by doing pretty much the same thing for cultural determinism, though with not much more persuasive evidence. In her somewhat desperate reliance on the transforming powers of "culture" she reminds one of the thrust Morris Raphael Cohen once made against John Dewey's use of the term "experience": it was hard, said Cohen, to know what in Dewey's system was *not* experience.[4]

[4] Were there space enough and time, I would want to write at length about Miss Millett's way of approaching literary texts—an approach that proves women critics can be as heavy-handed as male critics.

Thomas Hardy, in presenting Sue Bridehead, the charming and neurotic heroine of *Jude the Obscure*, shows himself "troubled and confused *vis-à-vis* the sexual revolution"—though Sue is one of the first and greatest portraits of the emancipated woman and nothing is said by Miss Millett about Hardy's still greater portrait of Tess, a magnificent figure transcending all of Miss Millett's categories. George Eliot is "stuck with the Ruskinian service ethic." Virginia Woolf "glorified two housewives." D. H. Lawrence, whose mystique of blood consciousness is read as if it were a social policy, is a virtual devil. His Lady Chatterley is never "given the personal autonomy of an occupation" (unlike all the other contemporary English ladies in both life and literature?). Mrs. Morel, the mother in *Sons and Lovers*, is "utterly deprived of any avenue of achievement" (as if that were somehow Lawrence's fault rather than an accurate reflection of what a miner's wife would have been like at the end of the nineteenth century—and apparently the raising of her family under conditions of hardship and with a drunken collapsed husband doesn't strike Miss Millett as an "achievement"). Paul Morel, "when his mother has ceased to be of service . . . quietly murders her"—a grotesque distortion of what happens in the book. And as if there had never been a domineering woman in the world, Miss Millett complains of "a curious shift in sympathy between the presentation of Mrs. Morel from the early sections of the novel when she is a woman . . . 'done out of her rights' [Lawrence] as a human being . . . to the possessive matron guarding her beloved son from maturity . . ." But this sentence itself gives a sufficient reason for the shift in narrative tone toward Mrs. Morel, as well as indicating, through the quote from Lawrence, that he did have kinds of sympathy for women which Miss Millett either won't allow or depreciates as tokens of male hostility.

It comes as a sign of Miss Millett's literary grasp that, outraged over Mrs. Morel's pleasure at ironing her son's shirts (as if Lawrence were here inventing a feeling utterly without precedent in human experience!), praise should then follow for, of all books, *Portnoy's Complaint* as "a healthy antidote to this kind of thing."

The one writer whom Miss Millett approves of as a spokesman for sexual health is Jean Genet, the portraitist of prison crime and homosexuality. His "explication of the homosexual code becomes a satire of the heterosexual one"—this on the dubious though popular premise that the extreme instance is the best illumination of the usual experience. Writes Miss Millett: "The

VI

It was the usual things of life that filled her with silent rage; which was natural inasmuch as, to her vision, almost everything that was usual was iniquitous.

This sentence was written a good many years ago by Henry James about Olive Chancellor, the femininist heroine-martyr of *The Bostonians*. Brilliant, it is also hard-spirited and a little unpleasant, for we sense a certain withdrawal of sympathy on James's part. Yet for those of us committed to the hope of changing the world, it is a sentence alive with challenge. Often enough "the usual" is iniquitous, and often enough, not to feel "silent rage" toward the complacence with which the idea of "the usual" can be employed to rationalize injustice is to abandon a portion of one's humanity. Yet in the history of modern intellectual life nothing has been more disastrous than this hatred of "the usual"; this disdain for what is called "one-dimensional"; this scorn for the inherited pleasures, ruses, and modes of survival by which most of us live; this nagging insistence that life be forever heroic and dramatic, even if ordinary humanity must be herded by authoritarian party bosses and ideologues to make it so. And in large measure this is the spirit that informs *Sexual Politics*.

Miss Millett's nightmare-fantasy of sexual lordship in which the man buys a woman as "sexual object" or household drudge and in which the woman submits to his ruling-class will; this parody of the Marxist vision of class dictatorship, with the woman as propertyless proletarian who can sell only her labor power or her sexual power—how much truth does it contain and what does it tell us about the realities of the life we lead? In the glistening towers of the Upper East Side of New York, in the country clubs of the O'Hara provinces, in Hollywood, in whatever places the rich enjoy their idleness, there are, I suppose,

---

degree to which eroticism and shame are inseparable in Genet is a nice illustration of how deeply guilt pervades our apprehension of the sexual, an unpleasant fact of sexual politics and hardly less true of heterosexual society than it is of Genet's." But *is it* hardly less true? Is the common range of human sexuality really "illustrated" by the world of Jean Genet?

women who have sold themselves as "sexual objects" and must slink and kitten before their masters. Among the millions of middle-class families living in suburban homes there are surely some—who can say how many? how does Miss Millett know? what has she *actually observed* of their lives?—that conform to this grotesque version of the human relationship. And among working-class families there are no doubt blunter and cruder variants of male bossdom and female submission.

But how can anyone with eyes to see and ears to listen suppose that this is the dominant and unmodulated reality of our time? Isn't Miss Millett guilty of the prime sin of the ideologue, which is always to forget that the scheme is at best an abstraction from reality and not reality itself, and that always the reality must be seen as more shaded, complicated, and ambiguous than any scheme can be? Caught up in a masochistic tremor of over-determination, Miss Millett sees only butterflies broken by brutes, drudges exploited by gang bosses.

Again, one must say, yes of course, there are such instances, just as blacks are still sometimes lynched and often brutalized; but to fail to see the improvement in large areas of black life in America isn't merely political obtuseness, it is the snobbism of those who will have nothing to do with the small struggles and little victories of human beings unless these are patterned to their ideologies and slogans. This is the very opposite—in spirit, in feeling, in political consequence—of genuine radicalism. It is, instead, a symptom of the contempt that rages today among our intellectual and professional classes: contempt for ordinary life, contempt for ordinary people, contempt for the unwashed and unenlightened, contempt for the unschooled, contempt for blue-collar workers, contempt for those who find some gratification in family life, contempt for "the usual."

You would never know from Miss Millett's book that working-class life can be marked by that easy warmth and fraternal steadiness in the relations between sexes that Richard Hoggart has sketched in *The Uses of Literacy*. You would never know from Miss Millett's book that there are a great many middle-class Americans who have struggled to find and perhaps in part found, terms of personal respect through which to share their lives. You would never know from Miss Millett's book that there are families where men and women work together in a reasonable approximation of humanness, fraternity, and even equality—as reasonable as one can expect in an unjust society, in a bad time, and with all the difficulties that sheer existence imposes on us.

I look about me and think of the people I know, the friends with whom I live. The women have it hard, since they try to be at one and the same time intellectuals or professionals (and they do suffer disadvantages here), mothers (and they do have to confront generational conflicts and confusions of value), attractive wives (and why not? since many succeed), and heaven alone knows what else. But in part at least the women have it hard because, and for the same reasons that, the men have it hard. Do they have it harder than the men? Probably so. Yet these women, who seem to me among the most interesting people in the world, are struggling and fulfilled human beings creating the terms of their freedom even as they recognize the bounds of limitation that circumstance, gender, history, and fortune impose on them. "Chattels"? "Sexual objects"? Submissive to the "master group"?

Perhaps, however, I am referring to a very special group, too "enlightened" to betray the stigmata of sexual politics as Miss Millett describes them. I think back, then, to the one other world I have known well, the world of immigrant Jewish workers. I recall my mother and father sharing their years in trouble and affection, meeting together the bitterness of sudden poverty during the Depression, both of them working for wretched wages in the stinking garment center, helping one another, in the shop, on the subways, at home, through dreadful years. And I believe, indeed know, that they weren't unique, there were thousands of other such families in the neighborhoods in which we lived. These people, less sophisticated than Miss Millett and her colleagues, were nevertheless animated by values of compassion, affection, and endurance. They lived under conditions of exploitation, and in consequence, no doubt, there was also injustice or at least unfairness in their personal relationships. But they were not merely passive agents or victims, not merely "chattels" or "oppressors." They struggled, within the limits of the possible, to make something of their lives, to make something *human* of their lives, together. And, like millions of other people in other cultures, other places, other moments, some of them succeeded. It it an outrage to reduce them to mere categories of ideology.

Was my mother a drudge in subordination to the "master group"? No more a drudge than my father who used to come home with hands and feet blistered from his job as presser. Was she a "sexual object"? I would never have thought to ask, but now, in the shadow of decades, I should like to think that at least sometimes she was.

DA